Collective Morality and Cr Americas

This study examines the ways in which the moral community is "talked into being" in relation to crime, and the objects of concern that typically occupy its attention. It explores collective morality with particular reference to the unease about rising violence, guns and gun control, gangs, and hate crime in North America; and the deep anxiety about crime and violence, organized crime, and drug trafficking in Latin America. Its source materials are commentaries about crime and criminal justice appearing in selected newspapers across the hemisphere.

Research on social problems, moral panics, and the sociology of morality has largely overlooked the type of moral discourse studied here. While emphasizing the culturally contingent nature of the findings, the conclusion reflects on their significance for understanding the nature of morality, the artifacts of talk, and the construction of identity.

Given its focus on the Americas, this book will be of great interest to students, researchers, and non-specialists in both Canada and the United States, especially those interested in criminology, cultural studies, social problems, and social movements.

Christopher Birkbeck is Professor of Criminology at the University of Salford, UK, where he has been based since 2006. He is also Professor Emeritus of Criminology at the Universidad de Los Andes, Venezuela, which he joined as a junior faculty member in 1980. Between 1987 and 2000, he also held several visiting positions as a teacher or research associate at the University of New Mexico, USA. He has researched numerous topics relating to crime and criminal justice in comparative perspective, many with a focus on Venezuela, and is currently working on collective morality and crime across the Americas.

Routledge studies in crime and society

1 **Sex Work**
   Labour, mobility and sexual services
   Edited by JaneMaree Maher, Sharon Pickering, and Alison Gerard

2 **Collective Morality and Crime in the Americas**
   Christopher Birkbeck

Collective Morality and Crime in the Americas

Christopher Birkbeck

LONDON AND NEW YORK

First published 2013
by Routledge
2 Park Square, Milton Park, Abingdon, Oxon OX14 4RN

Simultaneously published in the USA and Canada
by Routledge
711 Third Avenue, New York, NY 10017

Routledge is an imprint of the Taylor & Francis Group, an Informa business

© 2013 Christopher Birkbeck, selection and editorial material

The right of Christopher Birkbeck to be identified as author of this work has been asserted by him in accordance with sections 77 and 78 of the Copyright, Designs and Patents Act 1988.

All rights reserved. No part of this book may be reprinted or reproduced or utilized in any form or by any electronic, mechanical, or other means, now known or hereafter invented, including photocopying and recording, or in any information storage or retrieval system, without permission in writing from the publishers.

Trademark notice: Product or corporate names may be trademarks or registered trademarks, and are used only for identification and explanation without intent to infringe.

British Library Cataloguing in Publication Data
A catalogue record for this book is available from the British Library

Library of Congress Cataloging-in-Publication Data
Birkbeck, Christopher.
  Collective morality and crime in the Americas / Christopher Birkbeck. – 1st ed.
  p. cm. – (Routledge studies in crime and society)
  Includes bibliographical references.
  1. Criminology–America. 2. Crime–Moral and ethical aspects–America. I. Title.
  HV6025.B5397 2012
  174'.936597–dc23
                                                                    2012021671

ISBN: 978-0-415-64477-8 (pbk)
ISBN: 978-0-415-52981-5 (hbk)
ISBN: 978-0-203-09977-3 (ebk)

Typeset in Times New Roman
by Wearset Ltd, Boldon, Tyne and Wear

Para Marlene
And for Chris, John, and Howard

Contents

Preface ix
Acknowledgments xi

1 Collective moral discourse 1

2 Making crime "our" concern 11

The significance of the first person plural 13
Collective concern 15
Concern for others 17
Concern for ourselves 20
Concern for the collectivity 22
Concern for "our" response 24
Drawing back 26

3 "We the good" 30

Alterity 33
Identity 38
Collective and individual identity 44
Drawing back 46

4 The moral outlook 50

Anglo-America: a secure moral community? 51
Latin America: an insecure moral community 61
Morally significant certainties 69
Drawing back 74

5 Moral agency — 76

Stirring morality 80
Prosaic morality 81
Moral deliberations 84
The limits to effectiveness 89
Drawing back 91

6 American melodramas — 95

Melodramatic morality 97
Staging: the city's defenses 98
Props: facts and evidence 100
Characters: moralists and experts 102
Context and collective moral discourse 106

7 The artifacts of talk — 108

Six newspapers, five countries, two years 108
What if…? 111
What consequence? 115

Appendix — 119

Preliminaries 119
The set of texts 120
Coding 122
Analysis 126
Reporting 129
List of items—organized by newspaper and date of publication 130

Notes — 148
Bibliography — 190
Index — 205

Preface

The collective morality examined in this book is of a particular kind. It is not the *conscience collective* so influentially discussed by Durkheim—that constellation of deeply held sentiments which, possibly, bring the notions of crime and punishment into being. It is a collective morality that materializes in text and talk, through which people write or say things that not only have moral significance but also communicate the idea, often insistently, of a moral community. And in their episodic, frequently offhand, sometimes dramatic, and often clichéd utterances, people give off a much untidier and less robust image of the moral community than that evoked by Durkheimian mechanical solidarity.

Nor is this collective morality concerned with all of the possible phenomena that might attract social concern; it is studied here—perhaps rather artificially—in relation to the matter of crime and the "responses" to it. Neither is it a collective morality that might be found in TV studios, lecture theatres, legislative debates or street protests; it is studied as it appears in the commentary published in newspapers. Finally, it is not necessarily a collective morality with universal characteristics, independent of space and time; it is the collective morality that can be observed in commentary published in three Anglo-American and three Latin American newspapers during 2006 and 2007.

But for all its apparent specificity, this kind of collective morality is very interesting to study. Morality is, after all, expressed only through words or behavior; so a focus on words is always likely to bring rewards. Not only does this book explore the discursive creation of a moral community in relation to crime, it also examines some of the features of moralizing (moral talk) that are associated with that enterprise. It seeks to understand how moral matters are typically handled, and to examine their significance for identity and experience. Indeed, some of the characteristics of this moralizing seem so pervasive and important that it would not be surprising if they were also found in other media, other societies and, perhaps, the recent past.

Some social commentators allege a decline in morality, while the few sociologists that write explicitly about morality comment on a contemporary lack of interest in the subject among their peers. These alleged trends may look to be related, but the claims themselves may be questionable. If the exploration undertaken here is at all indicative, moral talk is a frequent ingredient in commentary on crime; and one result of this is that other ingredients of that commentary often become morally significant as well. It may not be that morality has declined but that its discursive appearance has changed, making it less obvious. And, where evident, perhaps the content of this moralizing does not please those who, nostalgic for the social critics of yesteryear or concerned to defend a particular ideological programme, dismiss it as of inferior quality. As for the marginal status of "the sociology of morality," it is the label that blinds. True, there are not many studies that explicitly orient and advertise themselves under this heading, but moral matters keep bubbling to the surface in numerous other specialisms within the field of social studies. Thus, the present inquiry has found itself particularly engaged with the literatures on social problems, moral panics, and social movements. Indeed, one of its intended contributions is to highlight the tangential manner in which morality has been treated in previous work and to suggest some benefits that can be gained by studying it more directly. If this book encourages readers to examine, and reflect on, the morality embedded in the largely unedifying talk that characterizes much of the public sphere, it will have served its purpose.

Acknowledgments

Pedro Vargas, the great Mexican singer, was famous for ending each performance with thrice-repeated thanks: "*muy agradecido, muy agradecido, muy agradecido.*" For invaluable help and support in relation to the preparation of this book, thrice-repeated thanks are wholeheartedly extended to the following organizations and individuals:

To the Center for Latin American Studies, University of Florida, for an invitation to spend the Spring Semester of 2009 as a visiting scholar; and in particular to Charles Wood for facilitating the visit. The Center's program on Crime, Law and Governance in the Americas was the catalyst for extending the scope of the present study from its initial focus on Latin America to the wider hemispheric perspective that is adopted in this book.

To the University of Salford, for granting a sabbatical semester in Autumn 2009, during which much of the data preparation and analysis for the present book was completed. Staff at The Library have diligently responded to requests for document delivery over the last three years; and colleagues in Sociology and Criminology have made generous allowance for personal unavailability as the project wound to a close.

To Gary LaFree, Eduardo Paes Machado, Greg Smith, and Charles Wood, for providing valuable comments on an early part of the draft; and to Steve Edgell for giving wise authorial advice throughout.

To Tom Sutton and Nicola Hartley at Routledge (Taylor & Francis), for providing excellent editorial support.

And last, but by no means least, to the Birkbeck family for providing unfailing encouragement with this project and for tolerating ever-lengthening absences as the book neared completion.

Muy agradecido, muy agradecido, y muy agradecido.

Permission to reproduce in English the article titled "Víctimas y Verdugos," by Alejandro Gertz Manero, and originally published in *El Universal*, Mexico, on March 22, 2006, has been granted by Servicio Universal de Noticias, S.A. de C.V.

Every effort has been made to contact the copyright holders of all articles that required permission for reproduction, but if any have been inadvertently overlooked the publishers will be pleased to make the necessary arrangements at the first opportunity.

1 Collective moral discourse

In its December 19, 2006, edition the *Los Angeles Times* carried an item about rising rates of violence in the United States.[1] The trigger for this article was a recently released report by the FBI that gave crime rates for the first half of 2006. Not surprisingly, a few of the numbers in that report made it into the text. Thus, readers were informed, for example, that "violent crime increased 3.7% compared with the first six months of 2005," while "the number of robberies increased 9.7%." In addition, three "criminal justice experts" were consulted about the figures. Their responses focused on plausible explanations for the increases in violence and, in particular, on the possibility that a national preoccupation with terrorism, combined with budgetary cutbacks for the police, had allowed violence to creep up again. This item was a typical example of routine news production: a government report about something of social interest or concern provided the core subject matter, and one or more experts were asked to comment on it. Indeed, at least one of the experts quoted in this article—the criminologist James Alan Fox—was regularly called on by newspapers in the United States to give comments about crime and criminal justice.

Embedded in this routinely generated item of news were the following segments:

> *Fourth paragraph*:
> Though criminal justice experts were cautious about drawing conclusions from six months of data, they found the report worrisome and said the country could be in a new period of slowly rising crime...

> *Final sentences*:
> They [the police] are having an increasingly difficult time in effectively trying to combat crime and provide for safer communities. It has been a struggle.

That the FBI report was found to be "worrisome" looks unexceptional. Rising crime rates would be seen by most people as a cause of concern, and very few indeed might try to argue that they were of no concern at all, or even to be welcomed. But it is interesting to see how the sentence begins: "criminal justice experts were cautious about drawing conclusions from six months of data." Here, they were focused on uncertainty: did six months represent a blip or a trend? Yet, within the same sentence, the article had them putting caution aside and entering a different terrain: that of morality. To say that rising crime is worrisome is to offer a moral perspective; it is, obviously, to declare that crime should not happen.

Mention of the "struggle" to "combat crime" at the end of the article similarly looks unexceptional. It brings in terms which are widely used, drawn from a narrow inventory of words and phrases that denote conflict with crime (the "war on crime" and the "fight against crime" being two other examples). But these terms also carry moral overtones because they cast the police as adversaries of criminality, as a force for good. Thus, a 694-word article that is mainly about numbers and explanations—about what is (or might be) known—also carries a moral dimension. In scarcely 13 words, it communicates a censure of violence (the "worrisome" trend) and imputes virtue to the police (who combat crime).

Critical readers of this same article, and the comments that have just been made about it, might question the validity of the moral word count. Some might bring it down to three ("worrisome," "combat," "struggle"); most would probably argue that it should be much higher. After all, the article is replete with words which, while obviously describing crime types, also carry a clear moral valence: "murder," robbery," "aggravated assault," "forcible rape," and "violent crime" are terms that designate highly objectionable behaviors. Could not the whole article be seen as a brief report on the nation's moral health, in which the numbers and explanations merely provide information for the more important reflections about progress or decline?

There is no doubt that it could; but this is precisely because of the handful of words highlighted above, which give the text that possibility. Morality seems largely to be called up by specific kinds of utterance. There are countless tracts that deal with crime (and its varieties) in a clearly amoral manner, that is, with no attention to its moral significance, yet full attention to what is (or is not) known about it, or to what might (or might not) be done about it. And while moral crusaders might take up the unassuming FBI report and weave it into a denunciation of the nation's ills, they would probably find themselves wanting to add some judgmental text—about "disturbing figures," "the threat to personal safety," or governmental "complacency," for example—as accompaniment.

Of course, with a topic such as crime, the possibility that commentary might wander into the moral domain is always present, which is precisely what happened—in a quite limited way—in this *Los Angeles Times* article. And just as this article included a couple of sentences of explicit moral significance, many others do exactly the same, whether it be through recourse to routine words and phrases (in a sort of "slippage" into normativity) or the conscious stride to a moral standpoint that is presumably felt to be necessary. Thus, an opinion column about crime prevention in Venezuela's *El Nacional* mentioned "the brutal magnitude of our crime problem" (seven words out of 774) in its second sentence;[2] while an editorial in Toronto's *Globe and Mail* began, very simply, with, "The problem is crime" (four out of 483 words).[3] In other cases, the moral perspective is dominant, as in another *Globe and Mail* editorial, this time on school safety, of which about 337 words of the 535-word text were given over to criticisms of the crime, disorder, and victimization that were claimed to exist in a Toronto school.[4] Similarly, an editorial in Mexico's *El Universal* was almost entirely devoted to denouncing the problem of juvenile alcoholism, sometimes with dramatic language.[5] At the opposite end of the spectrum, although quite difficult to find in these newspapers, are texts that are entirely devoid of moral comment, such as a brief item in the *New York Times* that reported on falling crime rates,[6] or an article from *La Nación,* in Argentina, about the use of computer technology in the criminal justice system.[7]

Newsprint has a markedly ephemeral quality, lasting only until it has been read and generally destined to be cast aside as attention moves on (although electronic archives are constantly growing). Yet this sometimes hastily assembled, and often skimpily read, material is shot through with morally significant utterances, at least in relation to crime. Along with information, knowledge, ideas, and blueprints for action, newsprint also conveys the moral stances of those who comment on this subject.

It is not, of course, the only site for moralizing about crime. Commentary on crime materializes in many different discursive domains. A political speech about rising crime, a police report on the latest crime statistics, a research paper on the causes of crime, an op-ed piece on juvenile delinquency, a neighborhood meeting about a recent spate of burglaries, a conversation between two acquaintances about unsafe areas of the city; all represent commentary about crime. Even private thoughts about these topics could be considered as a sort of commentary, although the only access to them is through words. And, just like newsprint, any of these commentaries could start from, or slip into, the moral domain.

Newsprint shares evident characteristics with other mass media, in its mechanical reproduction and wide dissemination.[8] It also shares commonalities with other kinds of public discourse, which may not be mechanically reproduced or widely disseminated (such as speeches, meetings, pamphlets, and specialist books), in that they are all understood to be accessible or potentially accessible to anyone. They stand in opposition to private comment, which is reserved for the self, or the few. Newsprint, therefore, offers a readily accessible route to the realm of public moral discourse, and that is the way in which it is used in this book.

The following study is an exploration of morality as it materializes in public commentary on crime. It is not a study of crime, nor a study of the way in which newsprint about crime is generated, disseminated, or consumed. Both of these latter fields, obviously, have been, and continue to be, amply researched, with criminology and media studies providing the respective disciplinary supports. In contrast, the following study uses public commentary on crime as a case study, as a means to access a particular kind of moral discourse. Commentary is one type of what linguists call "natural discourse," that is, discourse which has not been generated for the purpose of measurement. Its counterpart is what might be termed "experimental discourse," which materializes when a researcher elicits verbal or written responses to questions or requests for information. Morality also exists as experimental discourse when, for example, a sample of people answers a survey question measuring whether or not they are in favor of abortion, subjects give their opinions about hypothetical moral dilemmas, or a focus group discusses the pros and cons of health care reform.

Natural discourse is, obviously, often used as a source of data in the social sciences, particularly by linguists and discourse theorists (who are interested in understanding language and discourse), and ethnographers (who, except for linguistic ethnographers, are interested in something else). The ethnographic focus has often included natural moral discourse, but it is generally of the private sort, that which, for example, articulates the "code of the street" in Philadelphia,[9] or the dynamics of the *brigas* (violent encounters) during Carnival in Saõ Luís, Brazil.[10] Public moral discourse has been drawn on by scholars from diverse specializations—cultural sociology,[11] moral panic studies,[12] and social problems[13]—who are interested in the role played by morality in collective life. It has, however, been drawn on in a particular way, conveniently expressed through the notion of "framing."

In Entman's useful definition of the concept:

> Framing essentially involves *selection* and *salience*. To frame is to *select some aspects of a perceived reality and make them more salient in a communicating text, in such a way as to promote a particular problem definition, causal interpretation, moral evaluation, and/or treatment recommendation* for the item described.[14]

Frames have been invoked, directly or indirectly, to characterize ideational clusters that not only communicate meaning but also have consequences—measurable effects on social action and social life. Scholars have expended a great deal of effort on the identification of frames in relation to many social "issues" (including crime) and an exploration of their links to the decision-making process in public policy.[15] Frames have been an attractive concept for examining the big issues of the day: they touch on weighty matters of morals and politics, they highlight the public uses and misuses of research (of particular interest to researchers, obviously), and—very importantly—they signify conflict (a perennially popular topic for study).

Frames, however, are one step removed from public discourse. They exist first as abstract models in the minds of researchers, made up of such things as "roots," "consequences," and "appeals to principle,"[16] or "diagnostic," "prognostic," and "motivational framing,"[17] which are then populated with relevant bits of text selected from the discourses of interest. In this process, the natural quality of the discourse is broken down through dissection. In addition, as Entman's definition correctly contemplates, frames not only include morality but also other things, such as "causal interpretation;" hence, these sorts of discourse are as equally likely as morality to be cited and discussed in any given study, and there is often a corresponding failure to make sufficient distinction between them all. Thus, while studies of framing draw on public moral discourse, they do not reveal much about it.

Benford's study of the "vocabularies of motive" (or types of argument) used to mobilize action in favor of nuclear disarmament provides a pertinent illustration from work that makes explicit use of the notion of framing.[18] He identified four frames that represented the discursive tactics aimed at getting others involved in the movement: appeals to the *severity* and *urgency* of the nuclear danger, and claims about the *efficacy* and *propriety* of action to deal with it. Severity was mainly constructed through descriptive accounts, such as "statistics regarding the size of the superpowers' nuclear arsenals and the number of casualties expected in the event of a nuclear war."[19] Urgency was based on predictions about the imminence of a nuclear holocaust or, at the least, the impending development of a new generation of nuclear weapons. Efficacy involved claims that campaigning was capable of averting disaster and producing positive changes, while propriety addressed the duty to get involved for the sake of defending life, both immediately and for future generations. Propriety was, therefore, the moral component of the frames. While there are important linkages between each frame—severity and urgency, for example, give depth and immediacy to the repudiation of nuclear violence—Benford did not explore them or develop a comprehensive portrait of campaigners' moral stances in relation to nuclear war. He was much more interested in the discursive props and prompts to movement participation.

Benford's method involved the analytical extraction of his vocabularies from hundreds of pages of field and interview notes and more than 1,000 movement documents. Short quotes were included in the article as illustrations of each kind of motivating discourse. To the extent that it is present, morality comes alive in those quotes—"I'm here because I choose life over death," "We're concerned about what's going to happen to our families," and so on[20]—but just as quickly slips from view. A more systematic study of moral discourse would have required extensive exploration of the utterances contained in the source materials. It would have required a change of focus.

Similar comments (and others) apply to research on moral panics, a line of work which, on the face of it, might look to be particularly relevant for the study of morality. The literature on moral panics makes no explicit reference to the concept of framing and, in consequence, its ideational clusters of interest take on a fuzzier form. But the common roots of moral panics and framing studies in the social constructionist perspective mean that frames are identified in both, even if they are not so-named or clearly delimited in the first of these. For example, Cohen's classic study of events that happened in some English seaside towns in the 1960s described in considerable detail the portrayal (by the press, politicians, and other public figures) of youth subcultures as violent and unruly, the threats that these subcultures were perceived to pose to mainstream values, and the actions that were called for (some of them, in fact, taken) in response to the phenomena that were thus portrayed.[21] Moral discourse was obviously involved here—"grubby hordes of louts and sluts,"[22] "You have to deal strongly with this lot,"[23] and so on—but, once again, it appeared in snippets, extracted from a wide variety of texts for the purposes of illustrating particular points. Cohen was evidently more interested in panics than in morality. He developed some very insightful and influential analyses of collective behavior, the workings of the media, and the emotiveness and unreason that sometimes prevail in public discourse, all of which were taken up as themes in subsequent research.[24] However, when interrogated in relation to its own, rather idiosyncratic, rendering of morality, the moral panics literature is largely silent. How is indignation invoked and sustained? Is demonization the right word to describe the censure directed at deviants? How does moral discourse intersect with knowledge claims? What ethical stances underlie moral discourse? No systematic analysis or meaningful answers emerge.

Discursive morality is arguably one of the two directly observable forms that morality takes, the other being what might be termed "corporal" morality (physical behaviors with a moral content, such as a scowl, a slap, applause, an embrace, or avoidance). This does not mean, however, that either exists as a crudely objective phenomenon, waiting to be grasped by the researcher. Whether a slap is meant to calm down a hysterical person or degrade them is a matter of intent, which may not be clear to the slapper and even less so to the observer (although the person slapped may quickly formulate an interpretation). Whether calling juvenile violence "senseless" is an empirical observation about the meaninglessness of crime, or a particular type of censure (implying that crime committed for a reason is bad enough but that senseless crime is even worse), depends—again—on the speaker's intent and the observer's interpretation of it. Even natural moral discourse is mediated by the researcher; and experimental moral discourse obviously more so.

The study of natural moral discourse does not, therefore, stand entirely apart from the study of framing: both involve the selection and interpretation of text.[25] The difference between them lies in their focus. Framing involves the extraction of text for the purposes of illuminating and explaining social processes such as mobilization, political conflict (or political consensus), policy developments, and so on. The study of natural moral discourse involves the analysis of text for the purposes of illuminating morality itself.

Within the broad field that takes a sociological look at morality,[26] work on social problems, social movements, and moral panics has paid the closest attention to public (and therefore natural) moral discourse. Other studies have either drawn on that discourse in a much more schematic way through the interpretive construction (i.e., more abstract framing) of a particular "ethic,"[27] or have stimulated moral discourse through the careful measurement of values and normative orientations.[28] These diverse renderings of morality—the "capitalist ethos," "American values," "conformity," and so on—imbue it with greater gravitas than the routine, and sometimes dramatic, utterances—"bad news," "shocking development," "line in the sand," and the like—that are found in natural moral discourse. And, in addition, they work quite well as things that are to be explained, or which can be drawn on for the explanation of other phenomena, tasks which are rightly seen as essential to the social scientific enterprise. Public moral discourse is untidy in appearance, often trivial in content and seemingly irrelevant for understanding. What can be gained by examining it?

A first answer is that its pervasive presence indicates its social significance. That people routinely include morally tinged utterances in their public statements is further confirmation of what social scientists already grasp: that morality is a fundamental dimension of social life. A second answer is that, despite their episodic, imprecise, and frequently offhand textual character, public moral utterances can fruitfully be treated as a discourse with its own identifiable idioms and characteristic ways of feeding off, and feeding into, other types of discourse. To claim that moral utterances constitute a discourse is to assert (and demonstrate) continuities, duplications, and links between instances of these utterances that appear in a set of texts.[29] It is also to claim that moral discourse can be distinguished from other types of discourse, such as those comprising aesthetics, description, explanation, or technique.

In the present study, an utterance is considered to be morally significant if it communicates or implies a putative obligation or prohibition (a strong form), or desirability and undesirability (a weaker form), in relation to behavior. Obligations and prohibitions are expressed most strongly in the verbs "ought" and "ought not," but can also (along with desirability and undesirability) be communicated in a myriad of other ways: the "troubling" trend in crime (because crime ought not to occur); the "grubby hordes of louts and sluts" (who, as the antithesis of virtue, ought not to do what they are said to do); to "combat crime" (combat being a virtuous stance towards something which ought not to occur); "you have to [ought to?] deal strongly with this lot" (dealing strongly being a virtue); and so on.

Among the different lines of inquiry that can be developed in relation to public moral discourse, the focus of this study is on the imagined social world that it brings into being.[30] This is a world populated by morally significant actors (who can, therefore, be mapped) and its history is that of the relations between them (which can, therefore, be deciphered). It is a world that exists in newsprint and other public texts, but it is a world whose existence has not been recognized by those who, so far, have drawn on public moral discourse for data. It is a world centered on "the good," although necessarily inhabited as well by the unvirtuous. To chart its terrain and chronicle its history is, in fact, to explore morality rather than immorality. In the present case, it is to study moral virtue—or perhaps (and more precisely) the pretension to virtue—rather than criminality.

According to one of its meanings, virtue denotes efficacy, the power to get things done. Partly congruent with this meaning, morality has often been examined as a determinant of other social phenomena, which is precisely the way it has been treated in studies based on framing. Arguably, the greater the interest in the social process, the lesser the interest in the discourse itself—which would explain why frames are fuzzier in the moral panics literature than they are in the social problems literature. And, arguably, the greater the focus on the discourse itself, the more challenging it becomes to delineate its causal effects. In fact, the following study makes no attempt to study the role of public moral discourse in influencing other social phenomena. This is not simply an exercise in bracketing, in placing the lens on one bit of the social world as a prologue to exploring its relations with other bits. Instead, the imagined social world constituted by public moral discourse is treated as important in its own right. It is seen as playing an important role in the construction of identity and experience, irrespective of any other effects that it might have.

Most basically, public moral discourse affirms (or continually re-affirms) the existence of morality itself. The varied modes (speeches, essays, reports, etc.) and settings (politics, the media, community, and so on) in which this discourse materializes represent sites for morality—public social "spaces" in which the latter can be performed, legible, or aural reassurance that morality is, as it were, alive and well. Thus, for example, a report that labels crime trends as "troubling" is not simply (or perhaps even mainly) a cue for action, it is also a demonstration (however unobtrusive) that morality exists; seemingly called forth by the immorality that is crime. The symbolic importance of these sites for morality is not only reflected in the routine inclusion of morally significant language and the stylized, repetitive, forms that it often takes. It is also reflected in the fact that these sites are heavily policed (through censure, including self-censure, and sanction) to avoid the intrusion of immoral discourse—that which challenges or inverts the commonly affirmed order of virtues and vices. At these sites, no one declares themselves in favor of robbery, fraud, rape, or murder—it would be considered "unthinkable"—and even those who have committed these, or other types of crime, must deem that behavior unacceptable (through repentance, regret, apology, and so on) in order to participate as commentators.

A related characteristic of this discourse is its affirmation (or re-affirmation) of the existence of a moral community; its declaration that civil society is a moral society, made up of "right-thinking"[31] individuals who are on the side of the good. Whether or not this group is imagined to be the majority, it is always located at the center of the morally constituted universe, with immorality at the margins, somewhere else. Morality has to be strong because immorality is always perceived as a challenge, as threatening to weaken or replace it.[32] The notional existence of the moral community is, therefore, an affirmation of the strength of morality, derived from the putative sharing of similar values by its members.

And a third characteristic of public moral discourse is that it provides a means for the construction of individual identity, by allowing people to align themselves with this notional moral community through the use of appropriate vocabularies. To articulate public moral discourse is also to affirm one's own identity as a moral person. This strategy even includes individuals who may be highly critical of selected aspects of what they perceive to be the prevailing morality. They are often labelled as "moralists" or "moralizers," in explicit (and perhaps consciously sought) recognition of the particular attention that they pay to morality. The only danger for them is that, if their critique is too radical, they will be seen less as moral crusaders[33] and more as moral renegades.

These characteristics of public moral discourse are explored here through the imagined social world that it constitutes in relation to crime. Mapping that social world proceeds first by looking at the ways in which collective morality is "talked into being"[34] through the materialization of collective concern about crime. This is the subject matter of Chapter 2, which explores the ubiquitous and routine discursive orientation to a collective dimension (punctuated occasionally by criticisms of individualistic apathy and indifference), and the typical objects of collective concern (which can be varied). This is followed, in Chapter 3, by an examination of the identity of the moral community—an identity which does not simply emerge as a counterpoint to that of "criminals" (or whatever other word is used to designate those who commit crimes), but is also fashioned out of appropriate sentiments and significant virtues. It is an identity which is always implied to be that which is occasionally proclaimed as "we the good."

The coexistence of a moral civil society with the pole of immorality represented by criminals gives a history to this imagined social world, which is written in terms of their respective trajectories and the relations between them. It is this moral outlook which is explored in Chapter 4. Because any history has an empirical foundation, public moral discourse must draw on knowledge to build its account of the world. The inherent challenge is to do this in the face of uncertainty (understood as the necessarily contingent and provisional nature of knowledge), because it is difficult to formulate a convincing evaluation of a state of affairs which might not exist. Public moral discourse must, therefore, assume a certainty that is belied by other discourses, particularly that of science. How it does this, and how it utilizes empirical, poetic, and hyperbolic language to map the moral world, are also explored in Chapter 4.

Public moral discourse also writes history of a special sort, looking only occasionally to anything beyond the very recent past, and focusing instead on the present, and on some likely scenarios for the immediate future. It is a history which provides context as much as narrative, and which calls for moral agency, for morality as a seemingly necessary (and desirably potent) force in shaping the course of human affairs. This latter role is examined in Chapter 5, which looks at the incessant calls to action and the routine formulation of prescriptive statements within the apparently commonsensical framework of problems and solutions. Those prescriptive statements are not studied here as precursors to action (although they might be such), but as visions of moral agency, symbolic interventions in the history of the imagined social world, affirmations (or hopes?) that the moral community is endowed with power.

Cumulatively, the discourse presented in Chapters 2–5 reflects a melodramatic conception of the world, in which evil is pitted constantly against good. This was the discourse to be found in the sources used for this study: a set of 853 items published during 2006 and 2007 in six broadsheet newspapers across the Americas—the *Globe and Mail* (Canada), the *Los Angeles Times* and the *New York Times* (United States), *El Universal* (Mexico), *El Nacional* (Venezuela), and *La Nación* (Argentina).[35] Chapter 6 uses melodrama as a metaphor in order to look at some of the differences in moralizing that emerge when the two major cultural regions of the hemisphere—Anglo-America and Latin America—are compared. It notes important contrasts in the locus of concern, the salience of research, and the conspicuousness of moral talk,[36] which can be related to broader cultural processes in each region. And it underlines the need to see public moral discourse, wherever it might be found, as a combination of the general and the particular.

Chapter 7 continues the reflection on variability; first, in a methodological vein, by identifying some relevant correlates of the potentially differentiated character of moralizing: the type of medium conveying the discourse, the object of social concern, the cultural context, and the passage of time. It then moves on to consider some key dimensions of potential variation in moral outlook and moral agency: a tragic, as opposed to melodramatic, vision of criminality; moral agency based on something other than the virtue of determined action and the utility of positive results; and narratives built around empirical perplexity rather than certainty. These possibilities highlight the significant contributions of collective moral discourse to the construction of identity and experience, at least in part, through the artifacts of talk.

2 Making crime "our" concern

In late June 2006, Liliana Cánaves—a cultural activist in Buenos Aires—wrote the following letter to *La Nación*:

> Señor Director:
> I still do not have a family member who has been kidnapped.
> I still do not have a child killed by criminals.
> I still have not had the experience of being raped.
> I still have not been tortured for the coins in my pocket.
> I am still not a retired person who has been robbed, tortured and killed for nothing in her own home.
> But I cannot say that this is never going to happen to me.
> I watch and hear about the situation of national insecurity only through the media, and through them I feel vulnerable to an uncertain future.
> What do I do so that my freedom is not trampled on by crime? What do I do so that my human rights and those of my loved ones are respected?
> Nothing. That is the best thing that we know how to do, we who have not had the soul-hurting experience of being wounded for life by the insecurity that one breathes.
> But I also see that the struggle of those who were touched by the black wand of insecurity is not heard. The marches to Congress and to the Plaza de Mayo, the images and testimonies that are constantly circulated do not awaken the need for efficient action either from those who are in power (to deal with that), or from those who, like me, in spite of still being the majority, *never do anything*.
> What can we do? One more march? Twenty marches more?
> We are bound hand and foot by impotence and by the absence of exemplars that defend our human rights. That is what I feel. I ask myself: what can we do before anger and hate invade our soul because of an unwanted experience? We are still the majority. We are still in time to do something, even if it is writing a letter.[1]

This was an unusual letter to the editor of a newspaper. It was longer than most. It offered general reflection rather than the succinct or telling point that seems to meet with normal editorial approval. It suggested paradox ("even if it is writing a letter"). And it hinted at poetry ("I still do not have.... I still do not have...").

Interestingly, the first lines seemed to evoke Martin Niemöller:

> First they came for the Jews. I was silent. I was not a Jew.
> Then they came for the Communists. I was silent. I was not a Communist.
> Then they came for the trade unionists. I was silent. I was not a trade unionist.
> Then they came for me. There was no one left to speak for me.[2]

Cánaves was not watching other people being taken away by the regime; she was watching them fall victim to crime. But, like Niemöller, she was aware that she was not merely a bystander: "I cannot say that this is never going to happen to me." There was a situation of "national insecurity," articulated by the media, which made her "feel vulnerable to an uncertain future."

Her first reaction focused on the personal sphere: "What do I do so that my freedom is not trampled on by crime? What do I do so that my human rights and those of my loved ones are respected?" Her answer was immediate and negative: "Nothing. That is the best thing that we know how to do..." Here was a forceful indictment of inaction. It insinuated either fatalism or vain hope in the face of the inexorable probability of victimization. And its trenchant tone may divert attention from a subtle grammatical shift. Suddenly, the author was speaking as part of a community: nothing is "the best thing that *we* ... know how to do."

Who were "we?" Cánaves spoke of: "we who have not had the soul-hurting experience of being wounded for life," but reverted to the personal level to add an important idea to her reflection: "I also see that the struggle of those who were touched by the black wand of insecurity is not heard." This struggle was not heard by government or by those who, like Cánaves (and "still being the majority"), did nothing. The majority (by now, obviously, those who had not been victims of crime), becomes the unit of action: "What can we do?... We are still in time to do something."

This letter left many things unexamined. It conjured up crimes that are all the more infrequent because of their seriousness, but did not dwell on the more mundane breaches of social order. It imputed a struggle to those who have been "touched by the black wand of insecurity," but did not identify the nature of that struggle. With whom? (The government? Society? Criminals?) For what? (For justice? For vengeance? For help, or recognition?) It declared that the non-victim majority was doing nothing about crime, but did not define what would be recognized as doing something—beyond the minimal effort of writing a letter. It expressed concern for self and possible concern for others, but never explicated for *whom* something should be done. In short, it was a concatenation of vagaries.

Precision and detail, however, would have destroyed the character and force of this letter. There are plenty of prosaic treatments of crime that abound with specification. Cánaves' text is interesting, not for any contribution to understanding or intervention, but because it identified a moral space in the difference between the reactive attention to crime incidents and a proactive concern for crime in general. It was not enough for the individual to allow the happy avoidance of victimization to nurture unconcern and inaction. Whether it was for reasons of personal welfare ("I cannot say that this is never going to happen to me") or for solidarity with victims ("those ... touched by the black wand of insecurity"), something had to be done, "even if it is [only] writing a letter."[3]

This injunction was based on the recognition that concern about crime cannot be treated as a given; it has to be mustered. But Cánaves' letter was a relative rarity. True, in the set of texts compiled for this study there were several other calls for collective concern about crime. For example, a Mexican business leader reflected that: "It seems easy to think that as ordinary citizens it is enough to stay out of the line of fire in order to be reasonably safe, but that is not so;"[4] while a stained-glass artist in Savannah commented: "If you look at the numbers and you're not one of the numbers, we don't have a crime problem. But if your car's been broken into or your girlfriend's been hassled while she's walking around, then we do."[5] Perhaps these occasional calls for concern reflected some anxiety about the moral disposition of the average citizen, a fear that people are only attentive to crime when they have direct experience of it. But their infrequency suggests that there are several ways and numerous instances in which crime is routinely and unreflectively sustained as a matter of collective concern. This chapter seeks to identify and exemplify them.

The significance of the first person plural

Why, in her letter, did Cánaves move from the personal ("What do I do so that my freedom is not trampled on by crime?") to the collective level ("What can we do?")? There seems to be an inexorable logic that demands a collective stance towards putatively collective phenomena: individual concern is not enough. Speaking to mayors at a national meeting, the Mexican President said:

> Let us join forces and efforts ... I know that we can, because there are very many more of us who want order and peace in the country, than those who want to upset public life in Mexico. And Mexico is much stronger than a band of criminals; that is why we are committed to this.[6]

Referring to his own local band of criminals (gangs), the Governor of California said: "I'm calling for a big meeting. Everyone could get together and come up with ideas. We have to put all this together and not piecemeal it."[7] "*Unámonos y venceremos* [Let us join together and we will win]" declared a Venezuelan police chief, invoking a hackneyed revolutionary slogan.[8] These were all declarations of faith in the virtues of collective action. Individual efforts were obviously limited, sometimes nearly fruitless:

> [T]hree members of the Guardian Angels arrived in Montgomery for two days of patrolling and recruiting. They drove to a blighted neighborhood near downtown, where a house marked "Bad Boys Boxing Gym" leaned so badly it could have been doubling as the heavy bag. They parked, and walked about in red jackets and berets, their arms swinging stiffly at their sides, powerlifter style, and handcuffs clinking on their belts.
> They looked like grand marshals of a parade that no one was watching.[9]

There is no better or more direct manner of invoking the collective dimension than using the first person plural. The pronoun "we" creates a group, simultaneously gives it a spokesperson, and conjures up the foundations of unity. For Cánaves, "we" designated a majority: those who had not, so far, been victimized. Similarly, for the Mexican President, "we" were the majority who wanted order and peace. "Do we [law abiding people] allow sexually violent predators back into our community?" asked a criminal justice advisor.[10] "We [US society] do not have drive-by poisonings or drive-by knifings, but we do have drive-by shootings," wrote a researcher.[11] "We are [all] still hostages in our own city," complained a Mexican NGO.[12] The formulations were general but meaningful, nonetheless. They evoked large groups, sometimes referred to as "society," "the community," and "citizens,"[13] or designated by national/local identity (Canadians, Venezuelans, Angelenos, *bonaerenses*, [inhabitants of Buenos Aires], etc.).[14] And they gave them possessions: "our community," "our cities," "our children," "our police," "our safety," and so on.[15] As the terms of reference moved from the first to the third person, the emotive dimension of group cohesion was lessened—it is stronger to say "we are hostages..." than to say "Mexicans are hostages...," for example—but the notion of the collective was still solidly present: "these criminal groups are the 'most powerful' enemy that Mexico confronts," said the President;[16] "Canadians are growing concerned about the rate of youth criminal activity and the seriousness of these crimes," declared the Justice Minister;[17] "how long is the government going to play with the lives of the citizens of Buenos Aires?" asked another letter-writer to Argentina's *La Nación*.[18]

These different semantic devices were sprinkled through the texts, providing occasional, but important, invocations of the collective dimension. Even the following type of news item was not entirely devoid of collective significance:

> Metro Briefing | New York: State Crime Rates Continued To Fall In 2005
> Overall crime rates continued to decline in New York last year, as vehicle thefts dropped almost 13 percent, although robberies edged up from 2004, according to a F.B.I. report. The rate of violent crime in New York increased 1.2 percent, similar to the 1.3 percent increase nationally. The level of crimes tracked by the F.B.I. declined 3 percent from 2004, largely because of a 12.7 percent drop in motor vehicle thefts and a 3.8 percent decline in property crime.[19]

Its content was clearly of interest and potential concern to the paper's readers—New Yorkers—otherwise it would not have been published.

Most frequently, a text would include one or two direct references to the collective dimension, often at the beginning or the end. For example, a commentary by two law professors in the *New York Times* on proposals for the civil commitment of sex offenders focused nearly all of its 800 words on arguments against such a policy. The authors went into considerable detail about the costs involved, and the failure to consider alternative measures that are arguably more effective in reducing reoffending. These were academics who had clearly studied the matter and felt sufficiently strongly about it to write to the paper. But any possibility that readers would see this critical commentary simply as the particular hobbyhorse of the authors was dispelled by the penultimate sentence: "Everyone agrees that we have a moral obligation to prevent as many sex crimes as possible with the resources available."[20] Here, the existence of the moral community was partly assumed, partly called forth.

Similarly, an article in *El Nacional* combined anecdotes and statistics to provide a picture of the fear of crime among Venezuelans. While fear of crime might be seen as an individual trait (as someone else's problem), a comment from a leading researcher halfway through the 880-word text was enough to confirm what was elsewhere always implied: "Violence can take your life and creates a feeling of fear which makes us lose freedom. That is a generalized phenomenon."[21] Here, "your life" did not mean the reporter's life, or the reader's; it meant anyone's life. The "us" who lose freedom were not the researcher and the reporter, or the researcher, reporter, and readers; they were everyone. The allusion to a "generalized phenomenon" was also an evocation of the collective dimension, but without specification. Generalized among whom? Where? An answer did not seem to be necessary; precision might have been seen as pedantic. If pressed, the researcher would doubtless have fallen back on the types of term already identified: "Venezuelans," "society," and so on. The power of the first person plural to conjure up a community resides partly in the vagueness of its membership.

Collective concern

The "Metro Briefing" on New York crime rates, transcribed above, was written in the neutral tone that is typical of bureaucratic data reporting. (Its source was explicitly acknowledged as the FBI). There were no emotions, no value judgments, here. Although the text referred to "crime," "robberies," "motor vehicle theft," and so on (all terms with a negative moral valence), there was no hint of a moral stance. There was no satisfaction expressed that overall crime rates had declined, no lament that violent crime rates had increased. This briefing was based on the notion of a community, but it would be for New Yorkers (or others) to give it explicit moral significance by making its content their concern.

Evidence of such concern, for whether things were going well or badly, is easily found in other texts on the very same subject (crime rates in New York).

16 *Making crime "our" concern*

For example, at the end of 2007, the *New York Times* wrote an editorial on the police's "excellent year" (in bringing down the city's crime).[22] A criminologist wrote that New York had "*enjoyed* a decade and a half of steadily declining crime," which he characterized as "the largest and longest municipal *winning streak* in the recorded history of crime control in the United States."[23] On the negative side, reporters noted that: "...digging deeper into the city's numbers uncovers some *worrisome* trends. Crime committed by young people, including murder, is rising."[24]

Concern was not, therefore, ubiquitous in commentary about crime. It materialized in value judgments that varied in the form and force with which they were expressed. Liliana Cánaves, for example, wrote of "the black wand of insecurity," and "the soul-hurting experience of being wounded for life;" the *Los Angeles Times* wrote of "a plague of gun violence in California."[25] The *New York Times* referred to "worrisome trends;" a Mexican minister spoke of "the seriousness of the [drug dealing] problem."[26] These were terms of censure. "Excellent year" and "winning streak" were terms of approval (as was the more generic "good news"). But value judgements were also revealed in prescriptions, in statements about what should, or should not, be done. "We should not ... abandon ... [the insanity] defense," wrote two US legal experts;[27] "Toronto should learn from Boston's approach [to gangs]," argued a Canadian religious leader;[28] "the will to help has to be accompanied by a realization that it is not a problem for some ... but for all," urged a Venezuelan bishop.[29] The range of semantic variation was vast.

Moreover, as Cánaves' letter revealed, concern could be individual *as well as* collective ("What do I do.... What can we do...?"). And in some cases concern could be individual *rather than* collective: "*Señor Director*: As an ordinary citizen who does not want drugs to kill our youth, I propose..."[30] Granted, this writer spoke of "our youth" (a collective possession) and thereby made some connection with the collective domain, but his stance was explicitly personal: it was his concern (that drugs should not kill youth), not "ours." Even the use of the first person plural may refer to an organizational, rather than collective, concern. "What we don't like to see ... is the violence that erupts when they [drug dealers] can't come to a letter of understanding or memorandum of agreement," commented the Calgary Police Chief, referring to something that (apart from the dealers themselves) only drug enforcement officers would be in a position to see. Collective concern materialized only when value judgments were made in the name of a community. But collective concern was much more frequent, at least in this set of texts, than individual or organizational manifestations of concern.

Discursively, many instances of concern were superficial. Declining crime rates were "good news," a "winning streak," or something to be "enjoyed." Rising crime rates were "worrisome," "troubling," or "alarming." Crime was a "problem," or a "plague." And this was all that was expressed. But value judgments are implicitly relational propositions: crime is only a problem or a plague because of its negative effects on someone or something, or because it reflects some other situation that requires attention. Concern is as much about the entity affected as it is about crime itself. These brief manifestations of approval or censure were pointers to underlying objects of solicitude, to the social bases on which collective concern was established and nourished. This concern was variously directed to others, to "ourselves," or to the collectivity. It also extended to "our responses" to crime.

Concern for others

The death of Jane Creba, a teenager caught by gunfire between groups of young men on a street in downtown Toronto on December 26, 2005 (Boxing Day), shocked Torontonians. The outrage and concern were not because she was white, argued Margaret Wente (a columnist), but because she was an innocent bystander who "got shot in broad daylight, in the heart of mainstream Canada, on a day when millions of people go out to shop and have fun."[31] In other words, she was a conventional person, in a conventional place, doing a conventional thing. She was shopping with her sister. She had no moral stain, no connection with either of the groups in conflict, no plausible culpability for her own death.

There was renewed public reflection in Canada about the dangers of guns, particularly in the hands of juvenile gangs, and renewed criticism of the "gangsta culture" that was seen to breed violence. But the indignant censure of gangs and young people that can so easily follow an event like this hardly materialized (at least in the *Globe and Mail*). There was, instead, a conscious attempt to understand what was happening to young people in Canada's cities.

Almost two weeks after Jane Creba's death, a Toronto community worker spoke to the media:

> For nearly two decades, Monica Willie has fought to keep young black men in Toronto from crime by going into the streets and talking to them, building trust and challenging them to take charge of their lives. "They fear me, not police, because they know I respect them," she said at a news conference at city hall yesterday. "These are not animals. They are young black men that have been put into a vicious system that needs to change."... "I've been saying for years that this would escalate, and the violence would reach the other side," Ms. Willie said. Referring to the shooting death on Yonge Street of white teenager Jane Creba, she said, "Now that young girl on Boxing Day has paid the ultimate price, and people are making noise."... "We're going to ask... [young blacks] to put their guns down, to turn them in and plead with them to turn their lives around because they are valuable to us," Ms. Willie said. "Some of these kids are too far gone for help, but so many are just being initiated into this lifestyle and we need to rescue them. We have to." Taj Nelson, 27, is one of the men who turned his life around after meeting Ms. Willie three years ago.... "These kids are intelligent and have talent, but have too much time to themselves and need choices," Mr. Nelson said. "When I look at their faces, man, I feel like I've failed them, too. We all need to be in this together."[32]

This is just one, but undoubtedly the best, example of concern for the offenders, and others like them, in the instant case. That concern, fairly obviously, sprang from the perception that they, also, were victims: "These are not animals. They are young black men that have been put into a vicious system...," said Monica Willie; into "the social conditions that breed violence—unemployment, exclusion, disparity," said the Toronto Police Chief.[33] As Ms. Willie commented, "...so many [kids] are just being initiated into this lifestyle and we need to rescue them." While nothing could be done for Jane Creba, and perhaps not much for her family, something certainly could be done for the kind of young people who had caused the problem, and both Monica Willie and Taj Nelson were clear about the need for a collective commitment to this task: "We all need to be in this together."

The treatment of offenders as victims is the most striking manner in which concern for others is shown; but it is also the most infrequent, because it crosses the moral divide and converts the likely targets of opprobrium into objects of sympathy. Nevertheless, it also reveals the obvious underpinning for any expression of concern for others: their identification as victims. More typical expressions of concern for young people viewed them as victims (or potential victims) of crime and deviance rather than as victims of social conditions. For example, talking to a reporter about crime in Mexican schools, a government spokesperson commented: "Very young children come into contact with drugs. Therefore, we, as a society, including parents and the authorities, have to think through deeply to a position of the utmost importance in order to combat this crime."[34] *El Universal* editorialized that: "While the authorities and society in general focus on the growing problem of drug trafficking and its associated violence, alcoholism advances unchecked and preys on our adolescent boys and girls."[35] The Lieutenant Governor of Texas declared that the death penalty "sends a message to those monsters who want to hurt our children: 'Not in Texas,'"[36] while a doctor wrote that: "As a surgical resident, I see the ravages of this violence, which robs our young people of life and happiness."[37]

Throughout these newspaper items, children and young people were the most commonly recurring "others" about whom concern was expressed. But additional groups were also mentioned. Some were defined geographically by the area they lived in, for example, those in the North of Mexico,[38] or along its southern border;[39] those who were tied to Toronto's Kensington Market;[40] or who were living in Canada's Northern Territories.[41] The latter location highlighted crimes that particularly affected aboriginal groups. These, and other minorities (blacks, Hispanics, etc.), constituted a category that was of broader concern in Anglo-America, but not in Latin America. Thus, a letter writer to the *Los Angeles Times* explicitly articulated the relationship between the "empowered majority" and the minorities victimized by hate crimes:

> Within our society, hate crimes can be thought of as acts of war on a particular segment of the population, identifiable by the history of hostile treatment they received from the empowered majority. When the empowered

majority recognizes a population as having been victimized in such a manner, it is appropriate to grant it protection. It is also a statement that we as a society are serious when we renounce such crimes.[42]

If one regional difference was the absence of references to minorities in Latin America, another was the presence of concern for crime victims (either singly, or as a group) among Latin American commentators, something that was not frequently found in Anglo-American commentary. For example, a mayoral plan for preventing crime in Caracas was prefaced by the following principle: "So that the country turns a page on crime and this scourge ceases to put 44 families in mourning every day, society should involve itself in the oversight of criminal justice."[43] More dramatically, and referring to an incident not unlike that which killed Jane Creba, a Caracas resident referred to the death of a 16-year-old girl, also caught in crossfire, and asked: "Who will answer to these parents afflicted by the death of their daughter?"[44] Similarly, Liliana Cánaves' letter expressed solidarity with "the struggle of those who were touched by the black wand of insecurity."

These latter comments reveal most plainly a distinction between "us" and "them" that underlies the concern for others: "they" are victims and "we" are not. As such, "they" invite attention, sympathy, compassion, worry, help, and other solidary reactions. "The matter of weapons will continue to be a concern for many," reported *El Nacional* in relation to violence between children.[45] "Are we failing our most disadvantaged kids? Damn right," wrote one columnist.[46] "I have a five-year-old and have seen first hand some of the appalling conditions other children his age live in," said a Toronto resident; "If we just wait until after they have committed crimes, it is too late."[47]

That sympathy and solidarity can be the basis of concern was also used by some who saw themselves as particularly victimized to try to gain the support of the majority. This was a uniquely Latin American phenomenon. For example, the kidnapping, in one of Venezuela's southern states, of a prominent local cattle rancher moved the entire business sector to raise its voice in protest—"we are the raw material for crime"—and demand effective measures from the government. But appeals were also made to the public:

> Business leaders called for the whole collectivity of Guayana to join a motorcade today which will be called A Light for Life, and will set out from the Chamber of Construction.... Tomorrow, all the churches in Ciudad Guayana will offer prayers for the release of the rancher.[48]

Similarly, a trio of violent crimes in the Argentine city of Mendoza triggered local protests, together with demands for government to do more to prevent crime. In addition, a local businessman pressed the claim for national attention to the problem: "The whole country should know that they are killing us in Mendoza, because there are more and more murders with greater impunity."[49]

Changing tack, in Tijuana, Mexico, César Cázares, the leader of the local Chamber of Commerce, argued that business was the sector most affected by crime and kidnapping. But rather than simply asking for collective concern about the victimization of business people, he suggested that everyone should be concerned for their own safety:

> The leader of the Chamber of Commerce ... argued that business has been hardest hit by crime and that it now also suffers the ravages of kidnapping. He therefore recommended that citizens take care of themselves and even change their routines to avoid falling into the hands of kidnappers...[50]

This rather ambivalent approach revealed the ever present possibility, clearly anticipated by Liliana Cánaves, that victimization would not only affect others but also ourselves ("I cannot say that this is never going to happen to me."). As Margaret Wente commented in relation to Jane Creba's death: "...if she's not safe, who is?"[51] When the matter was framed as one of safety, it easily became a focus of both personal and collective concern. Now the worry was not about others, but about ourselves.

Concern for ourselves

An opinion column written by Rodolfo Tuirán, a Mexican academic, began as follows:

> Safety and public order are necessary conditions for guaranteeing both the adequate functioning of society and the exercise of civil liberties and rights. Nevertheless, from day to day we Mexicans see with annoyance how crime and violence have been able to spread themselves everywhere: they take over streets, stroll in parks and markets or roam along highways and byways. On their march, these social ills fracture community networks, lower sociability in communities and put people's lives, wellbeing and property at risk. As a result, insecurity has become one of the most important concerns of citizens.[52]

Of course, "insecurity" does not refer here to a lack of personal confidence, as often implied by the English usage of the term. Rather, it alludes to a lack of safety, to a crime-related strain of the ontological insecurity frequently discussed by social scientists.[53] Crime and violence are antithetical to safety, and "insecurity" becomes a shorthand reference to them—both in this article and many others in the set of texts compiled for this study.[54]

The semantic switch from crime to insecurity carries with it an important change in perspective. While crime refers to incidents, insecurity implies a condition. People are either the targets of crime, or they are not, but everyone is subject to insecurity: crime is a threat; everyone is at risk. Here is how Tuirán explicated the situation in his second paragraph:

> The Third National Survey on Insecurity undertaken by ICESI (the Citizens' Institute for Insecurity Studies [an NGO]), indicates that during 2004 there

were about 11.8 million alleged crimes (approximately 22 per minute), of which about three quarters were robberies. In essence, the available figures confirm that each year crime affects a significant number of victims (11 per 100 persons) and households (13 per 100 households), while they also suggest that the experience of suffering a crime incident could, sooner or later, reach all of us.

In other words, everyone is subject to insecurity; the only possible variance lies in whether crime will "reach ... us" sooner or later.

How, then, could crime *not* be linked to concern for ourselves? As if there were any doubt about this, Tuirán offered a portrait of generalized fear and anxiety:

> This painful reality feeds the perceptions of insecurity among millions of people who, today, live in a kind of citizenship of fear.... The almost generalized perception of insecurity has forced different segments of the population to construct ... a kind of agoraphobia, that is, a fear of public spaces. For Mexicans, to go out on the street has increasingly become an adventure. In fact, according to the same survey by ICESI, a considerable proportion of citizens thinks that public transport is the most dangerous place (59%), followed by streets, highways, markets and shopping malls.
>
> All of these realities and perceptions of insecurity in Mexico are a source of anxieties which have converted people into victims of their own fear. For fear of robberies and aggression, many Mexicans get home as early as possible or simply "don't do things" in order to avoid risks.
>
> Thus, people frequently avoid going out at night, visiting relations, taking a taxi, using public transport or carrying money or credit cards.

Here, the motivation for collective concern lay in the fact that many people shared the same fears and anxieties about crime—enough to be able to talk about "we Mexicans," as Tuirán did at the start of the article. It was a justification for commentary on crime that was frequently found in Latin America. For example, when *El Nacional* ran a series of articles on "Territories of Insecurity" and prefaced them with an editorial (subtitled "When no one is untouched"), its first line read: "A subject that affects each and every one of the residents of the Metropolitan Area and, in general, throughout the country, will be addressed in detail by *El Nacional* in forthcoming issues."[55] Unsurprisingly, it also included a reference to opinion surveys: "Insecurity occupies first place among the things that keep Venezuelans awake at night. Surveys repeatedly show this." Similarly, an editorial from *La Nación* took a very similar tack:

> Insecurity: Much More than Figures
> A recent research study showed clearly the horrifying situation of insecurity that we Argentines live in, beyond the heightened social-thermal sensation derived from some incidents which, because of their spectacular nature, have captured the attention of public opinion.

> In effect, according to a report from the New Majority Studies Center, the crime rate in Argentina has increased 53 per cent during the last year compared to 1995 and 121 per cent compared to two decades ago.[56]

An Argentine columnist expressed the case for concern even more dramatically: "For the fearful majority, the big national matters today begin with ensuring that life ends when decided by God, not by an outlaw."[57]

In Anglo-America, concern about crime based on collective self-interest was similarly constructed but much less frequent. In a miniature reproduction of the Latin American notion of insecurity, "danger," "threat," "fear," "risk," and similar terms were invoked to spread the problem to all. A Canadian columnist captured the essence of this mindset in two short sentences: "The public perception is that crime rates are rising. We should be vigilant and fearful."[58] "Considering the vile nature of sex crimes, the public is right to be concerned about its vulnerability to predators on parole," editorialized the *Los Angeles Times*.[59] Similarly, police chiefs attempted to garner political support for increased funding by arguing that crime would shortly be affecting everyone again:

> "We are here to say 'America, we have a problem,'" Los Angeles Police Chief William J. Bratton told the Police Executive Research Forum in Washington last month. "Crime is coming back and it has a new and troubling element ... a youthful population that is largely dissociated from the mainstream of America."[60]

And the Mayor of Trenton, New Jersey, told the same meeting: "We need a national movement which recognises that while homeland security is important, hometown security is equally important."[61]

Concern for the collectivity

At one point in his column, Tuirán introduced a rather different kind of concern in relation to crime. Following his comment that "people frequently avoid going out at night, visiting relations, taking a taxi, using public transport or carrying money or credit cards," he added:

> For the same reason, security measures proliferate in the cities and are most visible in gated residential communities. These communities not only restrict free access and privatize public spaces; they also turn cities into areas that are increasingly fragmented, divided and segregated.[62]

His argument was that self-interest (the search for protection from crime) at the neighborhood level produces its own problem: the fragmentation of social interaction. Here the object of concern was not "ourselves" (a collection of individuals confronting the same problem) but the social unit to which all belong, and which, in true sociological fashion, transcends its constituent parts. Not infrequently, concern about crime was expressed in relation to some form of collective entity, thereby providing the most direct and immediate foundation for collective morality.

In early August 2007, three young men were killed, execution-style, in a "quiet" Newark, New Jersey, neighborhood. The sister of one of the victims was also shot, but survived. These were people who were studying, or about to start, at university. According to the *New York Times*, the shootings shook the city of Newark, and the paper itself was moved to editorialize about this incident which had occurred in its own backyard:

> Newark has seen hundreds of senseless killings over the years, but few have shaken its weary residents like last weekend's brutal murders of three young people and the shooting of a fourth. One can only hope that the savagery of this latest crime will at last bring the city together in a new determination to end the bloodshed...
>
> Police have arrested a 15-year-old and a 28-year-old man. But the killings are a horrible reminder of how much more Mayor Cory Booker needs to do to deliver on his campaign pledge to reduce violent crime. Though shootings, rapes and many other major crimes are down significantly, the number of murders, 60 so far, is almost what it was last year, when Newark's murder rate was the highest in a decade.
>
> When Mr. Booker took office 13 months ago there were high hopes—in Newark and nationally—that he would bring the city together and turn it around. The killings have dimmed those hopes and further divided the city.... [H]e owes it to everyone to renew his efforts to end the mayhem and crack down on the underlying problem of gang activity.... The effort to end the violence will succeed only if everyone pitches in. And Newark cannot even begin its hoped for comeback until it is viewed as a safe city.[63]

The background to these killings was not given, except for a vague reference to "gang activity" towards the end of the text. Neither did the editorial dwell on the victims, although it mentioned their names, ages and educational aspirations. Similarly, little attention was given to the suspects who were arrested, except to mention their age and gender. This was not a text in the spirit of Monica Willie's comments following the death of Jane Creba; it was not based on a concern for either the victims or the aggressors. Nor did it reveal any fear or apprehension about the possibility of violence becoming a threat to Newark residents in general (a vicarious materialization of "ourselves"): the editorial confined the "mayhem" to gang activity, which was perceived to be a highly localized phenomenon. The concern was for Newark, an unfortunate city which had suffered "hundreds of senseless killings," and whose current murder rate was "the highest in a decade." That Newark needed to be "turned around" (to make a "comeback") clearly signalled its embarrassing trajectory: violence was a reflection of its moral ill-health, and needed to be curbed in order to restore a picture of well-being. This task could only be achieved "if everyone pitches in."

Other cities also became the object of concern when their moral course was in question. For example, a Canadian evangelist commented that: "If we tackle [drugs], we will have Toronto the Good again;"[64] while San Bernardino, California, was "edging toward unwelcome notoriety" because of a jump in homicides.[65] Sometimes, the concern was not so much for a disreputable image but for the negative consequences that could flow from it. For example, Alfredo Babún, another businessman from Tijuana, Mexico, felt that: "Press reports on violence, which are not few in number, surely reach investors in other places. Insecurity has been one of the main inhibitors of the state [Baja California] and has forced businessmen to abandon this border."[66]

As often as cities, the country provided the framework for collective concern. Speaking only days after Jane Creba's death, Canada's Conservative leader outlined its significance for the nation:

> Mr. Harper said Canadians deserve to be proud of the country's reputation for safe streets, safe communities and low crime rates. "But we are learning, even in the midst of this campaign, that these things cannot be taken for granted. The Canadian way of life and those proud traditions of safety and security are today threatened by a rising tide of drugs, gangs and guns."[67]

Another political hopeful, this time in Latin America, also called attention to his country's difficulties: "Venezuela is colored red, because they have allowed guerrillas and paramilitaries to operate here; they have let the mafia come in to rob and steal vehicles; they have let contract killings, protection payments and crime develop..."[68] Similarly, "One in three juvenile delinquents commits a further crime," editorialized *El Universal*; "One in three. If this trend continues Mexico's future is at risk."[69]

Alternatively, the collectivity may have simply been "society," "the country," or "the nation:"

> If all we elders can do is to keep reviving the century-old fear of youth and minorities while ignoring the serious crime threat in older generations, then maybe we would be better off turning the country over to young people.[70]

Concern for "our" response

Speaking of kidnappings and violence in the frontier region of Tijuana, Mexico, César Cázares treated them as a form of insecurity, as a threat to the whole community. Alfredo Babún saw them as a problem for business and investment in the city and the surrounding state. José María Ramos, a local researcher, had the following to say about them:

> ... he warned that it is time that society demanded that the authorities do what they are supposed to, otherwise the problem will get increasingly serious.... [He] said that the population should call for an efficient and

responsible government, one that deals with a problem that is getting more serious every day in the state, before incidents happen such as the assassination of three police officers, who were kidnapped by about a hundred men in plain daylight and were later tortured and beheaded. Ramos García insisted that the citizen plays a fundamental role, particularly because the creation of citizen councils for public safety coincided with an increase in insecurity.[71]

One thing of note here was Ramos' injunction for citizens to show concern—yet another testimony to the possibility, and reality, that collective attention is not a given. But the other interesting thing about his call is that the object of concern was not the victims of these crimes, the wider community, or the region. Rather, he was urging people to engage with responses to crime, either by demanding better governmental action or (more implicitly) by getting involved in citizen councils. The political system and the criminal justice system became the focus of concern.

In fact, both these domains were quite frequently treated as collective possessions. They were "ours," with the implication that "we" should be attentive to them. Here is an Argentine columnist writing about the difficulties of dealing with insecurity:

> Like all governments in the world, ours also has police and the military. But how does it treat them?... What feelings do our leaders have regarding them?... It is immediately evident that, with the growing audacity of criminals who daily kidnap, rob, rape and kill on our streets, we Argentines need a police force that is incomparably more effective than that which we have.[72]

Similarly, when Joe Domanick, a US researcher and journalist, published a critique of California's sentencing policy, he titled it "A prison of our own making."[73] How did "we" make this prison? Through votes for legislators and policies that brought in tougher and longer sentences, Domanick argued. That prisons and criminal justice could be a collective responsibility (and an object of reflection) for concerned citizens was confirmed by subsequent letters to the *Los Angeles Times*:

> Re "A prison of our own making," Current, Dec. 10
> Californians can see that "get tough on crime," if it means only longer sentences, is a cure worse than the disease. So, in 2000, we passed Proposition 36 for drug rehab by a large majority. Voters need to learn that "felony" nowadays means some politician trying to look tough by morphing misdemeanors—the same petty crimes with a punishment on steroids...
> *
> Joe Domanick is right on target, but our legislators and governors have ignored the experts for years and have kept the stay-the-course policies that have built the crisis in our prison system. Change will occur only when we

address the two badly needed solutions that can turn this disaster around: sentencing and parole reform. Wasted tax dollars could be returned to a cost savings, making our state safer by developing sentences that fit the crimes.[74]

The first letter visualized the collective response to crime in terms of voters ("Californians"), who should be wary of politicians. The second was equally critical of political representatives but nonetheless seemed to include them as part of the notional community ("Change will only occur when *we* address..."). Ramos, in Tijuana, envisaged a model in which government and citizens are separate entities, but each with a role to play in responding to crime. Politicians, meanwhile, generally included themselves within the collectivity: "...what we have tried [with gangs] for the last 25 years has not been working," complained a councilwoman in Los Angeles;[75] "[w]e have to deal with this issue that maybe we can't do anything with [sex offenders]," urged a state senator in New York;[76] "they [the United States] demand security on the border as much as we [Mexicans] do," commented the Mexican President.[77]

Discursively, concern with the response to crime was frequently self-contained, in the sense that its moral justification was not explicated. However, its roots in the other types of concern already explored in this chapter were readily evident. Recall, for example, the mayoral plan for preventing crime in Caracas, justified by a concern for victims ("others"): "So that the country turns a page on crime and this scourge ceases to put 44 families in mourning every day, society should involve itself in the oversight of criminal justice."[78] "[W]hile homeland security is important, hometown security is equally important," said the Trenton Mayor, invoking a concern for "ourselves." (In additional comments, the Detroit Mayor said: "We need a serious strong national engagement on this problem."[79]) Concern for Newark's image as a violent city led to hopes of "a new determination to end the bloodshed," to the call for "everyone to pitch in."[80] In sum, concern for "our response" was based on an underlying concern for others, for ourselves, or for the collectivity.

Drawing back

Discursively, collective concern for crime was conjured up in numerous ways. It was invoked most directly through the use of the first person plural; it was brought into play by allusions to "everyone;" it materialized in references to "society." These modes of expression were not omnipresent; indeed, in terms of overall word count they were quite infrequent. But they appeared with unfailing regularity in the sample of texts, confirming that these were habitual ways of talking (or writing) and thinking about crime. Rather like threads that occasionally appear in a fabric, they surfaced from time to time to reveal the collective warp that runs through much commentary on crime; one which commentators might have laid bare if pressed to account for their choice of words. Their conventionality and importance were underlined by the criticism that occasionally flared up against individualism and indifference.[81] While some commentators expressed individual concerns about crime, no commentator ever argued that crime should be treated as a private trouble.

Discursively, concern about crime materialized in expressions of censure and approval, or prescriptions about what should (or should not) be done. Many were perfunctory, involving nothing more than a passing reference to the collective dimension and to some troublesome, or welcome, news about crime, or the response to it. Somewhat fuller elaborations identified specific targets for collective concern—others, ourselves, the collectivity, our responses—and discussed them, either singly or in combination. The degree of explication was, however, always incipient: these texts were dotted with morally significant phrases and comments, but newspaper commentary was not the place for moral treatises. It was, nonetheless, an important site for the materialization of collective morality.

Perhaps because of the routine and unobtrusive manner in which collective concern is conjured up, the way in which crime (or any other social phenomenon) becomes "our" concern has been largely unexamined. Nevertheless, there are many points of resonance between the findings reported here and the materials and results produced by other researchers, particularly those working within the social problems and social movements traditions. Thus, when scholars have given space to public commentary about a particular condition, the discursive formulae identified in this chapter are readily found. For example, a US senator complained about "*our* ... lack of compassion and real understanding for [the] difficult problem [of runaways];"[82] a pro-life speaker in Scotland told his audience: "what *one* has to make up *one's* mind about on this issue, is, is the unborn child a fellow human or not?;"[83] a prominent social problems scholar even used the collective formulation himself: *Random Violence: How We Talk About New Crimes and New Victims.*[84] More generally, linguists,[85] discourse analysts,[86] and even legal scholars[87] have noted the use (and ambiguity) of "we-talk"[88] and associated terms.

Similarly, in the frames that emerge from scholarly analysis of social problems, the orientations of concern to others, ourselves, the collectivity, and our responses, can also be found. Sympathy and compassion for the plight of others is a common emotional stance,[89] which has been extended to, for example, runaway children,[90] children more generally,[91] boys,[92] youth,[93] prostitutes,[94] wives of abusive husbands,[95] the elderly,[96] and animals.[97] As Loseke points out,[98] and Clark implies,[99] sympathy will be extended only where others are considered to be blameless. Often, blamelessness is explicitly acknowledged through a focus on vulnerability,[100] and collective concern is buttressed by the perception that those affected are unable to fend for themselves: they need protection because they cannot protect themselves.[101] Such concern divides the community into two segments ("ourselves" and "others") while binding them together as one.[102]

Concern may also be expressed for the welfare or interests of all members of the notional community, including the speaker (i.e., "ourselves"). Risk is a direct way of expressing this concern[103] and is reflected in the attribution of randomness to troubling events,[104] the metaphoric reference to "epidemics," or the tense claim that "this could happen to anyone."[105] Some scholars have described this type of concern as "the democratization of the condition's occurrence,"[106] the "universalization of social problems,"[107] or the creation of "equal opportunity problems,"[108] rather cynically implying that a concern for all cannot be sincere because events are never randomly distributed. At bottom, this critique privileges statistical reasoning over subjective perceptions of risk; but the latter can be extraordinarily powerful. For example, Albert described how Rock Hudson's announcement that he had AIDS "transformed [AIDS] overnight from *someone else's problem*, a 'gay plague,' to a cause of international alarm."[109]

Concern is also expressed for the more abstract entities called "community," "society," or "the nation," which sometimes require care, protection or remedial work. "People who deviate" may be seen as "threats to the community;"[110] child victims of satanic cults are sometimes portrayed as "a significant threat to society at large during their adulthood;"[111] while conservatives have argued that the "gay agenda" could place the future of the nation at stake.[112] More symbolically, the moral health of the community may be in question: environmental contamination in Canada was described as "horrific ... it's a national issue and, quite frankly a bit of a national shame;"[113] abortion in the United States was seen as a "national sin;"[114] while drug use in Singapore was seen to reflect "the erosion of moral and ethical values."[115] Similarly, Girling *et al.* wrote of "[t]he development of reputations and place-myths ... [which are] materially crucial to the declining or ascending paths of neighbourhoods and towns..."[116]

Finally, concern may focus on the deficiencies in systemic or societal arrangements for helping individuals address the problems that affect them. Whether the individuals are others or ourselves, whether the problem is theirs or ours, the arrangements for dealing with them involve a collective dimension of responsibility. "Our schools are just not doing the job that we want ... we can't just take people off the street like they used to, we've got to have people we can train," said a Canadian business manager.[117] Toni Johnson argued that the criminal justice system was not doing anything about child sex offenders and insisted that "they can be ignored no longer."[118] She continued: "Perhaps with a better understanding of this population and their families we can create additional alternatives within the juvenile justice system which will benefit the community, the child and the families."[119] Similar postures are detectable in the mobilization to identify and respond to hate crimes.[120]

This rapid review suggests that the same entities appear as the focuses of collective concern in relation to a wide variety of phenomena. Nevertheless, the analysis of commentary from the Americas presented in this chapter also indicates that regional variations in focus or emphasis may exist. In this case, the key difference between Anglo-America and Latin America was the much greater prevalence of concern for others in the North and "ourselves" in the South. In Latin America, the discourse of insecurity universalized the impact of crime: "I cannot say that this is never going to happen to me." And based on that possibility, however remote, citizens (and commentators) saw themselves as individually *and* collectively confronting a common threat. The frequent reference to insecurity in Latin American commentary will cause little surprise to Latin Americanist scholars, who study societies that, in the words of de Sousa Santos, are "used to risk—with which [they have] lived for many years, long before the invention of the 'risk society'...."[121] Greater surprise will perhaps, come to those familiar with the literature on risk and post-modernity, which—on a superficial reading—suggests that individuals and collectivities in societies, such as those in Anglo-America, adopt a "calculative" or "actuarial" attitude to crime.[122] It could be that such an attitude was only weakly developed (or had weakened) in Anglo-America; it could be that, within an actuarial framework, the risk from crime was seen to be low. Either possibility might have lowered the concern for "ourselves."

Finally, if concern for responses is seen as an outgrowth of concern for others, ourselves, or the community, the existential anchor of this kind of morality in attention to one or more beings, whether real or imagined, is also made clear. While crime, or any other phenomenon, may be the immediate target for concern, it is the welfare of those people (or that society) affected by them which underlies the moral stance that materializes in emotions, sympathy, censure, prescription, and virtue. These are the stuff of which moral identities are made.

3 "We the good"

The website of the US Embassy in Mexico reports that Alejandro Gertz Manero is a lawyer and businessman who has spent his career between public life and the academe. He has been Secretary General of the National Institute of Anthropology and History, Secretary of Public Safety for Mexico City, and the first Secretary of Public Safety for the nation (appointed by President Vicente Fox in 2000). He has been a professor at several universities and is President of the University of the Americas in Mexico City. He is the author of various biographies and social or historical essays and writes opinion columns for several national dailies.[1]

There is a moral portrait here which the reader should bear in mind, and it is that of the *notable*—the Latin American term for those who have managed to blend substantive academic output with important public service, garnering sustained societal attention and considerable respect in the process.[2] To be a *notable* is not a formal designation. There is no selection committee, no award ceremony, nothing that can be put in a CV. *Notables* materialize only in conversations with power, being called upon by governments or spontaneously constituting themselves as groups to speak to power.[3] Individuals cannot elevate themselves to the category of *notables*; the label must be applied by others. But individuals can use presentational strategies that align with this culturally respected figure. The US Embassy's brief biographical sketch of Gertz Manero is one such presentation; his own entry in Wikipedia is another.[4] And his opinion columns are yet another.

In March 2006, Gertz Manero published the following essay in *El Universal*:

Victims and Victimizers
A great part of those of us who live in this country are harassed by a system that continually subjects us to its requirements, permits, licenses, authorizations, taxes on everything and for everything, together with a diabolical structure of verifications, certificates, identifications, identity cards and innumerable controls that have converted our existence into a merciless human servitude without defence.

In this universe of sieges, blockades and levies, woe to the "contributor" who fails to pay the water, electricity, Value Added Tax, Income Tax, road taxes, certifications, deductions, Social Security or the ISSSTE,[5] road tolls or airport "taxes," and all the tolls that we can imagine; while he is besieged by the premonition that very soon he will have to pay for the rarefied air that he breathes, for the ground that he walks on, before he is assaulted, or for the panorama that he sees, through the contamination, the propaganda and the graffiti.

In exchange for this ferocious net of levies and controls, the "public sector" practices irresponsibility as a system, and that is why the services of security and justice are truly deplorable, to say the least ... while at any window in a public office the lunatics in charge are loafing around in front of the immense "lines" of citizens, or they torture the "contributor" with tricks, requirements and obstacles, so as to convert every procedure into a bazaar for corruption and bribes...

[T]his multiplication of abuses, accompanied by an extraordinary waste of public resources, has been the daily reality of the country ever since the "Revolution" converted itself into "institutions", and that is how they have got us criminally into debt...

At the other extreme of this social spectrum, and as a result of this inequity and of the failure of "globalization" and the "neoliberalism" of the 80s, a new Mexico has been emerging, one that is energetic, unstoppable and augmented. A Mexico that is illegal, itinerant, *pirate* and informal, which now has many more workers than the captive formal sector employees, which *launders* its immense fortunes through mammoth construction projects, encouraging contraband, robbery, *piracy* and consumer fraud, while it enslaves its dependents, without the authorities daring to touch those "privileged" who have found in political clientelism and public corruption the perfect society for making progress, while they devour the country and annihilate the "contributors", who have to pay taxes for themselves and for those who do not "contribute" anything.

In that sector of privileged lawbreakers one also finds drug trafficking and organized crime, which represent another terrain of enormous wealth, of limitless corruption and immense social destruction, which settles its territorial quarrels and its relationships with official corruption through gunshots and on the street, transforming the country into a real battlefield, where each morning "law enforcement officials" and other competitors are found riddled with bullets.

This is how the country has been divided into two great universes, that of the victims and that of the victimizers, the first group being those who follow the law and remain within "the rule of law," receiving in exchange mistreatment, arrogance, insecurity and the gradual destruction of its wealth at the hands of the other growing and unstoppable social sector, which is that of illegality, drug trafficking and generalized crime, which nothing and no one can stop.

As one more result of this social schizophrenia, the elections for mayors and deputies were held in the State of Mexico, where the "victim" sector expressed itself through 5.5 million abstainers who did not vote or who filled their ballot slips with insults, while there were only 3.5 million "firm" votes, coming mainly from illegality and corruption, or from the never ending expectation of a change which never arrives...

Whoever believes that this is the way to design the political and social future of this country, has no idea what awaits us and of what will come when the exhaustion of our oil reserves and its fantasy prices, and the savings of our migrants, are drastically reduced and the "captive" sector is left in starvation, crushed by illegality, street businesses and organized crime.

(Doctor of Law)[6]

This essay was a sustained outpouring of moral indignation. Indeed, it was almost as if the indignation obliterated style, for the prose was very awkward, with interminably long sentences and a questionable use of punctuation. There was not the simplicity of words and the rhythm of repetition that could be found in Liliana Cánaves' letter to *La Nación*. Gertz Manero seemed angry, and his anger carried him along. Here was a social critic who might justify his style by the seriousness of the situation he depicted: law abiding people were in danger of being "crushed by illegality, street businesses and organised crime." The urgency of the threat might have precluded attention to eloquence. Moreover, Gertz Manero claimed a clarity of discernment that others did not seem to have: "Whoever believes that this is the way to design the political and social future of this country, has no idea what awaits us...." His was the voice of alarm among naïve believers in the status quo and the 5.5 million voters who had abstained in recent elections. In these circumstances he was nothing short of an oracle, truly a solitary, but highly prestigious, social figure—perhaps a *notable*.

Why, then, did he need to tell readers that he was also a doctor of law? Could it be that he thought that any institutional affiliation would undermine the singularity of his position as social critic? Or could it be the more mundane problem that he had too many institutional affiliations to fit at the end of an opinion column? Whatever the explanation, the fact that he signed as a doctor of law seems to suggest that he wished to reinforce his claim to respectability, one that was also advanced by the content and tone of his text.

Gertz Manero's portrait of Mexico was one of "social schizophrenia:" "the country has been divided into two great universes, that of the victims and that of the victimizers." The victims were the law abiding individuals who paid taxes, submitted to corruption, and witnessed violence and crime on a daily basis. The victimizers appeared to be everyone from the "lunatics" in charge of public offices and corrupt bureaucrats, through street sellers and purveyors of contraband, to drug traffickers and other organized criminals. And there was no doubt where Gertz Manero was located in this Manichean world; his first sentence spelled it out: "A great part of those of us who live in this country are harassed by a system..." He was one of the victims, not the victimizers; he was on the side of the good. The crucial and close relationship between morality and identity was made absolutely plain.

The division between victims and victimizers, between good and bad, was described more explicitly in this text than anywhere else in the set of items assembled for this study. But Gertz Manero was only articulating more forcefully than others a vision of the moral world that was very widespread. At the end of a two-week march to protest about crime, a Mexican business leader declared: "We live in an unbearable climate of insecurity. Only we are going to be able to free ourselves from the chains, we have to remember that we the good are more than they the bad."[7] A member of a Mexican NGO, who herself had been a crime victim, "[l]amented that society was not prepared [to deal with crime] because of fear: 'the bad people are certainly organized and we the good, who are greater in number, are not.'"[8] An Argentine opinion columnist wrote of "the challenge which lies in seeing how to deactivate crime and so allow honorable citizens to avoid living in fright;"[9] while *La Nación* editorialized about crime news that was "like a mallet which with very hard blows daily shapes the sense of impotence that overwhelms the honest in the face of the insidious battering of crime."[10]

Such explicit references to moral "universes" (to continue with Gertz Manero's term) were not frequent. Perhaps ten texts out of the 505 from Latin America included them. They were even less frequent in Anglo-America, where the single most direct allusions to moral universes in the sample were a Canadian pastor's comment that "If we tackle this [drugs], we will have Toronto the Good again,"[11] and a radio ad for guns which urged Houstonians to "arm against Katricians" (evacuees from Hurricane Katrina, some of whom were characterized as "liv[ing] off crime and getting the loot").[12] But, across the region, these brief and infrequent references to the good and the bad merely served to confirm what was everywhere always implicit: that those who wrote in, or spoke to, newspapers belonged to the realm of the good, while crime, and those involved in it, belonged to the realm of the bad. This chapter seeks to examine the nature of the "bad" and the "good," and the boundary that separated them.

Alterity

As reported in Chapter 2, Toronto community worker Monica Willie had the following to say about the accused in the case of Jane Creba's death: "These are not animals. They are young black men that have been put into a vicious system that needs to change in Toronto."[13]

"Not animals..." Why did she say this? Was it simply designed to make an argument by undercutting an overstatement? Would not the easy response be that she was merely saying the obvious; that creatures wielding guns have no place in zoology? But to do so would have been to elide the unsubtle portraits that were sometimes drawn of those who commit crime. No one may have actually called the accused "animals," but the repertoire of terms often used to describe those who commit crimes included some that invoked the imagery of animals, beasts, and untamed nature. Thus, on the same day that Ms. Willie was talking to the press, a political strategist commented that "*Feral, predatory*, brazen, inner-city gangs are something new to Canada."[14] Elsewhere, a columnist in Los Angeles described the city's skid row as "a place of ruthless predation and violence,"[15] while references to "brutal" crimes appeared in several items, including the report on murders in Newark featured in Chapter 2.[16] In a reptilian turn, the latest crime waves in the United States were also described as "more vicious and cold-blooded."[17] Similarly, in Latin America there was talk of "brutal insecurity,"[18] the "brutal murder of three police officers in La Plata,"[19] and the "brutal murder of the three Faddoul brothers" in Caracas.[20] There was even a Mexican insurance representative who likened those who commit crime to vermin: "The rats and cockroaches are emerging and coming to the state of Mexico…."[21] And several commentators characterized crime as a "monster," occasionally with a thousand heads.[22]

While these animalistic references were not particularly frequent, other commentators saw emotional, cognitive and behavioral qualities in perpetrators which would also seem to signal that they were not quite human either. If skid row was a place of "ruthless predation," in many ways it is the adjective that is more interesting than the noun. The "ruthless" individual is one without pity or compassion. The same commentator noted that: "Prostitution and drug use and trafficking were open and *shameless*."[23] Not only were the Newark murders "brutal," they were also "senseless,"[24] as was the violence affecting children and young people in some Californian neighborhoods[25] and in Canada.[26] The suffix "less," of course, denotes absence. These are words that portray those who commit crime as lacking important sentiments such as pity, compassion, and shame, and their behavior as actions that are devoid of any kind logic or motivation. As "vicious" actors,[27] they were devoid of morality.

Latin American commentators also spoke of "ruthless" crimes and criminals,[28] of "dissolute" individuals,[29] and of a "mentality [which is] always malignantly disposed."[30] Marcos Aguinis, an Argentine writer, explicitly invoked the notion of "barbarity" (that is, of inhumanity) to describe the occurrence of 22 rapes committed in one night in Greater Buenos Aires.[31] In so doing, he referred to one of the country's great literary figures, Domingo Faustino Sarmiento, who wrote a widely influential, and still much discussed work—*Facundo. Civilization and Barbarity*.[32] In it, Sarmiento counterposed the alleged "barbarity" of Argentina's mid-nineteenth century rural areas with the assumed "civilization" of the cities. Adopting this cultural lens, Aguinis argued that the situation was now reversed: barbarity had moved to the cities.

Powerful as these kinds of word were in depicting the lack of humanity attributed to those who commit crime, they did not appear with much frequency in the texts, surfacing only from time to time as samples of a semantic repertoire that was seemingly more fitted to other genres. Attributions of inhumanity to perpetrators may have been more likely in the consideration of specific incidents, such as the "senseless" and "brutal" murders in Newark or the "brutal" murder of the Faddoul brothers in Caracas. While mention of such incidents obviously arose in the course of more general commentary about crime, it was in the "spot reporting" devoted exclusively to a given incident that such vocabulary may have been used more frequently.

Far more prevalent in these commentaries was the use of one-dimensional referents to designate those who commit crime—so common as to appear normal and unremarkable. "Organized *criminals* are fuelling much of the crime problem," wrote the Canadian Minister of Justice and Attorney-General;[33] "*los delincuentes* [criminals] act with impunity" in the Caracas Metro, wrote a crime prevention expert.[34] "A black *gang member* shoots a Latino toddler point-blank in the chest," reported the *Los Angeles Times*;[35] "[y]oung people will protest about the 67,000 killed by *el hampa* [the underworld]," reported *El Nacional*.[36] "[S]top imprisoning these low-level [drug] *offenders*," urged the *New York Times*;[37] "the *narcotraficantes* [drug traffickers] on this [Mexican–US] border do not seek out God," observed a priest in Nuevo Laredo.[38] The vocabulary was not very varied,[39] and clearly had a pragmatic function in labelling those who committed crimes. But, to borrow a phrase from Foucault, these terms also became a "caricatural silhouette,"[40] empty of any content other than that of the criminal or deviant, as if a person could be the latter and nothing else.[41] If this vocabulary did not explicitly suggest inhumanity, neither did it recognize or acknowledge humanity.

The one-dimensional portrait of those who committed crimes—simply as those who committed crimes—was sustained by distancing and silencing. Proximity would have generated details that could all too easily have insinuated humanity and complicated the division between bad and good. "Criminals," "drug traffickers," and the like, were always somewhere else, never actually present in the physical or discursive space that was created or reproduced by newspaper text.

"There haven't been problems on this street, but it's all around us," declared a resident of San Bernardino, California.[42] "It's block by block around here," said a lab technician who lived in Brooklyn, New York. "The next block over can be a different world."[43] "According to ... Police Commissioner Carlos Capote, the majority of crimes reported in [Santa Mónica] are committed by people coming from El Valle and Petare," noted *El Nacional*, in Caracas.[44] Newspapers, and those who had a voice in them, sited themselves with the actual or potential victims, not with the perpetrators, even when the latter must have been very close indeed:

> In a neighbourhood notorious for poverty and street drugs, in a city reeling from gun violence, I have witnessed hope: a supportive housing project that peacefully rid its building of drug trafficking [wrote Joyce Young, a family mediator and circle facilitator in Toronto].
> Called in to help, I watched as a community circle was created—a joint effort by tenants, staff, police, a lawyer and private security. In six months, this diverse group became a team and the nightly number of people let into the building to buy crack dropped from 45 to five.
> The project, in Toronto's Regent Park, houses formerly homeless people who are trying to turn their lives around. They include survivors of childhood sexual abuse, people struggling with addiction or mental illness and

recent immigrants. They have all been on the street. They are people who share a street culture characterized by the despair of poverty and the victimization of violence. They also share fear and distrust, pain which they cover with the thin veneer of being cool and tough.

The director of the housing project asked me to co-ordinate a meeting between staff and tenants to deal with issues in the shared outdoor space, the courtyard. I suggested a circle process...

Our first meeting dealt with annoying issues of noise and garbage. But by the second, the fearsome issue of drug trafficking in the building was in our laps.

It began when a man, who had not attended before, swept in and said, "I just passed five junkies stoned out of their gourds. There are needles in the stairwell and people passed out in the laundry room. They're smoking up all over the place. And they're dangerous. I mean, you are good people, but I'm telling you: Don't mess with them. You get between a junkie and his stuff and you're dead, man. Real dead." He ranted for about five minutes and left...[45]

Drug traffickers and junkies were "in the building," but hardly in the rest of this lengthy article. The writer described the evolution of the meetings, the growing sense of empowerment, the consultations with the police and other agencies, the publicity given to the problem, and the involvement of a security firm. The apparent result was that the drug traffickers and junkies largely moved elsewhere and the tenants felt much safer.

The "major crack dealer" in the building never went to a meeting. "Two more tenants, whom I later learned were the small-time dealers, had joined the circle. One of them, whom I will call Tony, stayed for the whole meeting and did not say a single word. But he was listening." Listening perhaps, but voiceless.

[The other] small-time dealer, came in ... and started to talk. He had never been to the circle before.... He said, "I don't know many of you, but if I've ever frightened or intimidated you, which probably I have, I apologize. I'm trying to kick the drugs. I'm trying to turn my life around and it's really, really hard." Then he left.

Here was a voice of repentance, which spoke only briefly; but repentance was what it took to cross the divide between the drug dealers and the tenants.

"Trying to turn my life around" is a well-worn metaphor. It suggests a desire to stop moving away from the terrain of the good and an aspiration to move back towards it. Raising an intriguing moral ambiguity, the tenants were also described by Young as "trying to turn their lives around." Were they victims, or might they also have been criminals or deviants of some sort? Young's article worked hard to portray them as the "good people" (to use the ranting resident's phrase), not least because in "trying to turn their lives around" they could claim to have earned an entry ticket to the space and discourse of the good. Taj Nelson, who—in Chapter 2—accompanied Monica Willie at her press conference, was also described as having "turned his life around" after meeting her: "'She challenged me to change and I did. I was confused and not proud of who I'd become,' said Mr. Nelson, a youth worker who did not want to elaborate on his past troubles with the law."[46] Elaborating on those past "troubles" could have been enormously complicating for Mr. Nelson (it might have relocated him firmly in the terrain of the bad), or for the *Globe and Mail* and its readers (it might have provided a wealth of human detail, confusingly illuminating the convenient silhouette of "gang member"). Having "turned his life around," and become a youth worker, Mr. Nelson had re-crossed the boundary between bad and good.

Joyce Young's article aptly exemplified the position of "criminals" and "*delincuentes*" in commentaries on crime: widely mentioned, but rarely given a voice. A mere ten texts in the Anglo-American items and one in the Latin American items featured people who could be construed as criminal or deviant. In some cases, their problematic conduct was said to be behind them. They were "older" or "retired" gang members who were "through with shooting and all that,"[47] a convicted carjacker who now "wrote and published poetry" and had won a college scholarship,[48] or a "fallen judge," convicted of embezzlement, who wanted "to use his experience to promote the importance of rehabilitation in prison."[49] In others, they were still involved in crime, but could also claim some saving grace, as apologetic Tony did in Toronto ("trying to turn his life around"). A crack addict in Buenos Aires described how "The neighbors look down on you, they criticize and treat you like a *chorra* [thief]. Because *paqueros* [crack heads] steal, *but* they're not all alike; *I never stole.*"[50] "An alcoholic woman *smiles* at Officer Deon Joseph as he ambles down San Julian Street, once the heart of skid row depravity."[51] One report dealt with the vexed topic of shooting in self-defense, where citizens teetered between the roles of victim and offender and categorical moral judgments evaporated. Interestingly, even here, a man acquitted of attempted murder "could not be reached for comment."[52]

That they "could not be reached for comment" might be one way to explain the silence of "criminals" and "*delincuentes*." Pragmatic or moral concerns about the dangers of self-revelation would have played a role here, as might the practical difficulties confronting the media in finding and talking to those who would fit this label. But another explanation would see "criminals" and "*delincuentes*" as necessarily silent figures in this discursive portrait of the moral universe, the necessary representation of the bad which is functional to the identity and constitution of the good. "*These* are not animals," said Monica Willie, in an attack on the temptation to dehumanize the young men involved in Jane Creba's shooting; "these" "denoting things or persons actually or ideally *present or near.*"[53] They, the criminals and "*delincuentes*," existed somewhere else, beyond a boundary which could not allow them a voice. Because humanity is defined by nothing if not by voice.

Identity

As many scholars have pointed out, a portrait of alterity is an important means by which identity can be brought into being.[54] To speak (or write) of "them," the "criminals" and "*delincuentes*," is obviously to claim the virtue of law-abidingness for "me" or "us." If "they" are not fully human, clearly "we" are. But identity is not entirely achieved, as Corbey and Leerssen would argue, by "silhouetting it against a contrastive background of Otherness;"[55] indeed, in the present set of texts, it seems as if the Other was mainly a silhouette. Identity is also fashioned through attention to self,[56] through some indication—however fleeting and indirect—of who "we" are; otherwise "we" might be little more than reflections of silhouettes. In these commentaries on crime, identity was affirmed through sensibilities and the determination to act.

After the ranting resident had delivered his invective against junkies and left the meeting of Toronto's Regent Park residents:

> The group was in shock. A tenant (let's call her Jane) had been curled up in a fetal position, crying as the man spoke. When it was her turn to talk, she flew from fear into a rage—and bolted, in the process expressing the frustration many of the residents felt.[57]

"Rant," "shock," "crying," "fear," "rage." This meeting was a concourse of emotions. These were the reactions of people for whom drug use, and drug trafficking, evoked strong feelings of disapproval. Their moral sense was built out of sensibilities.

Similar reactions could be evoked by other crimes. Also writing in the *Globe and Mail*, Samantha Wilson reviewed a book about the "almost unbearable subject of child sexual abuse;" "a subject that is so shocking and disturbing that even a hardened true-crime reader would wince."

> From the beginning, this book charges at you by describing the horrific story of a six-year-old girl, caged, sexually abused and tortured at the hands of her father, who traded pictures and home-made movies capturing her pain to a community of pedophiles hiding within the Internet. But this is not the only stomach-turning case described. In fact, there are many.[58]

The references to "shocking and disturbing," to the "horrific story," and the "stomach-churning case," all confirmed that Ms. Wilson was not "hardened" and implied that no other reader would be. It was no coincidence that the author of the book being reviewed was described as a "passionate voice."

In Venezuela, the kidnappings and deaths (in separate incidents) of a prominent businessman, a reporter, and three upper-class boys and their chauffeur, produced nationwide outpourings of emotion:

The horror caused in the Venezuelan people by the killers of the distinguished businessman Filippo Sindoni, the Faddoul brothers and Mr. Miguel Rivas and the ... reporter Aguirre has not died away. While the spontaneous and legitimate protests have ceased, especially those from young people who shouted their indignation and demanded justice and security, the pain still remains like a burning ember in the hands of a people that feels threatened, unprotected, and betrayed.[59]

"Indignation" was a word used with some frequency across Latin America,[60] alongside more occasional references to "anxiety."[61] In Anglo-America, there was quite a lot of "shock."[62] Many of these words arose in commentary on specific crimes, as a reaction to vividly imagined events (however vague the details). When the focus moved to crimes in general, the level of emotional intensity dropped but did not necessarily disappear. Now, in both regions, there was "alarm" and "concern:"

> After reading Jeffery Simpson's article ... and the alarming statistic that 172 murders were committed with guns versus 205 with knives in 2004...
> (began a letter to the editor in Toronto)[63]

> One of the things that gives most cause for alarm is to see how the age for committing crime is coming down.
> (wrote a columnist in Mexico)[64]

> Of particular concern are organized-crime activities at airports.
> (said a Canadian police commissioner)[65]

> Insecurity is one of the principal concerns of *porteños* (inhabitants of Buenos Aires).
> (reported *La Nación*)[66]

> Despite a decrease in city crime, troubling signs emerge.
> (read a headline in the *New York Times*)[67]

> [T]he President announced that the crime problem is worrying him.
> (wrote the editors of *El Nacional*)[68]

These moral sensibilities were often accompanied by virtue:

> Mrs. Faddoul writes a wonderful letter to the kidnappers, dense with sincere and profound Christian feeling, in which she forgives the kidnappers and implores mercy from them and accepts with Christian resignation and profound faith what God wills. With this noble position of a sincere mother, brave and profoundly Christian, contrasts the small-minded attitude of government representatives...[69]

40 *"We the good"*.

In Toronto's Regent Park project:

> We discussed the value of humility. Jane said she learned humility "when I found out my five-year-old daughter was dying and there wasn't a damn thing I could do about it." The police officer said, "Every time I hug and kiss my kids before I go to work, I am reminded of my humility..."
>
> The value for [a later] meeting was empathy. The reading for the opening ritual began like this: "Longfellow wrote, 'If we could read the secret history of our enemies, we should find in each man's life sorrow and suffering enough to disarm all hostility.'"
>
> A guest, a young security guard, said, "When I was seven years old, a police officer took me away from my parents because they were beating on me. I'm training to be a police officer. I'm a security guard. Empathy is why I'm here. I don't want any of your kids to go through what I did. And, if we don't get the drugs out of this building, they will."[70]

"Sincerity," "Christian resignation," "humility," "empathy." These, and other positive qualities, such as "courage,"[71] described the stances taken in response to individual crimes and criminals.

By contrast, the stance toward crime in general could be fairly well summarized as one of determination. For example, a mayor in Caracas spoke of "the sustained work in integral security" being undertaken by the local police,[72] while the Secretary of Public Safety in Michoacán, Mexico, referred to the "consistent and emphatic work" in police coordination throughout the region.[73] "We are coming with everything we have," declared the Mayor of Los Angeles in a "gang-plagued" neighborhood;[74] while Samantha Wilson, in Toronto, wrote of "investigators who have dedicated their lives to rescuing children" from sexual abuse.[75]

Occasionally, the stance was described as "low key,"[76] giving the impression of quiet determination. Or the image was one of a slow, steady, but relentless advance, as in the notion of "one child at a time" being saved from sexual abuse.[77] But determination was much more frequently cast as forceful. Toughness was a quality widely invoked in Anglo-America. "In our system there is a place for tough sentencing," wrote a former New York judge;[78] "...Liberal Leader Stéphane Dion, attacked by the Tories as soft on crime, toughened his own stand in March;"[79] "Californians can see that 'get tough on crime,' if it only means longer sentences, is a cure worse than the disease," wrote Rex Styzens to the *Los Angeles Times*.[80] Mr. Styzens was correct in suggesting that being tough does not only mean longer sentences or harsher punishments: in Toronto, Monica Willie described the approach to her work with young gang members as "tough love."[81]

Across both regions, the language of conflict was widespread. Crime was to be "combated,"[82] "battled,"[83] "fought,"[84] or "struggled with."[85] Some commentaries explicitly couched the conflict as a "war." For example, the Mexican President "paid tribute to the soldiers and police officers who had fallen in this 'war' [against drug trafficking and organized crime] and declared that there will be no truce."[86] "Democrats stake out turf in war on gangs," read a headline in the *Los Angeles Times*.[87] In California, there were parallel materializations of aggressive poses: "'We're fighting a war on our streets,' declared a man whose sister had been murdered, 'We as crime victims are the soldiers who must take that fight to win the all-important political victory [concerning three strikes legislation];'"[88] while "Bratton ... has aggressively enforced misdemeanour violations in L.A.'s central district."[89]

But the bellic trope was not widespread. Much of the combating, fighting and struggling involved tenacity or resolve rather than aggression. Just as Monica Willie "fought to keep young black men from crime by going into the streets and talking to them,"[90] so the Regent Park project, in Toronto, was "The building that fought back" with "a quiet but effective way to reduce crime,"[91] and Liliana Cánaves wrote of "the struggle of those who were touched by the black wand of insecurity.... The marches to Congress and to the *Plaza de Mayo*, the images and testimonies that are constantly circulated..."[92] It was determination that was important, helped by vigor,[93] aided by efficiency,[94] and demonstrated by forward movement.[95] Public expressions of this determination were often couched as vows or pledges, as a determination to be determined: "We vow to do whatever it takes ... to make this a safer city," declared the Mayor of New Orleans,[96] while a new governor in Argentina "pledged to combat crime."[97]

If there was an alternative virtue to determination that appeared in these commentaries, it was that of reason, but its presence was infrequent. A US psychiatrist wrote of "the effort to interpose rationality between public fear and legislation" in the matter of sex crimes,[98] while a criminal justice advisor to the New York Governor argued that, "If there are reasonable steps to take [in relation to sex offenders], we need to take those steps."[99] In Argentina, *La Nación* described a proposed cash-for-guns amnesty as "unimpeachable in terms of its principles," although it also noted that "its degree of efficacy is debated."[100] The same newspaper also wrote of "the need to safeguard and defend the system of general crime prevention, on which obviously rest the principles of legal causality and social security."[101] But these were rare appearances in a cumulative commentary across the hemisphere that highlighted action, dedication, and emphaticalness.

"Now's the time to show some muscle and make something happen," wrote a board member from a black organization devoted to reducing violence in Los Angeles.[102] With this phrase he nicely summarized the spirit of determination, but also called attention to its absence. His criticism was directed partly at Latino leaders, partly at black leaders. His comment hinted at moral shortcomings. If the community could be identified by its moral sentiments, its law abidingness, and its determined stance towards crime, there was also recognition that this latter virtue was not shown by all who should show it. A few other commentaries in Anglo-America were in the same spirit. "He talks the talk, but does not walk the walk," charged the leader of Canada's Liberals in a reference to the Conservative Prime Minister.[103] "It's past time for the Guard to be here.... I'm

42 *"We the good"*

fed up with all that New Orleans is not doing to help its people," fumed a victim of Hurricane Katrina.[104] Some criminal justice experts felt that the recent rise in reported cases of violence "reflect the nation's complacency in fighting crime."[105] But such criticisms were infrequent, suggesting that Anglo-Americans felt themselves and their governments to be active and determined in relation to crime. For them, charge and counter-charge —on the comparatively rare occasions on which they appeared—focused almost exclusively on the content of policies, in a debate between the punitive and legal measures dear to the right, and the ameliorative social interventions favored by the left.

By contrast, criticism of a lack of determination to act against crime was readily evident in Latin America. Following the torture and murder of Lucas Ivarrola, a 15-year-old boy in Argentina apparently killed because he was accused of stealing a TV set, Fernando Rodríguez, writing in *La Nación*, immediately saw a clear symbolic significance in the incident. Not only did it "speak" of a "sick society," but also of a "questionable State:"

> a State that, when it comes to dealing with those conflicts, can seem to be lazy when it should listen to people's demands and lagging behind when it comes to the urgent need to rescue street children in order to separate them from drugs, and crime...[106]

A "lazy" or "lagging" state, an inactive or indolent government, indifferent or incompetent authorities. These were frequent criticisms in the Latin American press.

> [T]he authorities that are responsible for preventing and, when necessary, repressing it [crime]—among others, the police and Justice—only manage to minimize or deny it, instead of designing plausible solutions and resolving to apply them to this extremely serious problem of national proportions.
> (editorialized *La Nación*)[107]

> In cities that are identified as mafia territory, the *capos* [mafia bosses] are widely identified by the inhabitants and their scandalous lifestyles and sumptuous gatherings make them very visible. Only the police fail to see them. Crime grows and the bureaucracy holds meetings.
> (echoed an editorial in *El Universal*)[108]

> The Government is the only one with responsibility for what is happening in relation to personal insecurity. We can only think two things: they have either been incapable of solving this problem or they turn a deaf ear to the increase in the number of criminals...
> (declared the leader of a Venezuelan opposition party)[109]

A widespread subject for critical comment was the perceived level of impunity resulting from the criminal justice system's failure to act.[110] "Underneath the growing intensity of crime ... lies impunity, crime without punishment," wrote *El Universal*;[111] "There is no prevention, there is a high level of impunity," declared a former police chief in Caracas;[112] "Criminal impunity" was the title of an editorial in *La Nación*.[113]

A political objective was often evident in these kinds of comment, notably when specific public figures (the President, a governor or a mayor) were alleged to be inactive or ineffective in dealing with crime. However, the politics of crime and control in Latin America were a little more complex than a simple polemic between government and opposition. In some cases, the government criticized the criminal justice system (usually the police),[114] or one branch of that system criticized another.[115] More generally, all of these commentaries revealed a widely shared vision of the state as separate from "society" and entrusted with its safety: "the State [has] an undeniable obligation to defend society and preserve social coexistence;"[116] "[t]he maintenance of a secure environment and the avoidance, as far as possible, of threats to societal freedoms and goods is an inescapable duty of the Mexican State;"[117] "the matter of security is an exclusive responsibility of the State."[118] Or in the more down-to-earth language of a Venezuelan columnist: "... death from a bullet, a knife, a fight, spurious passion, a kidnapping, a robbery, or getting caught in a gunfight is not normal. Call it what you will. It is not normal. And the State is there to avoid it striking us."[119] Inability or unwillingness to act was, therefore, seen as a moral failure of the state. In an attempt to spread responsibility, some public functionaries vainly reached for the rather empty phrase that crime is "everyone's problem,"[120] but these were feeble counters to the torrent of criticism. Indeed, the same words were sometimes turned back on the government in denunciation of its imputed lack of concern and failure to act.[121]

Failure was compounded, in some commentaries, by depictions of corruption and criminality within the state itself. Gertz Manero wrote of the "bazaar for corruption and bribes," and "the authorities [not] daring to touch those 'privileged' who have found in political clientelism and public corruption the perfect society for making progress."[122] In Venezuela, "The secretary of government [in Zulia state] ... admitted that a large number of police officers were involved in crimes...;"[123] while a journalist (interestingly, with links to the government) wrote that "little has been achieved in purging the police and eradicating vices such as extortion, [and] the use of officers for collecting 'contributions' which gambling dens [and] betting shops ... give to police chiefs."[124] In Argentina, a gubernatorial candidate in Buenos Aires declared that, "The lack of results in the fight against crime is not only inefficiency; there is some level of complicity [between criminals and functionaries]."[125] In these, and similar, commentaries, the state seemed to be succumbing to criminality, critically reducing the distance that it was supposedly designed to maintain between crime and the moral community. As Gertz Manero put it, because of a compliant or impotent state "the 'captive' sector [that of the victims] is left in starvation, crushed by illegality, street businesses and organized crime."[126]

To write of a "captive sector" was to give a pessimistic assessment of the balance of forces in the conflict with crime (a topic that will be examined in the next chapter). Nevertheless, Gertz Manero shared with other Latin American commentators the implicit reliance on a notional civil society, whose members combined moral sensibility towards crime with the virtues of being "honest," "honorable," or "hardworking." A charge of indolence against this "captive sector" would not stick because, in this view of public responsibilities, it did not fall to civil society to struggle against crime, only to suffer its ravages. And in this view, the moral failings of the state necessarily separated it from a civil society that was wholly virtuous.

By contrast, in Anglo-America, not only was the state generally granted the virtue of determination, it was overwhelmingly portrayed as law abiding. Throughout the sample of texts, the only mention of wrongdoing and collusion with crime came in three brief references in the *Los Angeles Times* to the Rampart Scandal of the 1990s, which involved police "corruption,"[127] "officers framing and beating suspects,"[128] and "dope-stealing ... false arrests ... [and] ... perjured testimony."[129] This scandal was treated as an isolated incident that had occurred in the past, with no hint of the possibility that such practices might be more widespread and persistent. For the rest, commentators might disagree, sometimes quite strongly, with a course of action taken by the state, but they did not harbor doubts about its determination and integrity.

Nor did they make a clear division between the state and civil society. "No one disputes society's obligation to protect the innocent," editorialized the *New York Times* about sex offenders; "it is fair to ask whether the state's limited resources might be better deployed at the front end of the problem."[130] "When the empowered majority recognizes a population as having been victimized in such a manner, it is appropriate to grant it protection," argued a letter writer to the *Los Angeles Times*; "it is also a statement that we as a society are serious when we renounce such crimes."[131] Through these and other comments, government was made part of the larger society, not separate from it. Its determination and integrity contributed to the collective good. Governmental failure was simply not seen, or was not egregious enough to be seen.

Collective and individual identity

Criticism and censure slice up the social universe into tracts of differing moral valence. "Crime follows civilization, just as the shadow follows crime," wrote a Venezuelan criminologist, misquoting a "criminological precept" that is popular with Latin American criminal lawyers.[132] He should have written "just as the shadow follows the body," but this would merely have been a correction of the analogy. The broader point—that crime and civilization are different—was still made clear, as was the criminologist's location in that universe (an observer of crime, but a part of civilization). This basic division, between crime and "civilization," or "society," was everywhere evident. In Anglo-America, "society" generally included the state, such that the terrain of "the good" was notionally ample and institutionally complex. In Latin America, frequent and severe criticism of the state set the latter apart from civil society, which was thereby reduced (in this image) to a mass of suffering and defenseless, but virtuous, "citizens."

Occasionally, however, across the region, a severely critical eye was trained on "society" itself. Following the killing of three young men in Newark, New Jersey (see Chapter 2), a columnist for the *New York Times* reflected that in six years, nearly 100,000 people had been murdered in the United States. Continuing, he commented that "No heightening of consciousness has accompanied this slaughter.... The news media and the politicians have hardly bothered to notice." He quoted the Director of the Police Executive Research Forum, who charged that "We have become numbed in this society."[133] In a similar vein, the Attorney-General for British Columbia remarked that "We had plenty of warning ... that gangs were a part of our culture and we as a society have ignored that."[134] In Argentina, a crime victim declared that "we don't do anything more than get used to living in a society that is increasingly insecure. We should not get used to that."[135] These were the occasional calls to arms that were mentioned in Chapter 2. They were infrequent because collective concern about crime was seen as widespread and natural.

But when the censorial eye was thus turned inward, even the notion of a moral community could weaken, leaving only the individual as a moral beacon. Writing after the death of Lucas Ivarrola in Argentina, Fernando Rodríguez had not only seen the incident as testimony to a "questionable state," but as evidence of a "sick society:" "A society infected with the germ of violence, with difficulties in resolving its conflicts and disagreements pacifically, and with a dangerous tendency not to believe in its norms and institutions."[136] This was a rare critique of the social body, but one which emphasized a moral divide between the commentator and the community. Criticism devalues the status of the criticized, but raises the status of the critic. Whether or not these occasional manifestations of moral individualism were a conscious attempt to bolster personal identity, they inevitably raised that possibility.

More explicit work in creating a personal moral identity was arguably found in other sorts of commentary relating to crime. One type was simply that which employed strong and abundant critical language, as did Gertz Manero in his tract on "Victims and victimizers." Although written in the name of "the victims," his column also seemed to be an exercise in self-affirmation, in which the force of his indignation was perhaps called up as testimony to the clarity and depth of his moral concern. Indeed, nine of his opinion columns fell into the set of texts compiled for this study, each of them filled with similar critique and invective.[137] While his formal profile was that of an academic and public functionary, his projected persona was that of the social critic, the figure who points a finger at society's ills, and who, in so doing, inevitability insinuated (and may have hoped to claim) respectability. Some other commentators in Latin America displayed a similar penchant for strong criticism. One was Norberto Firpo, an Argentine journalist who wrote a column on "Damned insecurity," the title aptly setting the tone for a piece that railed against the politicians and described the dramatic plight of ordinary people:

For the fearful majority, the great national matters today begin with managing to reach life's end when God decrees it and not when an outlaw decides it. So shameful and perverse is reality when the usual daily stress is the result of sudden fear and uncertainty rather than of overwork.[138]

Another was Eugenio Burzaco, an Argentine politician who was moved to write a column about youth violence following the death of a 16-year-old. "I shuddered anew along with society," he wrote in testimony to his own moral sensibilities, before launching into a critique of contemporary social and political arrangements: "…the flaunting of ill-gotten gains, the manipulation of police authorities, political cooptation through clientelism and the deterioration in behavior flood the message with its apology for the strongest and least principled over citizens who respect the law."[139]

In his conclusion, Burzaco turned from criticism to peroration:

The violent death of a young person is always a terrible failure of society, all violence is. Its consequences last beyond the circumstance, degrading coexistence in freedom, strengthening the perception of the other as a possible enemy, exacerbating paranoid and egotistical behaviours. It is time for we Argentines to commit our will to the resolution of our ethical dilemmas and renew the mystique of love for our fellow human beings and compliance with the law, on which civility is founded.

Here, explicit attention to morality joined a strong vocation for criticism in the presentation of individual identity. In a similar vein, an Argentine congressional politician levelled a charge of inaction at the legislature and the government ("It cannot be that we are discussing whether or not the criminal law is useful in combating crime in the midst of a fiesta of impunity organized by the criminals") before appealing to "ethics:" "An ethical attitude is not only seen in not stealing public funds. The ethical attitude of the political leader and public office holder is that which shows a real commitment to the people and maintains it over time."[140]

Neither of these expressions of individual moral identity—strong criticism or the explicit reference to ethics—was much in evidence in Anglo-American commentary.

Drawing back

Across the hemisphere, crime and criminals provided the basis for a clear division of the imaginary moral universe. While few commentators referred explicitly to "we the good" and "they the bad" (or the "victims" and "victimizers" as Gertz had it), this division was almost everywhere implied. Crimes, and the people who committed them, were alien; something that characterized others, for whom criminality was the totality of their identity. Newspapers, and the public domain that they created or drew on, were the site of "the good," a terrain for the performance of morality and virtue. "Criminals," "gang members," "offenders," and "delinquents" could enter this terrain only if they had attached the prefix "ex-" to their label, or if they expressed repentance for what their label implied that they did.

This Manichean vision of crime and criminals is widely mentioned in other studies. For example, Best observed that "We tend to view crime as a melodrama in which evil villains prey on innocent victims."[141] Later in his book, a citation from Moscovici nicely captured the lay of the land: "On the one hand, everything normal, lawful, that is native; on the other hand, everything abnormal, unlawful, and hence, alien. The opposing groups belong to two distinct universes: a region of daylight and clarity versus an opaque and nocturnal milieu."[142]

Among Latin American scholars, Vasilachis de Gialdino has noted that "while in 'them' is concentrated the illegitimate, that which violates norms and social customs, in 'us' reside the opposite attributes."[143] More broadly, Alexander has argued that there is "a highly generalized symbolic system that divides civic virtue from civic vice in a remarkably stable and consistent way" and which is relevant to "every study of social/sectional/subsystem conflict."[144]

Just as criminals and offenders had little presence or voice in the sample of texts compiled for this study, so other research on crime in the media confirms or implies their absence.[145] In Ericson *et al.*'s study of crime in the Canadian media, individuals accounted for only 7.4 percent of newspaper sources and all seemed to be either citizens, who figured as commentators on crime, or victims and their relatives.[146] No specific mention was made of offenders as sources. More recently, Thompson *et al.*'s study of a large sample of articles on gangs in the *Dallas Morning News* found that only 5 percent of them could be classified as "gang accounts"—possibly the category of texts that would most likely look directly at gangs and their members.[147] But even here, the examples given suggest that the spokespeople typically featured were not gang members. Similarly, Frost and Phillips found that, although 22 percent of spokespeople on crime incidents in cable news segments were "experiential guests" (known to the victim, the accused, or at the scene), no offenders were featured.[148] In like manner, Sacco commented that "crime news tends to provide only sparse details about victims and offenders."[149]

Criminals and offenders are, thus, a work of alterity. Some researchers have turned a critical lens on the "demonization" of offenders, the putative process by which the moral condemnation of people who commit crimes deepens, often wildly and emotively, into a panicky portrait of evil.[150] Demonization, however, was a relatively rare phenomenon in the set of texts compiled for this study. Very occasionally, offenders were alluded to in animalistic terms; more frequently they were portrayed as lacking the moral sentiments of humanity. But most frequently it was the simple use of terms such as "criminal" and "offender" that performed the necessary moral work. These habitual one-dimensional categorizations of people who commit crime were wedded to practices of distancing and silencing that kept them out of the social spaces built or occupied by newspapers, and gave them no voice.

Writing within the claims-making tradition of social problems studies, Lowney has argued that "Frequently ... claimsmakers may choose to let the villain remain under- or unconstructed ... in the hopes of not diminishing audience support."[151] Here, the superficial portrayal of the problematic individual or agency performs the strategic function of advancing the claimants' cause by providing uncomplicated censure of the other. More detail might reveal mitigating circumstances or saving graces which render moral judgments more difficult. A similar process seems to operate in the terrain of alterity. The distinction between "the bad" and "the good" exists by discursive fiat, under which the former are nothing more than their crimes and the latter are nothing less than their virtue.[152] That crime is a behavior which only sporadically figures in what people do, but which, at some point or other, figures in everyone's behavior, are empirical inconveniences that are banished by talk. To speak of "criminals" as "they" or "them" is, obviously, to make a claim to one's own moral integrity.

While previous research shows considerable similarity (but not, it should be noted, complete coincidence) with the present findings on crime and alterity, it has been largely inattentive to the matter of crime and identity. Identity is not simply the consequence of alterity, but also an active affirmation of the self. Across the Americas, crime created identity through the sentiments it provoked and the virtue it called for. The sentiments were those of shock, horror, and fear caused by individual crimes, and the expressions of alarm and concern in relation to crime in general. The virtue was that of determination—the "toughness" of the Anglo-Americans, the resolve conjured up by many, the widespread references to the "struggle" against crime. Prior research has not looked at these phenomena, except to fix a critical eye on the appeal to the metaphor of war.[153] But although the "war on crime" made occasional appearances across the hemisphere, this and similar aggressive poses were a relatively minor feature within a broader scenario of conflict and struggle with crime. While there was talk of "surge and purge" in Los Angeles,[154] and the military "crusade" against drug trafficking in Mexico,[155] the struggle against crime encompassed every type of strategy and tactic, including the empathy and humility of Toronto's Regent Park residents and similar stances in Caracas.[156] Even Liliana Cánaves' letter to *La Nación*, in Argentina, was written within the paradigm of struggle and action.

Lakoff pointed out that "One can *know* what is moral and immoral and still not have the ability to *do* what is moral."[157] This difference between knowledge and action carries potential implications of some magnitude for identity: the fully moral person must not only have the right values but also put them into practice, and inability to do the latter becomes a sign of lesser moral worth. In the present commentaries, this kind of inconsistency did not reveal itself in the basic division between "we the good" and "they the criminals" because that distinction was based precisely on the putative ability of the former and the inability of the latter "to do what is moral." There were no doubts here. But matters were more complicated when it came to the determined stance regarding crime that was widely seen as necessary and desirable. In Anglo-America there was little doubt that society and the state were united in the determination to deal with crime, even as there were diverse opinions about how to deal with it. In Latin America, society was generally cast in the role of the passive victim of crime, while the state was criticized for its inability or unwillingness to act.

The contours of the moral collective were shaped by censure which, in finding targets for criticism, created divisions and separation. To the basic distinction between criminals and others which prevailed throughout the hemisphere was added, in Latin America, a separation between civil society and the state, as the latter was unceasingly criticized for its moral failings. Occasionally in Latin America, criticism was even turned on civil society itself, leaving the commentator as the lone representative of morality in a social world populated by criminals and those who were either complicit with them or, most commonly, complacent about them. Here, personal moral identity was built at the expense of an imaginary moral community, even as it tried to invigorate the latter through criticism. More frequent in Latin America were those who wrote in the name of the collective but who also seemed to be bolstering their own identity through persistent and forceful censure or the appeal to moral principles. If everyone across the region who wrote of "criminals" (or some such category) was signalling their own moral identity, it was these Latin American commentators who could be thought of as moralists—hoping not to be deprecated, as moralists often are in other cultures, but to be accorded the respect they claimed. Newspapers allow commentators to show that they know what is moral; they do not require them to do what is moral.

4 The moral outlook

"We are here to say, 'America, we have a problem,'" Los Angeles Police Chief William J. Bratton told the Police Executive Research Forum in Washington last month. "Crime is coming back, and it has a new and troubling element ... a youthful population that is largely disassociated from the mainstream of America." According to Bratton, the nation needs to "refocus on this gathering storm of crime."[1] Undoubtedly, William Bratton said much more than this when he spoke to the Police Executive Research Forum (PERF) in August 2006. But these three sentences provided a usefully succinct bulletin on the moral outlook for the nation. "America," "mainstream America," the America to which Bratton self-assuredly belonged ("America, *we* have a problem"), faced the "new and troubling [criminal] element" of disassociated youth.

Like all bulletins, Bratton's comments provided a snapshot of recent developments. They offered a history of the present[2] ("crime is coming back") and a notional landscape on which that history was being played out (under "this gathering storm of crime"). Moral outlooks seem only expressible in terms of time and space, charting the trajectories of good and bad and the relations between them. In this case, the prospect for the moral community was given by what was happening with crime. Trends in crime, both quantitative and qualitative, were measures of the community's security or insecurity. Increased rates, or a turn to greater viciousness, were definite threats or, at the very least, developments of concern. Decreases gave grounds for cautious optimism. Similarly, alarm bells sounded when crime broke out of its imaginary haunts and began to appear at sites of assumedly solid conventionality. Across the Americas, bulletins that spoke to the moral outlook were a staple ingredient of news and opinion items:

> Bullets are flying in Vancouver as part of a wave of gangland violence that has raised concerns about public safety.[3]

> While citywide statistics show small bumps in interracial attacks, some neighborhoods are seeing troubling increases.[4]

"In many places—both cities and increasingly suburban and rural settings—things never got as good as they did nationally," he said. "Even if things got better, they didn't get as better as they did in Los Angeles or New York. In many places, they're getting worse."[5]

Kidnapping, protection payments and assassinations are the most frequent crimes which threaten the inhabitants of Alto Apure.... The mayor ... maintains that criminality is one of the most serious problems that the municipality faces.[6]

This time the crisis which opens the six-year presidential period is not economic, it is a crisis of security. The risk is not of losing our pesos, as happened in 1982 and 1994. The risk is greater: it is to lose peace of mind or worse, to lose even one's life in a Republic in which there are ever more spaces outside the law.[7]

In recent weeks, those who live in the metropolitan area have witnessed a troubling increase in crimes of the most varied type.[8]

Bulletins like these, and the text that accompanied them, revealed not just the anxieties of the moral community, but the "facts" on which they built them. Thus, a study of the moral outlook not only helps to delineate those anxieties; it also provides insights on the interface between moral and factual discourses. Which facts were used? With what degree of certainty? What role was played by research? These are matters of considerable interest when reflecting on the relationship between knowledge and moral claims, or evaluating the quality of those claims. Marked differences in the moral outlook between Anglo and Latin America demand that each region be examined in turn. Within that examination, the interface between moral and factual discourse will draw comment from time to time, but a systematic review of the topic is reserved for the final part of the chapter.

Anglo-America: a secure moral community?

Although they were his words, Bratton's bulletin as reported above was not strictly, or entirely, of his own making. It was put together by a researcher, Mike Males, who drew these elements from a lengthier set of statements for the purposes of critical comment: Males disagreed with Bratton's assertions about the trend and nature of crime. There was no "gathering storm of crime," argued Males, but a much sunnier outlook:

> go to the Los Angeles Police Department's website and you'll see a different story: "Crime has been reduced 15% in the past year," it beams. The LAPD's Sept. 9 report shows drops in homicide (down 4%), rape (down 4%) and overall violent crime (down 1%) compared with the same period in 2005, on top of a 28% decline in violent crime from 2004 to 2005.[9]

52 *The moral outlook*

To this he added statistic after statistic that indicated declining crime rates. For example:

> the figures show the least criminal and violent younger generation since accurate statistics were first compiled. Rates of criminal arrest of L.A. youth in 2005 were staggeringly lower than 30 years ago: Homicide is down 55%; rape, 81%; robbery, 21%; assault, 44%; property felonies, 83%; drug offenses, 52%; and misdemeanours, 60%...

And so on.

Given this data, Males asked: "How can law enforcement, interest groups, academics and the news media continue to ignore such striking trends?" And he answered by charging them with artifice:

> The subterfuge is accomplished simply: Even when crime is down and youth arrests are plummeting, there is always some offense in some city in some year that rose when compared to some previous year. For example, Los Angeles' teenage homicide and assault rates dropped sharply from 2004 to 2005, and robbery arrest rates have plunged 50% in the last decade—but robbery rates did rise by 3% in 2005. Bratton, law enforcement and other interests ... hype imaginary epidemics of "youth violence" as cynical political ploys to win attention and funding...

The allegation was that Bratton and others had seized on a minor countertrend to substantiate the much broader claim that "crime is coming back." This was a tactic that, if it had been used, would have been a case of fitting the facts to the claim rather than fitting the claim to the facts.

It is not clear, however, that Bratton had engaged in subterfuge. Quite simply, he and others were probably referring to other data when making their claims. Thus, a report published in the *New York Times* on the day after the PERF meeting appended different figures to Bratton's claim, and not the sort of statistic cited by Males:

> "Crime is coming back," said Chief William J. Bratton of Los Angeles, who was formerly police commissioner in New York City. Violent crime increased last year for the first time in four years, up 2.5 percent from 2004. The biggest increases in murder were reported in medium-size cities and the Midwest.[10]

Later in the same article, it was mentioned that:

> A preliminary crime report for 2005 that the Federal Bureau of Investigation issued in June said murders increased 4.8 percent over 2004. St. Louis, Houston, Philadelphia and Milwaukee reported increases, and cities including New York, Los Angeles and Miami had declines. Among violent crimes, the lone decrease was in rapes, which fell 1.9 percent. Robberies

increased over all 4.5 percent.... In Boston, murders increased 28 percent in the first six months of 2006, compared with the same period last year. Robberies soared 37 percent in Minneapolis and 35 percent in Denver. Assaults increased 24 percent in Charleston, S.C., and 26 percent in Atlanta.

The inferential link from these figures to the claim that "crime is coming back" was made plain by Chuck Wexler, the Executive Director of PERF: "We see this as the front end of an epidemic, if you will, of violence that seems to be gripping many parts of the country."[11]

This line of argument resonated with other bulletins that were being delivered with similar sorts of figures. Thus, the headlines to an item in the *Los Angeles Times*, reporting on the FBI's crime statistics for 2006, ran as follows: "Violent crime is up for 2nd year in a row—but it's still 'at a relative low'; The rise, 1.9%, is higher than expected. Property crime is down 1.9%. And overall crime is at its lowest in 30 years."[12] As a Justice Department spokesman noted: "While there's encouraging news in the latest crime rates ... violent crime remains a challenge for some communities."[13] Similarly, a Canadian academic noted that "... violence in general is not sharing the decline that property offences are, and within violence there's some shifting. There is an increase in some of the more severe categories."[14] And in Toronto it was reported that "When it comes to violent crime, the chief's greatest concern today is the sharp increase in domestic murders."[15] In other words, some crime may have been decreasing but violence, or certain types of violence, were not.

There were a few broader claims that crime in general had increased, or might be increasing, but these were carefully put. Thus, the Canadian Prime Minister (Stephen Harper) declared that:

> Even if Canada's crime rates are low by international standards, they are still very high by our own historical standards.... When I was a boy growing up in Toronto, we knew nothing of street gangs or crack houses. And gun crime was almost unheard of. That began to change in the 1960s. And during the next three decades, the violent-crime rate in this country more than tripled.[16]

In quoting this, a reporter grudgingly noted that "While it's true that reported crime rates are far higher than when Mr. Harper, born in 1959, was a child, he didn't mention that they have been declining relatively steadily since 1992." In other words, the observed increase was based on a simple comparison between the beginning and end point of the ideologically significant period that was a person's life experience.

Alternatively, a general increase in crime was heralded in cautious terms. For example, a US criminologist remarked that "The 2005 figures are not necessarily the beginning of a trend upward for everyone ... but the potential does exist."[17] Invoking that "potential" acknowledged the necessary element of uncertainty, but did not invalidate concern.

Overall, there was plenty of "good news" about crime in Anglo-America, plenty of data which depicted it as declining or stable. Causes of concern were almost always more focalized. They could materialize as worrying trends in specific types of crime (usually violence), not only in terms of rates, as exemplified earlier, but also in terms of alleged changes for the worse in its character. Thus, violence could be portrayed as turning increasingly gratuitous, or as losing any sense of instrumental justification. For example, according to a *New York Times* columnist:

> Law enforcement officials believe there is something more vicious and coldblooded, and thus more deadly, about the latest waves of crime moving across the country. Robberies involving juveniles with little regard for the lives of their victims are becoming more prevalent.[18]

A police officer in Halifax, Nova Scotia, noted that "police are concerned about the increasing brutality of crimes committed by young offenders. While the number of youth crimes may be dropping, they are more severe."[19] Then he added a slightly different claim: "What concerns us is the degree of violence ... and the random acts of violence—violence for the sake of violence." One such apparently random act of violence was described by the reporter who wrote the article:

> on Monday night, a woman in her mid-60s was viciously beaten by three teenage girls wielding metal table legs as she strolled near her home. When the woman asked what they wanted, they said nothing and struck her repeatedly before a witness with a dog chased them off.[20]

This vision of crime without reason was echoed in the occasional references to "senseless violence" perpetrated by the young.[21] It was, perhaps, a particularly worrying phenomenon because it implied that nothing potential victims could do would insulate them from its possible occurrence. Although one researcher did cite a motive for some youth violence, his depiction of it in subcultural terms meant that its operational referent ("what counts as being dissed") was probably a mystery to readers:

> Criminologists attribute the spurt in youth crime in some places to what they call an evolving subculture among juveniles and young adults that encourages violent responses to seemingly trivial disputes. "What everybody sees is street rules saying if you're dissed you have to do something," said David M. Kennedy, the director of the Center for Crime Prevention and Control at the John Jay College of Criminal Justice. "And what counts as being dissed is getting more and more minor."[22]

This kind of history of the present was one of a brutal turn across the country and particularly among its young.

"Senseless violence" was sometimes linked to certain neighborhoods in a spatial perspective on the crime problem. Thus, "experts" spoke of "a resurgence of senseless violence among young men in impoverished neighborhoods"[23] and a report on gangs in Los Angeles observed that "residents of Los Angeles' most dangerous neighborhoods continue losing children to senseless violence."[24] Casting crime in an areal framework was, in fact, another common way in which it was constituted as a problem: crime rates might be declining, but crime could still be some region, city, or community's particular headache.

"The biggest increases in murder were reported in medium-size cities and the Midwest," reported the *New York Times* in relation to Bratton's headline bulletin; and the same article noted that "St. Louis, Houston, Philadelphia and Milwaukee reported increases, [while] cities including New York, Los Angeles and Miami had declines."[25] In Washington, D.C., officials were trying to "calm fears that the city was returning to the crime-infested days of the early 90's;"[26] in Calgary, people had "the impression that the city is rife with social disorder and beset by crime."[27] Meanwhile, "Residents of the Canadian North are three times more likely to be victims of sexual assault, physical assault or robbery than their southern counterparts..."[28] and in the region centered on New York:

> In most smaller cities and even in some quiet suburbs ... violent crime rose last year, according to preliminary statistics released Monday by the Federal Bureau of Investigation. The increases were such that New York City, with a slight decline, appeared to be an oasis of relative calm.[29]

Rather similarly, the *Los Angeles Times* announced that "As L.A. violent crime drops, the desert becomes a hot spot."[30]

The perception of crime as a localized problem was strongest within cities—the ecological units with which commentators were most naturally familiar. Cities provided social landscapes that were not merely a foundation for discussing crime but were somehow bound up in its genesis and appearances. These were the places that reporters could visit to get a view on the ground and from which they could file "dispatches." As they moved physically out of the newspaper office to report back from these low-intensity conflict zones, they moved symbolically from the heart of conventionality to a latter-day frontier where the local residents contended with crime. More than one article spoke of the "Wild West."[31]

> When 13-year-old Elijah Henderson rode a bicycle onto a stretch of Fulton Street early on Monday—and was then killed by a gunshot to the back of the head—he crossed a perilous boundary not found on any map. To the west there is the endless rush of the New Jersey Turnpike. To the east, there is the Arthur Kill and cargo-container cranes that loom as high as skyscrapers. Overhead, there is the drone of airplanes headed to Newark Liberty International Airport. But that part of Fulton Street, on the edge of this

struggling town, is known to residents as a "Bloods block," turf claimed by the notorious street gang. It was there that Elijah and two other boys were shot at as they rode their bikes on the darkened street on their way home shortly before 1 a.m. "There ain't nowhere to go," said Fiedel Taylor, 30, who lives here in the neighborhood known as Elizabethport. The children "are out in the street," he said.[32]

That "there ain't nowhere to go" seemed to be the predicament not just of the children, but also of the neighborhood that they lived in:

> The sound of gunshots and police sirens is not uncommon in this city of 125,000, where residents live in the shadow of Newark and share some of its ills. It is a city of rapidly changing demographics, where new arrivals have added about 1,000 residents a year since 2000. And it is a place that has the 10th-highest rate of violent crime among New Jersey's 15 largest cities. Fulton Street alone has averaged a shooting a day this week, two as recently as Wednesday a block from where Elijah was killed.... One law enforcement official said that even by Elizabeth's standards, it was a rough week. "It was quiet for a while," the official said. "Now it's starting to look like the Wild West."[33]

These were neighborhoods that struggled with drugs and gangs, or at least they thought they did. In Elizabethport, no one quite knew why Elijah had been shot. "Friends, family and classmates insisted that he was not involved in gangs or drugs," although other residents thought that the shooting could have been a possibly misdirected retaliation from a rival Crips gang. Even the police did not know: "We're looking at every possibility, and gang involvement is one of them," said an officer. Here and elsewhere, criminals did not reveal themselves to the media. One resident of Elizabethport charged that "most of the area is infested with Bloods," but the reporter either did not look for them or could not find them. More commonly, as a resident of San Bernardino, California, put it, "There haven't been problems on this street, but it's all around us,"[34] as if crime was always one street over.

Significantly, these frontier zones were sites of struggle. A middle school principal in San Bernardino told the reporter that "There's almost no kid in the neighborhood who doesn't know somebody who's been shot or killed.... But there's also a culture of faith and a culture of learning—so you have competing forces, and we just refuse to give up."[35] And in relation to nearby Los Angeles, a think tank fellow wrote of "the everyday struggle among neighbors who break the law and those who obey and even grow up to uphold it."[36] This was a moral battle zone where the lines between contenders could not easily have been drawn on a map. In the most critical cases, residents were simultaneously the beneficiaries of a local drug economy and the victims of its violent accompaniments.[37]

As frequent as dispatches from neighborhoods that were deemed to be impregnated with crime were reports from areas where it was threatening an imagined peace or longed-for progress. For example, in one Toronto suburb a reporter found a considerable amount of anxiety:

> The area that some have begun calling Danforth East—roughly bounded by Danforth Avenue to the south, Cosburn to the north and bracketed by Pape and Coxwell—would seem, to many, an ideal mix of suburban calm and urban convenience at relatively low prices. Kids play ball hockey on the streets and set up skateboarding ramps. Dog-walkers wave at porch-sitters. If you look for them, you'll even spot a few lawn gnomes. Meanwhile, Riverdale and its bustling restaurants, bakeries and boutiques are only blocks away. But a summer of violent crime that has included sexual assaults, stabbings and shootings has left many residents wondering just which way the neighbourhood is headed.[38]

A police sergeant identified several developments that could give "the makings of a real hot zone": a youth center that "draws some bad kids into the area;" the presence of one of the city's biggest homeless shelters; and the relocation of residents from Regent Park (featured in Chapter 3), all of which were "going to increase your crime a little, reshuffling people." For residents and developers, the threat was that the neighborhood was "on the brink [of] tipping over."

Similarly, in Los Angeles, while "To the casual eye, Koreatown is thriving, ... behind the glitz, anxiety is building.... A series of high-profile slayings in the community over the last year ... have heightened concerns about crime."[39] And in Jersey City (New Jersey), "...glimmering towers now poke into the sky, newfound prosperity is trickling from the Hudson waterfront to the traditional downtown neighborhoods.... And for every resident, more and more, there is a crime story to tell."[40] As one resident put it: "We're waiting,... The area is becoming so great. But if crime keeps happening, and no one does something, the neighborhood could decay again." Could crime be spreading?

More than one report conveyed such anxieties:

> Los Angeles faces a crisis of gang violence that will continue to spread into previously safe neighborhoods unless the city adopts a Marshall Plan-like initiative to provide young people with jobs and other alternatives in gang-plagued communities, a city-financed study warned Friday.... Last week, city officials said that gang crimes, including assaults and robberies, rose 14% last year. Fifty-six percent of the 478 homicides last year were gang-related. Noting that nearly 75% of youth gang homicides in California occurred in Los Angeles County, the report said the violence would continue to spread without effective countermeasures.[41]

A similar concern emerged in the hinterlands of Los Angeles, where "The trend [in property crime] has become an increasing topic of debate and concern among law enforcement agencies, which are studying patterns to see if it is spreading."[42]

In some cases, the imagery was more dramatic:

> It would be easy to write off the murders of eight men connected to a vicious biker gang known as the Bandidos as an ugly internecine war that has nothing to do with the rest of society [editorialized the *Globe and Mail*].... But what the outlaw biker gangs get up to has a significant and increasingly costly impact on society.... In a few short years, [they] have become the dominant criminal organization in Canada, spreading their tentacles from coast to coast, and carving out a large and lucrative niche in a variety of criminal enterprises.[43]

Similarly, Stephen Harper warned that "The Canadian way of life and those proud traditions of safety and security are today threatened by a rising tide of drugs, gangs and guns."[44] Here was a vision of the moral community on the high ground, imperiled by an iniquitous flood.

Hydrostatic metaphors were, in fact, the most prevalent literary devices employed in expressing concerns about crime. Cities, or neighborhoods, could become "havens" for crime.[45] The latter could "rise" or "spread" as a "surge"[46] or a "wave"[47] and, like fluids, it had a "level,"[48] it could "spill onto the streets."[49] The nearest metaphorical contender was disease, when commentators referred to crime as an "epidemic,"[50] or occasionally as a "plague."[51] But just as animalistic references to offenders were relatively infrequent, so crime itself was rarely portrayed as animate, except on the few occasions when it was considered to "infest"[52] an area.[53]

Tides, waves, or disease require containment and control. Against a backdrop of stable or declining crime rates, there was some anxiety that, in some areas or in relation to some kinds of crime, these defenses were failing. Thus, William Bratton had the following to say about "the gathering storm" of crime:

> Philadelphia and Baltimore are having horrendous problems.... You just had that awful shooting in Newark. What we'd like to do is bring this issue of crime back into the national debate in this election year. What you don't want is to let it get out of control like it did in the late '80s and early '90s.[54]

And the study on gangs in Los Angeles warned that:

> This epidemic [of gang violence] is largely immune to general declines in crime.... And it is spreading to formerly safe middle class neighborhoods. Law enforcement officials now warn that they are arriving at the end of their ability to contain it to poor minority and immigrant hot zones.[55]

Congruent with this anxiety, and perhaps an important contributor to it, were explanations that anchored crime in otherness, with an autonomous capacity to develop and proliferate. Shallow accounts for rising crime focused on changes in its character and dynamics. Thus, a Canadian criminologist, somewhat tautologically, affirmed that "The illegal drug industry ... is a huge multimillion-dollar corporate enterprise that operates less and less in the shadows.... It's the primary driver of crime...;"[56] police in Houston "attributed some of their increased violent crime to New Orleans gang members who evacuated there along with thousands of other victims of Hurricane Katrina;"[57] and a county sheriff in New Jersey had "his own theory about why homicides remain high": "Guns are plentiful ... and those who own them have little compunction about settling disputes with weapons."[58]

Deeper explanations in this vein adopted the language of control, whether it was through containment, repression or prevention. Not surprisingly, this was a popular viewpoint among police and other representatives of government. Bratton, for example, credited "the Los Angeles Police Department's assertive policing for reducing crime by about 10% ... for the third year in a row;"[59] the International Association of Chiefs of Police attributed the "increase in crime, violent or otherwise,... to the substantial decline in funding for local and state law enforcement from federal government assistance programs;"[60] and the Solicitor-General of British Columbia commented that "a robust police presence is what reduces overall crime rates."[61] More broadly, criminal justice "experts" estimated that "as much as 25% of California's—and the nation's—decade-long crime decline is attributable to [a] punish-all-criminals strategy;"[62] while "years of crime reduction efforts all over the country are credited with lower crime rates almost everywhere."[63]

Indeed, although some commentators doubted the validity of this kind of explanation—one researcher, for example, took specific aim at Bratton's broken-windows-based strategy[64]—many were willing to include policing on the list of factors that might account for both the general decline in crime since the 1990s and the more recent increases in certain types of violence. For example, one researcher credited "three policing changes introduced after 1990" for producing "between a quarter and a half of [New York's crime] decline,"[65] while another linked recent increases in violence to a 10 percent drop in the number of police on the street.[66] Looking across the range of explanations advanced for "the astonishing drop" in crime rates, another researcher offered a list of "usual suspects": "a decline in crack use, aggressive policing, increased prison populations, a relatively strong economy [and] increased availability of abortion," to which he added a new candidate for consideration: immigration.[67]

Lists like these reveal that control was not the only perspective in play. Immigration, a relatively strong economy, and the increased availability of abortion locate the causes of crime in economic and demographic factors, and there were plenty of commentators who cited these, or social variables, in their accounts. For example, a Canadian researcher listed "being young people; being in lone-parent families; being aboriginal; unemployment and heavy drinking" as the factors that accounted for higher rates of violence in the Canadian North;[68] "experts" attributed the declines in crime in Los Angeles to "many factors, including an improving economy and a drop in the number of older teenagers and young adults;"[69] and a sociologist explained Baltimore's high crime rate in terms of "concentrated poverty in racially homogeneous, isolated neighborhoods and a brisk drug trade."[70] These explanations were not anchored in visions of crime as otherness; they focused on the processes which pushed people into crime. Here, the underlying moral issue was not that crime might break through the barriers set up to contain it, but that society was somehow failing. From this perspective, it was potentially harder to see criminals as a problem, easier to view their genesis as the real problem.

The vision of how "some of us" could turn into "them" was nicely illustrated by the Kansas City Police Chief, who was moved to put himself in the place of those who purportedly turn to crime:

> If I don't have skills, I don't have training, my socioeconomic situation looks desperate, do I really have hope?... I think that ties into the anger. If the only thing I have is my respect, that's what I carry on the street. If someone disrespects me, they've done the ultimate to me.[71]

This anecdotal explanation resonated with the portrayal of offenders as victims, with Monica Willie's charge (see Chapter 2) that "young ... men ... have been put into a vicious system that needs to change."[72] It was the system that was vicious, not the young men.

Portraying crime as a symptom of deeper social ills, however, turned the critical gaze on society itself and thereby invited censure closer to home. Interestingly, this rarely materialized. For the most part, contributory factors were mentioned in neutral tones and the possibilities for critical self-examination went unremarked. "Poverty and lack of opportunity breed crime," wrote a reporter from the *Globe and Mail*; but his article focused on the effect rather than the causes.[73] Similarly, a columnist for the same paper mentioned the roots of gang violence in "broken families, no male role models for young teenagers, widespread violence and disorder within the community itself [and] low levels of education," but that was not the "story" that interested him. It was, instead, the story "told by the numbers": "our streets are safe."[74]

The New Orleans District Attorney took a step closer to social criticism when he charged that "poverty, a near-absence of youth programs and a failing public school system"—"the root causes" of crime—"had festered for decades."[75] But he did not elaborate on this, or indicate who exactly was responsible. Taking an exceptional inward-looking stance, Orlando Patterson, from Harvard University, cited "the crisis in relations between men and women of all classes and ... the catastrophic state of black family life, especially among the poor" as the partial explanation for high rates of violence among African-Americans.[76] Elsewhere, he referred to a decline in "respect for traditional social norms."[77] And Canadian researcher Anne-Marie Ambert explained problematic juvenile behavior in terms of "everyone" (as the *Globe and Mail* put it): "parents (particularly single parents), other children, society, genetics, poverty, materialism, individualism and ... the media's violent programming."[78] That she had brought her criticisms too close to home for comfort was evident in the paper's reaction to her study, complaining that she had delivered a "moral lecture" that sought after an impossible set of social and ethical arrangements. Throughout Anglo-America, it was easier to treat crime as something pressing in from the outside than to view it as something growing within.

Latin America: an insecure moral community

> After being hounded by two men who followed her, one Sunday afternoon, in the stairways of Caracas' University Hospital, Lidmar Ruiz, a resident doctor, only walks with an escort on nights and weekends. At those times, this huge ten-storey building changes its appearance of a shopping mall and becomes a crossroads of lonely passageways and dark stairs. "I went into a consulting room and I didn't know if they wanted to rob me or attack me. Even if it's an emergency I don't go alone. They've already stolen my handbag while I slept in the domestic quarters on the third floor and, last week, they took 60,000 *bolívares* from my purse," says Ruiz.[79]

That an unclear encounter (perhaps the men were desperate for a medical opinion) and two episodes of theft should make it into a national daily paper is testimony neither to the type of crime or gender of the victim but to the significance of the location. Hospitals, and the people who staff them, are generally thought to be benign: they cure rather than cause harm. When crime makes its appearance in such morally benevolent environments it is a sign that something is seriously wrong, for even the spaces devoted to care are not free from risk. As *El Nacional* editorialized, "in the places we go to seek life, there awaits us a dangerous step towards death."[80] In a similar vein, a Mexican writer commented that, although public spaces and public transport are the most risky environments for crime, "the church, hospitals and private homes cannot be ruled out."[81] Back in Caracas, Eduardo Mayorca and his wife were tragic illustrations of his point:

> That particular wedding became a wake. It was not the typical scene in which the mother of the bride sobs with emotion. In this case, the bride and groom also cried, along with most of the guests.... Eduardo Mayorca, 68, and his wife Cristina Martí, 67, were to be the godparents of the wedding. They were parking their Ford Lancer when three men, pistol in hand, ordered them out of the car.... Mayorca, a plastic surgeon and retired ship captain, pulled out the weapon he was carrying and fired at the muggers to prevent the crime and wounded two of them. His response aroused the anger of his attackers. The car was hit by at least eight bullets. Mayorca and his wife died inside, with their seat belts still on.[82]

A focus on the violation of sacrosanct spaces was one of a number of ways of elaborating the theme that crime was everywhere. To declare its omnipresence was another. There is no place where one feels safe, editorialized *La Nación*:

"it has taken over public space, [and] ... also invaded private spaces.[83] Crime and violence in Mexico had managed to spread "everywhere: they take over the streets, go for a stroll in the parks and markets, or roam the roads and byways."[84] A particular cause of indignation was that many crimes happened "in broad daylight," suggesting that they were somehow impudent enough to show themselves in plain view rather than skulking in the shadows: "Murders by hit men, muggings in broad daylight, kidnapping and vaccination [protection] payments demanded by the police have become the most frequent crimes in the region during recent weeks," reported *El Nacional*;[85] "the murder of three police officers, who were kidnapped by about a hundred men in broad daylight and then tortured and beheaded," was mentioned by a Mexican researcher;[86] while "the rapes of women in broad daylight and in public places" was but one example of a "worrying increase in crime" cited by *La Nación*.[87]

Not only was crime happening everywhere and all the time, but—something that perhaps particularly irked the producers and consumers of these news texts—"it does not recognize social classes;"[88] "any mortal from the different social classes or of different political creeds can be converted into a victim of the underworld;"[89] and "random crime in the street can affect anyone."[90] These different claims—that crime was being committed everywhere, at all times, against anyone—were sprinkled through the texts assembled for this study. Individually, they did not appear with sufficient frequency to suggest that each was particularly common currency, but collectively they pointed to the widespread perception that current levels of crime were exceptional: "crime has gone beyond all known limits;"[91] "now, there is no respect for anyone or anything."[92] There was, in fact, a "crisis of public safety,"[93] and "the crime crisis continues to spread in the streets, neighborhoods and meeting places in every city and town."[94]

Indeed, crime seemed so intertwined with daily activity that it converted the territories of the ordinary citizen into "territories of insecurity." Such was the title of a series of nine articles published by Venezuela's *El Nacional* which depicted crime as the ever-present accompaniment to urban life:

> We are referring to violence and insecurity in their most varied and changing forms, spaces, tactics, modalities.... Following today's [article titled] "Violence also goes to school," will come holdups in traffic jams, muggings and express kidnappings in parking lots, robberies and violence in nighttime venues, robberies on the street, at the exits to the Metro, violence in hospitals, crimes in residential neighbourhoods, robberies at automatic tellers...[95]

This vision of crime as ubiquitous and threatening was bolstered by the focus and form of many of the statistics incorporated into commentary. One source of data were opinion surveys in which respondents were asked to rate the seriousness of the crime problem. For example, surveys in Argentina[96] and Venezuela[97] found that more people rated crime as the country's most serious problem than any other issue, such as unemployment or the cost of living, while a survey by

The moral outlook 63

El Universal in Mexico found that 60 percent of respondents felt that violence and drug trafficking were getting worse.[98] In Buenos Aires, a political think tank periodically measured an Index of Fear of Crime which indicated, in mid-2006, that "72% [of respondents] believe that they are at risk of becoming a crime victim;"[99] while another survey in Caracas found that "67% of Venezuelans cut back on going out at night because of the fear of becoming a victim of violence."[100] Many of these surveys also asked about victimization itself, reporting findings such as the following: "in 47% of Mexican homes at least one person was a victim of crime between January 1999 and June 2004;"[101] "83% of respondents [in Buenos Aires] ... reported being a crime victim or knowing someone who had been a crime victim during the previous year;"[102] and "45.87% [of passengers in Valencia, Venezuela] reported having been a victim of some type of crime on public transport."[103]

In line with this focus on actual and potential victims, a frequent technique of numerical presentation was to report the rate at which crime was occurring. For example, a state police chief in Venezuela claimed that there were about 60,000 criminals operating in his jurisdiction: "... common criminals are responsible for five murders a day and ... cause daily losses of 263 million *bolívares*. Meanwhile, organized crime causes 45 deaths every day ... and its members make 2.36 billion *bolívares* per day."[104] In Mexico, it was reported that there were "at least six violent deaths every day in the conflicts between organized crime groups,"[105] and two murders a day in Mexico City during the years of the Fox government (2000–2006).[106] In Buenos Aires, during the first eight months of 2007, "74 young offenders were arrested each day, in other words, three per hour."[107] In the same city:

> In recent weeks, and in an area of 16 blocks, 30 pedestrian lights were stolen. This number is added to the more than 50 traffic lights that have been damaged or stolen so far during 2007, as well as 10 vehicular traffic lights, 10 control boxes and more than 1500 meters of underground cable.[108]

This narrative technique brought immediacy to the numbers, implicitly inviting readers to visualize the individual events that ceaselessly appeared. It also evoked a randomness of occurrence and heightened the sense that victimization could fall on anyone:

> In 2004 nearly 12 million crimes were committed in [Mexico]: eight times more than the figure acknowledged by the authorities [wrote a researcher]. This means that 11 of every 100 people were victims of crime that year. At that rate it means that if you have not been a victim of crime in the last nine years you can consider yourself very lucky: you should have been a victim by now.[109]

Where crimes were not averaged out across days, years or people, their absolute numbers could give a sense of the size of the problem. In a few instances, these numbers were quite large: 7,702 people who, in a period of only ten days, contacted a Mexican agency after being threatened with extortion by phone;[110] or the "more than two thousand violent deaths and an unknown number of kidnapped and disappeared" attributed to organized crime in Baja California, Mexico, during 2006. This latter toll was likened by the authors to the grim contents of a "war dispatch," adding that "the number of victims is similar to the war in Iraq."[111] Mainly, however, the figures were much smaller: "During only the last weekend, there were 29 murders and seven on Monday and Tuesday.... And during the first three months of the year 10 people have been kidnapped,"[112] came the report from one of Venezuela's frontier states; "this year ... the number of robberies and thefts in *countries* [upper middle class neighborhoods] has risen to 48," reported *La Nación*;[113] while "this year there have been nine murders of women [in Sinaloa, Mexico] ... [i]n four cases the women were shot to death," reported *El Universal*.[114] What these numbers lost in size, they gained in their capacity to bring the reader closer to crime. Who, for example, were the four women that had been shot to death? How had they met their fate? Why had crime chosen them rather than others as its fatal victims? Questions such as these were neither asked nor answered in the text, but lurked under its surface, inviting readers to ponder on the circumstances in which they had died, thereby connecting themselves in some way with the world of crime.

All of these histories of the present were confined to a relatively thin slice of experience, detailing the distribution of crime in the here and now. Only trends invoked a clear sense of the passage of time; but trends were cited much less frequently here than in Anglo-America. In one example, *La Nación* reported that:

> In case Argentines do not want to feel unsafe: during the last ten years, the volume of crimes grew by 70 per cent—from 710,467 incidents in 1995 to 1,206,946 last year—while the population affected by them increased by only 10 per cent...[115]

In another, a spokesperson for Venezuela's Chamber of Commerce declared that "Venezuela is currently one of the most insecure countries in Latin America. Between 1986 and 2005, the homicide rate increased by 564%, kidnappings increased 426% and deaths in shootouts 253%."[116] Statements like these located their respective countries on trajectories of increasing crisis, offering incipient narratives of deterioration.

Nevertheless, just as in Anglo-America, trends were seemingly more malleable statistical artifacts which could be selected to suit a given political or moral objective. While claims that crime had decreased were less frequent than claims that it had increased, they were occasionally put forward by politicians, bureaucrats, and police chiefs as evidence of effective policies. Thus, a Venezuelan government minister affirmed that crime had declined "13.29% in four years,"[117] and the outgoing Mexican government claimed that serious crime had declined 23 per cent during its period in office,[118] a reduction curiously similar in size to that claimed by the Ministry of Security for Buenos Aires province between 2004 and 2006 (22.41 percent).[119] Almost without exception, these claims about decreases in crime were shrouded in polemic. Either those advancing them did so in a conscious attempt to refute claims that crime had increased,[120] or those reporting them added sceptical comments about the validity of the data.[121] By contrast, claims about increased rates were always presented uncritically, easily aligning themselves with the general perception that crime was everywhere.

Indeed, crime was seen to be so widespread that it could also be found in the institutions that were supposed to serve as the primary bulwark against it, particularly the police. On November 27, 2007, the Secretary of Public Safety in Tijuana, Mexico, was the target of an attempted assassination, which he survived unscathed. (More than 220 rounds were fired at his house—mainly his bedroom—and he apparently fired a few rounds in return.) In statements made after the incident, he linked the attack to organized crime operating in the city and, in particular, to the way in which it had "infiltrated" the police. He saw himself on one side of a "war in which spaces and regions are conquered for the commission of illicit activities and suddenly those spaces do not belong to citizens anymore." In this symbolic rendering of the moral struggle, one of the significant "spaces" succumbing to crime was that occupied by the police. In part, there seemed to be a process of corruption from within ("senior officers ... were exacting quotas and daily payments from line officers"); in part, there was the "infiltration" by organized crime already alluded to, coupled with an unholy alliance between the police and "common crime:" "For organized crime and common crime to be successful, they need institutional support," he commented. Much of the force had been corrupted: "(the percentage of corrupt officers) is high, but I don't know how high."[122]

This concern for the moral condition of the police, already mentioned in Chapter 3, was particularly acute in Mexico. "History shows us with frequency that he who today is a police officer can tomorrow end up as a *capo*, henchman, or hit man, with the added value of having been trained at the expense of the State," editorialized *El Universal*.[123] A candidate for the governorship of Baja California spoke of police officers who "sell themselves because of need, and those who sell themselves because they like to."[124] And the Governor of Nuevo León, announcing the suspension from duty of 113 municipal, state, and federal officers, charged that "organized crime has penetrated all the security forces."[125] Indeed, organized crime was seen to have gone beyond the police to affect other public agencies, perhaps to the point of competing with government:

> In Mexico the drug traffickers represent a power structure that developed under the tutelage of political power and has been protected by it [wrote the director of a prominent think tank]. This has functioned as one of the best informed hypotheses about the relation between the sphere of politics and that of drug trafficking.... However, the most recent information obliges us to review that position.... Are there now sectors of drug trafficking operating directly to capture State structures?[126]

Elsewhere in Latin America, similar concerns were expressed, but mainly in relation to the police and with a lesser degree of intensity:

> To the insecurity generated by the underworld, by criminals armed and drugged who do not hesitate to kill whoever resists their intentions, is added, and not recently but since a long time ago, the decomposition of police organizations [wrote a Venezuelan human rights activist].... It would not be imprudent to say that not a police force in the country is safe from having officers in its midst who are in league with the underworld, drawn by the easy and unsightly earnings derived from extortion...[127]

In Argentina, police corruption was named by *La Nación* as the second most important dimension of the crime problem (the first was overcrowded cities), and was attributed to "its marriage with the worst of Argentine politics, with the suburbs where it has fed on public resources, it has got involved in drug trafficking, prostitution, illegal gambling and led to highway robbery, bank robbery and burglary."[128] "Last week, in the province of Buenos Aires, two police officers stole an automatic teller machine. That's a snapshot of the reality in terms of safety," commented a politician.[129] Police deviance was one more proof that "Insecurity in Argentina's cities and rural areas has breached all known limits."[130]

As in Anglo-America, the metaphors most commonly used to dramatize crime came from the aquatic domain. References to the "level" of crime often depicted it as a kind of malevolent flood: like water from a swollen river, crime had "overflowed;"[131] "levels of violence are high,"[132] and "the level of insecurity is increasing."[133] Or crime came as a "wave that falls daily on the country."[134] Less cataclysmic, but more insidious, crime could "infiltrate" the police, other institutions of criminal justice, and even the political system. Also similar to Anglo-America, although comparatively less frequent, were depictions of crime as a disease, be it an "epidemic,"[135] an "endemic disease,"[136] a "social illness,"[137] or a "cancer."[138] By contrast, portrayals of crime as animate were more frequent: it was a "monster;"[139] it had "unleashed itself;"[140] it could "multiply"[141] and "grow;"[142] monarch-like, it "ruled" a particular territory,[143] and like a beast it could swoop on its "prey."[144] It could even "ride a motorbike,"[145] or "go to school."[146] Such descriptions added an unmistakable tone of drama to the moral outlook.

As in Anglo-America, the most frequent explanations for crime cast it as a product of otherness. At the most superficial level, crime fuelled itself. Mexican commentators attributed much violence to organized crime and drug trafficking, seeing them as the outcome of "struggles for the control of strategic points of the drug shipment routes;"[147] "the concentration and diversification of organized crime,"[148] or "the struggles among gangs that have been decapitated to decide who are the new leaders."[149] Sometimes, it was not drug traffickers but drug users who were cited as responsible. Thus, violence in the city of Mexicali was attributed to users in the *picaderos* (drug houses),[150] while in Argentina "There are many reasons that would explain the growth in criminality [editorialized *La Nación*]. One of them ... is the use of that infamous substance called *paco* [cocaine paste], which has grown 300% during the last five years."[151] One Argentine commentator cited "the easy access to drugs" as one of two causes of violence; the other was "easy access to guns."[152] Easy access to firearms was also mentioned in Venezuela.[153]

Given the anxieties, already described, about the moral fiber of the state, it is not surprising that the most frequently cited explanation for crime was that of an insufficient governmental response to it. The less critical version of this viewpoint located the cause in a failure to act, either to punish or to prevent crime. Thus, "impunity" for criminals resulting from the indolence of the authorities was mentioned on more than one occasion as the propitiating factor.[154] Similarly, an "absence of forceful measures,"[155] and a "lack of interest or negligence"[156] could explain the increases in crime, just as "operations"[157] or "the coordination between the community and the municipal police,"[158] could lead to decreases. On a different tack, the lack of preventive measures[159] or "the lack of continuity in public policies for citizen safety"[160] could be the cause of crime. In a more critical vein, it was not simply the inefficiency of the state, but its own turn to corruption and criminal activity that contributed to the problem. In the eyes of two academics, "the evident decomposition of the police forces"[161] and "inefficient, violent and corrupt"[162] officers accounted for the increase in crime in Venezuela. In Mexico, "the corruption of the police who specialize in combating drug trafficking,"[163] and "the corruption and complicity of the authorities"[164] were just two of the numerous references to the same kind of explanation. In Argentina, it was not so much the police who were cited as active causes of crime, but more nebulous phenomena, such as "corruption" and "clientelism"[165] emanating from the body politic.

To the lack of efficient or effective responses were sometimes added social or structural factors that pushed people into crime:

> There is an increase in young boys of 13 or 14 who commit armed robberies [commented a juvenile judge in Argentina] and the law prevents us from taking them under our tutelage.... This situation [added the provincial Minister of Public Safety] is encouraged by the absolute lack of measures to contain them. Minors who run away from home, minors who are outside the educational system, who have not been to school, who have no job training, who have no expectations or perspectives.[166]

It was as if they had gone to the margins of society, from there to prey on those who lived at the conventional law-abiding center.

Other commentators focused exclusively on these social structural factors. For example, a Venezuelan columnist attributed crime to a governmental failure to provide food, housing, and work, with the consequent frustration and violence that accompanied the increase in "insecurity."[167] Mexican businessmen cited

68 *The moral outlook*

poverty and inequality as "the structural causes of crime;"[168] while a political analyst saw the primary cause of "Mexican public insecurity" in "the precarious living conditions of the majority."[169] According to a BBC reporter in Argentina, "few doubt that inequality seems to one of the principal causes—albeit not the fundamental cause—of crime."[170]

The notion of multiple causes of crime was as prevalent in Latin America as it was in Anglo-America, made manifest in the lists of factors that, in both regions, were seemingly compiled on the spur of the moment. For example, the director of a treatment and intervention center for female adolescents in Mexico cited drug use, teen pregnancies, sexual abuse, neglect, delinquent male role models, the economy, low levels of education, and poor family relations as causes of crime among this group.[171] The president of an Argentine political party had an even longer list of causes of crime: impunity, poverty, marginality, injustice, exclusion, lack of education, the daily images of televised crime, morbidity, bribes, clientelist politics, and drugs.[172] A Mexican reporter captured a similarly long list in interviews with different experts, one of whom emphasized cultural forces:

> some of these young people [he said] want material possessions and to be someone in society; however, they have not been taught that to get these things it is necessary to make an effort. Thus, moral development does not keep up with social development...[173]

The focus on culture—something rarely found in Anglo-America—was shared by a number of commentators in Latin America. Thus, the director of a community social work agency in Caracas attributed much juvenile violence to "distorted values;"[174] a Mexican researcher cited "social resentment" as a cause of auto theft;[175] and *La Nación* saw "neglect, indolence, the lack of education, the lack of adequate supervision and irresponsibility" as the causes of vandalism.[176] It was here, in relation to culture and values, that societal responsibility for crime was potentially most evident. While, as in Anglo-America, social structural explanations of crime were rarely followed through into critiques of contemporary social arrangements, cultural explanations were sometimes accompanied by critical comments directed at civil society. Thus, a Mexican columnist called on readers to reflect in the following terms:

> Blaming the government for insecurity is not entirely correct, neither is it correct to say that it arises because of a lack of education or work, because, although it is true that the principal function of government is to offer security to we who are the governed, we must also recognize that we have failed as a society. To search for culprits without looking at ourselves in the mirror is the easiest and most comfortable thing to do. We have difficulty admitting our own responsibility, because, although it is true that there is unemployment, this is not the only factor that leads to insecurity. It should be seen as a multi-factored problem of education, corruption, impunity, lack of values,

family disintegration, lack of social security and the absence of community, to mention some of them.[177]

In a rather similar vein, a survey in Buenos Aires found that 49 percent of respondents attributed crime to cultural factors, summarized by the researchers in the following terms: "The crisis of values in education, the lack of a culture of work, Argentinians are taught *facilismo* [looking for the easy way], or they are not taught to value and respect social norms."[178] With these sorts of explanation, commentators joined the social critics who featured in Chapter 3. While they were relatively few in number, their presence suggests that, in addition to the perceived external threats to the moral community, the latter's claims to virtue might be hollow: "we have failed as a society." In more than one way, therefore, the moral community in Latin America might be insecure.

Morally significant certainties

A striking sense of certainty pervaded many of the statements about crime and its causes: "...violence in general is not sharing the decline that property offences are, and within violence there's some shifting;"[179] "a robust police presence is what reduces overall crime rates;"[180] "...common criminals are responsible for five murders a day and ... cause daily losses of 263 million *bolívares*;"[181] "public insecurity in Mexico has different causes, but the precarious living conditions of the majority stand out."[182] In some cases, that certainty was explicitly affirmed: "There is no doubt that the existence of some 260 million guns ... increases the death rate in this country," wrote a US researcher;[183] "The nexus between poverty and crime is clear," wrote a New York lawyer;[184] "few doubt that inequality seems to be one of the principal causes ... of crime," wrote the BBC's correspondent in Argentina;[185] "there is no doubt that the Pacific ports are one of the routes that is being prioritized for the entry of cocaine" commented a spokesperson for the Mexican Federal Public Safety Agency.[186]

Any of these, or hundreds of other similar statements, could have been challenged on their validity. What evidence existed to support them? How had it been collected? How interpreted? A questioning attitude regarding data and inferences, of the type commonly held to underlie good science, would have introduced a considerable degree of uncertainty and forced commentators to speak in much more provisional terms.

For example: "A robust police presence ... reduces overall crime rates."[187] This was the belief of British Columbia's Solicitor-General. But on what did he base that belief? Had he examined comparative data for areas with weak and robust police presence? Had he been able to rule out the influence of other variables on crime rates? Had he looked at what the research literature reported? If he had done the latter, he would have found that things are by no means as simple as his claim implied. In the words of one team of researchers, "It is far from clear ... that adding police does in fact reduce crime."[188] According to another team, "increases in police manpower will not increase

70 *The moral outlook*

general deterrent effects and decreases will not reduce these effects."[189] He would, in fact, have found that there are considerable methodological challenges to testing his claim and that, as a putative research finding, it needs to be accompanied by a large number of conditional statements regarding the types of crime it applies to, the level of analysis adopted and the type of statistical procedure employed.[190]

Or take the following: "The nexus between poverty and crime is clear."[191] "Few doubt that inequality seems to be one of the principal causes ... of crime."[192] Claims such as these stand in marked contrast to the more cautious statements found in the research literature. "What is the relationship between crime rates and the economic conditions of social areas?" asked one researcher. His reply was equivocal: "After more than a century and a half of empirical and theoretical investigations ... this question remains controversial."[193] More recently, another researcher reported that "studies testing the effects of income inequality and poverty on crime rates at various units of analysis yield mixed results,"[194] a situation that is not untypical of many areas of scientific interest. Once again, the research literature offers a much more complex and notably less categorical position than that found in the newspapers.[195]

Even moving from the more complicated realm of explanation to the apparently simpler task of description, consider the following: "...common criminals are responsible for five murders a day and ... cause daily losses of 263 million *bolívares*. Meanwhile, organized crime causes 45 deaths every day ... and its members make 2.36 billion *bolívares* per day."[196] How were these figures arrived at by the police chief who gave them to the press? Putting aside the difficulties of distinguishing between "common criminals" and "organized crime," were police investigatory resources sufficient to identify the persons responsible for each of *50 deaths per day*? How were the costs of common crime (lost property, time off work, etc.) calculated, particularly for incidents that were not reported to the police? How were earnings from organized crime computed in the very probable absence of comprehensive data about its operations? The solidity of the claims easily weakens under a cursory methodological scrutiny.

The certainty with which most empirical claims were made in the press, including those offered by researchers, contrasts strongly with the uncertainty that attaches to most results deriving from systematic inquiry.[197] Considering the dissimilar worlds of science and mass communication, Quarantelli attributed this trait to a journalistic striving for simplicity, particularly through an avoidance of jargon and the omission of qualifiers.[198] Titus wrote that "scientific uncertainty and contingency are mutated into journalistic conviction and dramatic simplicity."[199] This may well be part of the explanation. Science, obviously, has its specialist participants and publics. Among scholars, researchers, and students; in classrooms, conferences, and academic books or journals; the complexities, limitations, and significance of theories, methods, and results are discussed, and, sometimes, debated. These discourses are not for general consumption; they have developed around particular sets of information, terminologies, and patterns of thought.[200] They are self-evidently not material for the non-specialist readership catered to by newspapers; hence, the challenge for researchers to say something intelligible and convincing when speaking to the general public.

But there is also a practical need to "fix" knowledge for the purposes of social action. As Lindblom put it: "[The sciences] often shrink from giving answers when answers are desperately needed.... Meanwhile, ordinary people and functionaries are compelled to go on making commitments on how to live and how to solve social problems without waiting for answers..."[201] Indeed, "ordinary people and functionaries" were the bulk of commentators on crime across the Americas, their declarations far outnumbering those of researchers.[202] They provided their own answers to questions about crime (its characteristics, causes, and consequences), just as the researchers who entered this discursive domain were compelled to do the same, in implicit acknowledgment that all of this commentary was directed at the business of living (and solving social problems) rather than at the realm of understanding.

Moralizing, an activity very much bound up with "how to live and how to solve social problems," eschews uncertainty. If it did not, it would be in danger of becoming an empty exercise. No meaningful censure can be invoked against a problem that does not exist; no virtue deployed to deal with it.[203] Putative certainty was not just instrumental to moralizing but seemingly a requirement for it, and, where doubt was present, remedial discursive action had to be taken by alluding to possibilities, probabilities or potentialities: "The 2005 figures [for US crime] are not necessarily the beginning of a trend upward for everyone ... *but the potential does exist*;"[204] "Though criminal justice experts were cautious about drawing conclusions from six months of data, *they found the report worrisome.*"[205]

Hypothetically, these certainties would not preclude disagreements: one commentator's factual claim may be objectionable to another. Indeed, this was precisely the genesis of Males' critical attack on Bratton—his charge that crime was not, as the police chief had affirmed, "coming back." The variety of statements made about crime and its causes, amply evidenced in the foregoing analysis, created the potential for many such argumentative exercises. Yet disagreements over factual claims were rare in this set of texts, and almost all of them were, like Males' article, concerned with trends in crime rates. Were they going up or were they going down? The emergence of controversy on that point, albeit infrequent, probably reflected a perceived simplicity and efficacy in the functioning of crime trends as indicators of the moral outlook. Statements about the increase or decrease in crime were the most readily accessible indicators of the nation's moral health, a convenient reference point for satisfaction or concern, and therefore a crucial object of social and political attention. For the rest, factual claims were brought unchallenged (and usually unsubstantiated) into the discursive arena.[206] Their function was not to further understanding, but to provide a necessary prop for the business of living (and attending to crime).

Even where disagreement arose about matters of fact, there was little debate beyond a few brief rebuttals in letters to the editor.[207] This was a discursive domain in which factual claims went largely unexamined, their content limited not by critical empirical scrutiny but by the powerful influence of convention on public knowledge, by the availability of a common, but fairly restricted vocabulary, for talking about crime and its causes: drugs, gangs, guns, "senseless violence," "good news," the economy, and so on, in the North; the crisis of public safety, the number of murders per day, the corrupt police and organized crime, etc., in the South. Such vocabulary provided the themes around which relatively minor idiosyncratic variations were composed.

The factual certainties asserted in these texts thus provided a context which was supportive of the moral discourse. But the moral segments themselves also contained normative and literary elements which made them much more refractory to empirical critique. Perhaps, as befits a researcher, Mike Males was one of the more assiduous critics of someone else's factual claims. Indeed, he even went so far as to engineer a sense of debate by predicting a likely (and imputedly disingenuous) reply from Bratton to his own counterclaim that crime was declining: "even when crime is down and youth arrests are plummeting, there is always some offense in some city in some year that rose when compared to some previous year."[208] In so doing, Males attributed his disagreement with Bratton to their respective focuses on different sets of information: Males was looking at the sustained declines in general crime rates during recent decades; Bratton was looking at a very recent countertrend in selected crime rates. Yet this disagreement was hardly about matters of fact, for both commentators had data to support their positions; this disagreement was about a moral claim. "America, we have a problem," declared Bratton, citing one set of information; "no, we do not," effectively replied Males, citing another.

But it is obvious that what constitutes a problem cannot be resolved by empirical research alone; a normative judgment is also required, a declaration that the situation is in some sense undesirable.[209] There was no such normative debate in Males' article, and if he *had* taken that route things would have quickly become complicated. Should the countertrend in violence be dismissed as a problem because other crime rates were declining? Should the increases in violence be seen as a problem only for its victims, or for the cities where they lived, rather than as a problem for civil society? Is some violence trivial, or is all violence serious? These, and other matters, would have needed resolution in order to decide whether or not America had a problem. And, in the solidly conventional moral domain of the newspapers, it would have required a valiant and morally creative soul to argue that increases in violence were not a problem. It is not that Bratton's claim was irrefutable, but it was a much more demanding task to refute it than Males perhaps realized, and one which required engagement on the moral terrain as much as the empirical. Moral claims also require moral critiques.

Metaphor was also present in Bratton's moral bulletin, among other places in his rallying call to the nation to "refocus on this gathering storm." Here was a vision of crime preparing to rain down on the good, to beat at the doors of convention and wreak damage on civil society. Males did not choose to counter this claim directly, perhaps assuming that his evidence was sufficient to reveal its hollowness. Or perhaps he felt, very wisely, that it was answerable only in a laborious fashion. For, in using metaphor, Bratton had insulated himself from much empirical critique. To demand a definition of "storms," or to seek operational indicators of their presence or proximity, would be to miss the point. Bratton had used the term in what Kenneth Burke called the "poetic" rather than the "semantic" sense.[210] Poetic meanings cannot be promptly judged as true or false, but must be evaluated for their capacity to convey a valid idea. They are statements about the world of experience, but not factual claims of the sort researchers are used to making. To question the validity of "this gathering storm of crime" would have required Males to address its "scope, range, relevancy, accuracy [and] applicability."[211] He might have had to propose a different metaphor (after all, researchers were as likely as anyone else to speak of crime "waves," "levels," "blips," and so on); or he might have rejected the use of metaphor in descriptions of crime. But if he had done the latter, he would have had to engage in detailed discourse analysis to banish poetic meanings from Bratton's utterances, and from his own.[212]

Given that certainty seems to be a prerequisite for moralizing, it is not surprising that poetic language (in Burke's sense of the term) often accompanies segments of text that denote censure. Metaphor, of the sort seen above (and earlier in this chapter), was one kind of trope found in the sample of texts, but hyperbole was the more frequent exemplar. "We are turning the country over to our young people, and they are killing each other," charged a police chief quoted by Males;[213] "Jesus, nothing but stabbings, shootings, B and Es," exclaimed a resident of Toronto's Danforth East;[214] "When you're in a gang, you have three things to look forward to: prison, the hospital or death," warned a church youth leader.[215] With its exaggeration and excess, hyperbole, in the apt words of Ritter, "stretches and strains facts and ... elicits a constructive, transformative ambiguity for alternative possibilities of meaning and being."[216] These portrayals of critical situations would certainly give pause for thought.

Hyperbole was a particular feature of Latin American commentary, being more frequent, extensive, and strident than anything found in the North. As seen earlier in this chapter, for example, crime and violence were "everywhere;"[217] "now, there is no respect for anyone or anything;"[218] "criminals armed and drugged ... do not hesitate to kill whoever resists their intentions."[219] But it is in Chapter 3 that the Latin American moralists showed their capacity for sustained outpourings of hyperbole:

> This is how the country has been divided into two great universes, that of the victims and that of the victimizers, the first group being those who follow the law and remain within "the rule of law," receiving in exchange mistreatment, arrogance, insecurity and the gradual destruction of its wealth...[220]

> For the fearful majority, the great national matters today begin with managing to reach life's end when God decrees it and not when an outlaw decides it...[221]

74 *The moral outlook*

> The violent death of a young person is always a terrible failure of society, all violence is. Its consequences last beyond the circumstance, degrading coexistence in freedom, strengthening the perception of the other as a possible enemy, exacerbating paranoid and egotistical behaviours...[222]

This was a discursive style absent in the North. It portrayed the moral outlook in terms that were elusive to empirical critique. But it was not a work of fiction, for it self-evidently expressed the realities that appeared to its authors. Its exaggeration and excess were the key to its urgent tone. This was the platform for righteous indignation.

Drawing back

Mike Males' article in the *Los Angeles Times* exemplifies much of the researcher's approach to collective commentary on crime. His objective was to debunk the idea that crime, particularly juvenile crime, was on the increase; and to do so he offered an extended presentation of crime statistics. Similarly, in the voluminous and ever-expanding academic literature on crime in the mass media, one prominent theme has been some sort of debunking. Focusing on the "construction" or "framing" of crime, researchers have sought to put distance between themselves and the representations that they identify, working to reveal their ingredients of myth, exaggeration or ideology.[223] Although most of this research is seen only by other researchers (and their captive students), its general tone, if not its style, implies that a wider audience ought to see it; indeed, more than one academic has urged that criminologists should actively seek to get themselves read, seen, and heard in the mass media.[224] In pitching their work as socially relevant, criminologists engage in the social construction that they are simultaneously studying, although they often seem not to be aware of it.[225] As a result, they have been implicitly or explicitly competing to write histories of the present, as much as thinking about how those histories are elaborated and imbued with moral significance. Rather than asking what the moral outlook looks like, criminologists are more likely to have an opinion about what it should look like. Much research could be cited that complements or contradicts the outlooks described here; indeed, this is necessarily so since researchers and their outputs were one source of knowledge that appeared in commentaries about crime. But research has rarely approximated a depiction of the collective moral outlook as a composite product of commonsense ideas, politically driven knowledge claims, research results, anecdote, and so on. Thus, the Anglo-American vision of crime as hopefully contained, and the Latin American vision of crime as largely unchecked have previously gone unremarked.

In providing their own view of the moral outlook, criminologists and other researchers are constrained to deal in certainties, however provisional they might be. From the congeries of data and ideas available they must select some as the foundations for their own histories of the present. Of course, they hope (and will often claim) that the knowledge claims they advance would also be accepted by other researchers and by a wider audience. They cast their comments largely in terms of "evidence." But evidence is not the only resource for constructing morally significant knowledge claims; poetic uses of language and hyperbole can also accompany much moral talk. The seemingly axiomatic requirement for moralizing to be based on some kind of empirical certainty, and the manner in which poetic language and hyperbole can readily fulfill that imperative, have so far gone unnoticed in studies of social problems' "rhetoric."[226] In this way, as with histories of the present, a focus on the moral outlook suggests lines of inquiry that have not, previously, received much attention.

5   Moral agency

"We can't just throw our hands up in the air and say we can't do anything about this problem."[1] These were the concluding words to an article about violence, and responses to it, in the city of Baltimore, Maryland. They were spoken by a trauma surgeon who worked at the University of Maryland Medical Center. He had been consulted by a reporter from the *New York Times*, who was writing an article about new moves by the city's recently elected Mayor, Sheila Dixon, to deal with crime. She had convened the press to announce the formation of a task force on illegal guns, together with the installation of a system "to track where and when guns had been used in crimes."

> "Attacking gun crime," Ms. Dixon said, "means cracking down on gun sales and arresting, prosecuting and putting in prison criminals who carry and use guns." The city has had 93 homicides so far this year [continued the journalist who wrote this piece], compared with 88 at the same time last year. Last weekend alone, six people were killed.... Ms. Dixon spoke at a news conference where the police displayed 260 guns and rifles that officers had confiscated last month alone.... "Just an incredible amount of firepower coupled with a bulletproof vest," [said a deputy police commissioner]. "It really does speak volumes about what we're encountering."

Employing a typical reportorial technique, the journalist sought an independent opinion from a professional who might know something about the topic, in this case the doctor:

> Dr. Carnell Cooper, a trauma surgeon at the ... University of Maryland Medical Center here, said some form of gun control was needed to quell the violence. "Nationally, we're up against individual rights versus the health and safety of our citizens," Dr. Cooper said. "We need to somehow come to a compromise." Dr. Cooper said that locally something had to give. Last year, Baltimore recorded 275 homicides, up from 269 in 2005. "We can't just throw our hands up in the air and say we can't do anything about this problem."

Cooper's depiction of the tension between individual rights and health and safety was a workable portrayal of one dimension of the conflict over gun ownership in the United States. What is the appropriate balance between the right to bear arms and the need to control access to firearms in pursuit of lower rates of lethal violence? But this journalistic rendering of his comments gave greater weight to that which appeared last. The auxiliary verb "can't" was repeated twice in his final statement, but with very different meanings. In the second instance, "we can't do anything" was a description. It simply meant "we are unable to do anything." In the first, "we can't just throw our hands up in the air" was used as an injunction. It meant that "we ought not to throw our hands up in the air." It gave a particular moral significance to the doctor's parting comment. It was a call to action.

The virtue of action was an important dimension of moral identity in the set of texts compiled for this study. A determined stance, the disposition to confront crime, a readiness to do something; these were the requisite qualities to accompany sentiments of disapproval and concern. Censure of crime and empathy with its multiple victims were not enough; something had to be done. "The situation [of insecurity] needs to be faced with measures that overcome the perception of stagnation that exists," wrote an Argentine lawyer, "we believe that action is the mandate for overcoming the sensation of paralysis."[2] Indeed, a prime source of moral weakness would be the failure to act, as if moral integrity were founded not only on emotions but also on doing the right thing. In this sense, the demand for action sprang as much from the collective conception of what morality required as it did from the nature of events. The injunction to do something was a call for collective morality to manifest itself.

Calls to do something were very frequent in this set of texts, and extremely varied in content. For example, "About 1,500 people who took part in the final day of the March Against Insecurity ... demanded a 'halt to violence' and 'police corruption, '" reported *El Universal* in Mexico;[3] while "It is time for concrete actions and not for more vain and unfulfilled promises," editorialized Argentina's *La Nación*.[4] A Canadian advocate called for the creation of an ombudsman for victims at the provincial and territorial level;[5] an Argentine legislator urged that the capital's subway company should hire security guards and install closed-circuit cameras;[6] and Democratic politicians in California "unveiled a package of bills" for dealing with gangs.[7] A community activist in Caracas called on the Minister of the Interior and Justice to "address the serious problem of insecurity, which stains hundreds of homes with blood every day."[8] "We believe that all violent crimes should be prosecuted vigorously," declared the White House Press Secretary, "and that all people should be protected from violent crimes."[9]

Alongside these calls to action were criticisms of current arrangements for dealing with crime. For example, Argentina's *La Nación* disagreed with a recent judicial decision that removed the use of a weapon from the list of aggravating factors to be applied in sentencing.[10] The *New York Times* lamented "a particularly woeful crime statistic from the Federal Bureau of Investigation: nationwide, nearly 40 percent of all homicides go unsolved each year."[11] And a Mexican researcher declared that the outgoing Fox government had left various aspects of crime and insecurity unattended, including prisons which were "a true disaster zone."[12] In each case, the criticism clearly implied some specific or generic course of action that should be taken.

Other commentary straddled the fuzzy border between what is effective and what is desirable as responses to crime. Thus, nearly 50 percent of respondents in a Buenos Aires survey felt that crime would be better addressed if the city's police were under local, rather than national, control;[13] specialist prosecutors in the United States commented that the Internet could be an important resource for solving crimes;[14] and the Mayor of Mexicali argued that "if we want to stamp out crime, more resources have to be devoted to crime prevention."[15] Whether these, and similar, declarations were comments about what would work, or prescriptions about what should be done, was unclear from the texts themselves.[16]

If to these are added commentaries on what could or could not be done in relation to crime;[17] on how crime-oriented measures function;[18] on what was being done in relation to crime;[19] or what was about to be done in relation to it,[20] in this set of texts there was more commentary about measures for dealing with crime than about crime itself.[21] The drama of crime was outweighed by the practicalities of dealing with it, and never left to play itself out alone.[22] Even the lengthy depictions of rampant insecurity from someone like Gertz Manero were mindful of the importance of action: "Whoever believes that this is the way to design the political and social future of this country, has no idea what awaits us," he wrote in conclusion to his diatribe on "Victims and victimizers."[23] In another piece, on "The insecurity that annihilates," he concluded that, if his "testimonies" did not "move the three powers and the leaders of the nation," and if they continued to think that the "ungovernable monster can be combated with aspirins and good intentions, our present and future will be gravely affected."[24]

Gertz Manero was writing histories of the present. They were melodramatic and hyperbolic, but histories nonetheless. He was taking stock of recent events and looking to the immediate future. He was warning that things were getting worse, pointing to the importance of action. Strictly speaking, he was calling for a *reaction* to the developments that he portrayed so dramatically. And while few commentators in this set of texts shared his literary style, all were similarly writing histories of the present, however selective or specialized, and all proceeded in some manner or other to write the next chapter as a response to what had recently been happening.[25]

> Maybe the best holiday gift Los Angeles received this year was the news that fewer of its citizens are being murdered [commented the *Los Angeles Times*]. As *The Times* reported this week, the city is on track to end 2007 with the lowest homicide count since 1970, when L.A. had 1 million fewer residents. Public officials, police and academics give differing reasons for the drop in violence, but it's a phenomenon to be celebrated regardless of its cause. And it's evidence that police efforts to crack down on gangs—the source of most of L.A.'s killings—should be continued and strengthened; despite the good news, the war on gangs isn't anywhere close to being won.[26]

As is often the case in newsprint, this opening paragraph to an editorial strategically summarized the rest of the item: homicide rates were continuing to decline (for reasons that were not entirely clear), but to maintain this trend into the future the police should continue and strengthen their response to gangs. The rest of the text was divided about equally between comments on the possible causes of the decline in gang homicide and censure of the "senselessness" and trivial precipitators of many fatal incidents. The editorial concluded that "New strategies from [the police] have undoubtedly played a part in the reduction in street killings. They aren't a cure for the social ills that breed gangs.... But they're part of the solution. Keep them coming." Here, the final, imperative, sentence was a prescription for action; a call for the police to keep doing what they were already doing.

In these histories of the present, crime was always an antecedent problem that required a subsequent "solution" or "response," from the state, civil society, or both. "Combating the organized crime groups which *have taken over* the majority of states in the country" was a task facing the newly elected Mexican President, according to a researcher consulted by *El Universal*.[27] "More than 1,500 people marched Thursday through Riverside, carrying poster-sized photographs of relatives *lost to violent crimes*, and rallied for tougher penalties for California's offenders," reported the *Los Angeles Times*.[28] "Gang violence is a serious challenge but it requires a pointed response," wrote a Canadian columnist;[29] "national and provincial authorities should make a response" to the "drama of insecurity suffered by millions of Argentines," editorialized *La Nación*.[30] Even crime prevention, which has a forward-looking focus, was triggered by phenomena that had already emerged. The Toronto police chief proposed to use prevention for domestic violence incidents, which were "higher this year than in several years;"[31] the authorities in Mexico City set up a Violence and Addiction Prevention Program in 23 neighborhoods that were heavily affected by drugs, crime, and domestic violence;[32] citizens in Mendoza, Argentina, outraged by the "barbaric" number of murders, demanded more crime prevention.[33]

The extent to which the discursive pattern that inhered in these histories rewrote the temporal order, that is, the number of times that the "solutions" shaped the "problems" (rather than vice versa),[34] is impossible to determine from the texts themselves. More interesting here was the persistent focus on the stream of events; the latter packaged into short segments by commentators who figuratively paused to depict the moral outlook and make calls to change the course of affairs, to redirect these histories, to effect new social or institutional arrangements (or improve those already in existence). This historical framework was integrally linked to the conception and form of the prescriptions that were advanced. And it is the characteristics, existential doubts, and significance of this conception of moral agency which are explored in this chapter.

Stirring morality

Calls to do something varied greatly, not only in their content but also in their style. Some commentators set out proposals in fairly concrete detail, others formulated prescriptions in only the vaguest of terms. Some got involved in the minutiae of legislative proposals; others merely urged change. Indeed, there was a marked difference between calls for action, in and of itself, and calls for a particular type of response to crime. The former were much more prevalent in Latin America, where widespread perceptions of inaction or criminal behavior on the part of the state were the prologue to injunctions to get something done.

> In these three articles on insecurity [wrote a Venezuelan columnist] ... I have tried to present a general view of the insecurity that we experience in our country which is a strategy planned by a government more interested in obtaining power than using it for the good of the people.... As a response, I propose that we do not get disheartened, we do not give up hope, and that we persevere. Unamuno already said it: "For consistency, resistance; for subsistence, assistance; and for existence, insistence." Let us insist, therefore, in our ideas, let us assist and help our fellows and the institutions that represent or might represent us and, being congruent with our ideas, let us be consistent in our actions, resisting the unsettling onslaughts of the violent and terrifying policies of a leader and his group...[35]

> It matters little to the family of someone who has been savagely murdered whether the crime rates increased or decreased [editorialized *La Nación* while denouncing the complacency of the Minister of the Interior], what really matters to them is that justice be done and that ways be found to prevent and repress any criminal behavior.[36]

> We firmly demand energetic action and immediate results [editorialized *El Universal* after criticizing the corruption and inefficiency of the government].[37]

Here, and in similar sorts of statement, no particular line of action was envisaged; the call was merely for a better future but without any detailed vision of some more secure or beneficent society. Indeed, in some cases, action seemed to be little more than alerting to the need for action: "It is time to draw the attention of all social sectors," wrote *El Universal* about the problem of juvenile alcohol consumption;[38] "each one, in his own sphere, must be concerned about the present and future of our children and adolescents," wrote an Argentine columnist;[39] "We are still in time to do something, even if it is writing a letter," wrote Liliana Cánaves, in a spirit of epistolary idealism.[40] The tone was often poetic, the narrative often dramatic, and the corresponding call to action more important than any practical detail. These were commentators who seemed more concerned with the act of invoking morality itself than they were with setting the parameters for the future; hence, their injunctions looked idealistic, quixotic, and unanswerably vague. Barely seen in Anglo-America, and by no means the primary idiom in Latin America, these calls to action could be usefully seen as *stirring morality*: they sought to bring it to life, and often in high-flown terms.[41]

General calls to action such as these did not evoke disagreement. "The battle against that scourge [crime] affronts the whole society," wrote Mexican journalists, "and in this fight no effort can be spared."[42] No one said otherwise, either in this piece or in other texts published by *El Universal*. "Deputies agreed that to fight effectively against crime it is vital to have all citizens involved, irrespective of their ideology," [reported *El Nacional*]; and, in a country as politically polarized as Venezuela, even opposition governors and mayors joined in the discussion.[43] Such was the importance assigned to action that no one proffered an alternative formula; no one counselled resignation (or merely patience); no one depicted crime as a misfortune rather than as a problem to be solved.

Underlining this imperative, it was the failure to act that was taken as a sign of moral weakness and which could be used as a gambit in one kind of political polemic. Opposition legislators in Mexico, blaming the president for "the brutal insecurity" in the country, charged that there was a lack of "readiness, will and commitment" on the part of the government;[44] while the president himself was asserting that "the government has not given a truce to organized crime."[45] A police chief in western Venezuela attributed recent incidents of violence to Colombian paramilitaries who were crossing an "open border," and the commander of the National Guard (the agency responsible for border control) replied that "a frontal attack is being kept up against armed bandits who cross the border."[46] The Mayor of Mar de la Plata, in Argentina, charged that "no go" zones were appearing in his city, where "it seems that crime can operate with absolute freedom," to be countered by the police chief who affirmed that "we have officers and we are working."[47] This occasional trading of general accusations and counter-claims was as far as stirring morality led in terms of creating disagreement.

Prosaic morality

In contrast to the above, much prescriptive text was concerned with specific actions, especially in Anglo-America.

> About a year ago, the New York State Legislature made a number of revisions to the Rockefeller drug laws [began an opinion article published in the *New York Times*].... These measures were a step in the right direction, but unfortunately they fail to take into account drug kingpins. As the new legislative session begins this month, the priority should be to retain severe sentencing for major drug dealers while providing more alternatives to incarceration and more treatment options for low-level addicts and small-time dealers. To do this, we must provide judges with greater discretion in determining which defendants should be placed in alternative sentencing and treatment programs. We must pass legislation that provides for more such programs. And we must enact a kingpin statute to ensure that major

and violent drug predators are sentenced appropriately and cannot have their sentences reduced.[48]

The language was replete with terms that marked the writer's vision of new institutional arrangements as a moral agenda: "step in the right direction," "the priority should be," "we must provide judges," "we must pass legislation," and so on. The list of actions was fairly extensive, and its elaboration took up most of the rest of the article, avoiding the technical detail that would interest only lawyers and legislators, outlining briefly how each proposal would work, and providing some anecdotes in support of key recommendations. Because of its language, the moral tint was a little stronger in this text than in many others, but any piece that was concerned with proposals or recommendations was similarly performing normative work: "Republican Rep. Frank R. Wolf... said *he would support* additional federal funding for crime control in the district;"[49] "Among the *proposed* amendments, the Tories want to impose two-year mandatory prison sentences on people convicted of trafficking hard drugs;"[50] "Ms. Bath of Security on Campus says ... [h]er group is *pushing for* the Enhanced 911 service, which allows emergency dispatchers to pinpoint the dorm room where a call is made."[51] Similar sorts of call were also made in Latin America: "he *demanded* that a checkpoint be installed, or that the existing one be activated because it is not operating;"[52] "the police at all levels *need to be* given firepower;"[53] "crime statistics are public information and for that reason *should be* made available."[54]

With its orientation to specific actions and measures, the practical content of this kind of injunction gave it a much more mundane, occasionally tedious, tone. This was the prosaic morality relating to sentencing, treatment, policing, checkpoints, weapons, federal funding, crime statistics, and a host of other topics. It could not be expressed in the rousing terms of generic calls to action—it is difficult to put poetry into legislative proposals or policy blueprints—but it far outweighed stirring morality in abundance and extension.

In the detail of these prescriptions, some well-established differences emerged. A large number of proposals focused on the business of controlling crime and offenders. For example, a state-sponsored commission in New York called for DNA samples "to be collected from anyone convicted of a crime;"[55] a civil rights activist demanded "a federal crackdown on hate crimes and a more vigorous response to incidents of noose hangings;"[56] Canadian crime victims "urged the country's next elected government to move forward with an aggressive plan to remove handguns from urban streets;"[57] the Caracas Chamber of Commerce proposed that a new emergency number be set up "to help in the fight against the scourge of insecurity;"[58] a Mexican researcher proposed the creation of a special investigatory unit for computer crimes and new federal legislation to "combat cyber criminals;"[59] and Argentina's *La Nación* wrote that "over and above the need to adapt the legislation to new exigencies, it is not a matter of drawing up new reforms or more laws, but of ensuring compliance with those that already exist."[60] Some such calls also proposed a more punitive stance towards offenders, usually by putting more people in prison, and for longer.[61]

Another approach focused on the mitigation of factors that were seen to push people into crime. Some of these proposals addressed social conditions such as poverty or unemployment. For example, a retired police chief in Venezuela recommended "education, more employment, and saving neglected children" as measures to deal with youth violence;[62] the Attorney General of Mexico's Federal District argued that "social programs are needed to combat crime ... [such as] economic support for single mothers, health plans, construction of schools, training;"[63] and a letter written to the *New York Times* supported birth control ("the criminals of tomorrow are being born at lower rates") and social services ("And when born, have more social services available").[64] Other proposals centered on individuals at risk of offending or re-offending. For example, a Canadian lawyer argued for "increased funding for correctional programs so that those who are incarcerated are released with skills;"[65] a New York judge convicted of embezzlement advocated "the importance of rehabilitation in prison;"[66] and a Mexican researcher urged that "young [offenders] should not be stigmatized, instead they should be given comprehensive treatment."[67]

Collectively, these sets of recommendations pursued either greater control or greater welfare, a difference that has potentially important ideological and political significance.[68] But, while most prescriptive statements involved only one of these approaches, ideology and politics did not arrange themselves to fit neatly with this analytical distinction. So, for example, a Mexican researcher supported measures to improve the control of drug trafficking, while also calling for "the restoration of social, employment, educational and food security;"[69] demonstrators in Buenos Aires urged both the "upgrading of shanty towns," and "the creation of juvenile detention centers and jails which restrain those who are held there;"[70] the Canadian Minister for Public Safety declared that "We want to have [a] balance of enforcement and prevention;"[71] and the Director of a Californian NGO proposed a "Marshall Plan of sorts that would mix law enforcement with gang intervention and job programs, community outreach and newly created community oversight groups."[72] No one seemed to think that these eclectic prescriptions were fatally riven by ideological antagonisms. And, when it came to explicit ideological or political frameworks, the situation was equally confused. For example, in Argentina, the most frequently recognized ideological encounter was between the notions of *mano dura* ("firm hand") and *garantismo* (individual rights)—both pertaining to questions of control—but commentators were unanimous in rejecting this as an unhelpful dichotomy.[73] In Canada, newspaper readers witnessed both the Liberal and Conservative parties competing for the most politically appealing approaches to crime control, rather than debating the relative merits of welfare and control.[74] And in California, a "Democratic gubernatorial candidate ... threw his support behind a Republican ballot measure ... to toughen the penalties for sex crimes."[75]

Most proposals for dealing with crime did not elicit an immediate or direct response from anyone. They merely remained in the never-ending flow of texts as signals that actions were being sought by commentators and, in that sense, as symbols that identified the moral community. To the extent that debate emerged, it focused on specific topics, such as safe zones for the sex trade,[76] what to do about gangs,[77] whether to collect DNA from all convicted offenders,[78] the use of preventive detention,[79] and whether to publish crime statistics.[80] But these were fuzzy debates, often one-sided and without an answering opponent, or played out in a very perfunctory way across different texts with no explicit connections between them. It was only when a commentator engaged in deliberation, and weighed up the pros and cons of some specific proposal, that clearer lines of argument emerged. And these were interesting for what they revealed about the instrumental character of the morality that they reflected.

Moral deliberations

Some of the more specific proposals purveyed by prosaic morality opened the door to differences of opinion regarding what should be done because, as one newspaper put it (citing a well-known phrase), "[t]he devil ... is in the details."[81] But a devil was seen there only because debaters and deliberators presumed a powerful link between prescriptions and results, and assumed an unfailing societal capacity to effect change (for the better or for the worse). Without these suppositions, proposals and objections might have seemed a waste of time. So what sort of devil did these deliberations in moral engineering unearth?

Sex offenders

During 2006 and 2007 various proposals for dealing with sex offenders were mooted and discussed in the United States, and some of them were implemented. For example, the governor and legislators in New York proposed and managed to secure the votes for a bill that provided for the civil commitment of sex offenders who had completed their criminal sentence. Details of how the new law would function were very scarce in the available news reports, but it appeared that sex offenders who were still considered to be at risk of reoffending after completing a prison sentence would be committed to a residential facility for treatment, and released only when that risk was considered to have disappeared.[82] Similarly, many jurisdictions were contemplating or implementing measures to restrict and monitor the movements of convicted sex offenders. For example, the governor of California proposed measures to prohibit sex offenders from residing within 2,000 feet of a school, or a park frequented by children, and to require the majority of them to wear—permanently—a device that would be tracked by satellite.[83] Cumulatively, the proposals constituted blueprints for new ecological arrangements in the management of sex offenders, involving greater or lesser degrees of spatial confinement.

These very concrete visions of the future attracted debate, which extended over days, weeks, and months in the pages of the newspapers just as it evidently did in other public domains. But it was not a debate about the gravity or levity of sex offenses or the need to do something about sex offenders, for there was general agreement on those points. "No one is suggesting that sexual crimes should go unpunished," wrote a psychiatrist.[84] "Everyone agrees that we have a moral obligation to prevent as many sex crimes as possible," observed two legal scholars.[85] "Considering the vile nature of sex crimes," wrote the *Los Angeles Times*, "the public is right to be concerned about its vulnerability to predators on parole."[86] And the *New York Times* acknowledged that politicians were "[s]ickened by highly publicized crimes against children," and worried by "allow[ing] men who seem likely to repeat terrible crimes back onto the street."[87] There was consensus on these matters, a basic agreement that defined an essential foundation for the moral community. The disagreement was about specific prescriptions for dealing with the problem, about means rather than ends. "If they can't be treated and they are dangerous, you have got to come to grips with the fact that they should be put away," concluded a Republican legislator who sponsored the New York bill for civil confinement.[88] "This is a bad idea," responded those who felt that there were other solutions.[89]

Interestingly, a *New York Times* reporter wrote that "[t]he effectiveness and fairness of the [residence] restrictions has become a matter of great debate."[90] There was, indeed, debate about these restrictions, just as there was about the proposals for civil confinement. But in this version of moral engineering it was the effectiveness, rather than the fairness, of the proposals that occupied attention. Both sides appealed to facts rather than to principles. "[P]roponents of [civil confinement] say that sex offenders are likely to commit the same kinds of crimes again after their release from prison," reported the *New York Times*.[91] "In Arkansas, a 2001 study found that sexual offenders of children often lived near schools, day care centers and parks. Those results suggested ... that residency restrictions could be a reasonable deterrent."[92]

Countering this were empirical claims that pointed in a different direction:

> in Washington State, a study by the independent research office of the Legislature showed that felony-level sex offenders had a recidivism rate of 2.7 percent—lower than the rate of repeat arrests for felony-level drug violations and several other categories of crime.[93]
>
> [D]espite the popular perception to the contrary, recidivism rates for sexual offenders are among the lowest of any class of criminals.[94]
>
> Research shows that treatment can reduce sexual recidivism. And offering treatment in prison to sex offenders soon after conviction is far more effective than delaying treatment until the end of their prison terms.[95]

The core of this debate involved different perspectives on several interrelated empirical questions. How many sex offenders respond to treatment? Which sex offenders respond to treatment? What proportion of sex offenders reoffend? Proponents of measures for greater confinement generally claimed that few sex offenders respond to treatment, that it is difficult to identify those who will respond to treatment and that the proportion of reoffenders was unacceptably high. Opponents generally claimed the reverse, and added other claims about the costs and unintended consequences of measures for greater confinement.[96] The specific configurations of arguments and counter-arguments are less important here than the manner in which these claims were endowed with certainty. They had to be, for just as censure seems to require empirical certainty so, too, does prescription. For example, the opposition to civil confinement was built on the putative certainty that sex offenders have a low rate of reoffending. With regard to the latter claim, here is how opponents of civil commitment "fixed" one doubt so as to support their own position:

> The impetus for civil commitment laws, of course, is the fear that freed sex offenders will assault again. But the data on sex-offender recidivism is *unclear*. For instance, a Justice Department study of 9,700 sex offenders released from prison nationwide in 1994 found that their overall re-arrest rate was much lower than that of other released convicts. Most experts, however, say that like sex crimes in general, sex-offender recidivism is vastly underreported. *Still*, the available evidence shows that sex offenders have a reoffense rate lower than all other serious criminals except murderers.[97]

Here the operative word "still" was used to counter admitted unknowns and signal the use of official statistics as a source of provisional certainty. Those numbers were pitted against similarly constructed "facts," but with diametrically opposed pragmatic implications, adduced by the proponents of civil commitment.

But even more striking than the requirement, shared with censure, to build prescriptions on certainties, was the primary attention to "facts," however weak their foundations, rather than to principles in these debates. There were a few brief references to the normative dimensions of responses to sex offenders: on the one hand, the avowal that "individuals who commit sexual crimes should be punished," and that sex offenders "deserve what they get;"[98] on the other, the claims that civil commitment laws "could easily be abused and ... could represent a threat to civil liberties,"[99] or that residency rules "may have created some hardships for sex offenders."[100] But these went largely unexplored, and were far outweighed by the focus on empirical claims and counterclaims. Indeed, more than one commentator thought that research would, and should, provide the resolution to debates about what ought to be done: "Everyone agrees that we have a moral obligation to prevent as many sex crimes as possible," wrote the law professors. "Only a public policy based on sound research can accomplish this important goal."[101] "It is time to reexamine our approaches and develop empirically based, scientifically sound measures and treatments to bring rationality back to this discussion," wrote the psychiatrist.[102] A cynic might see too much self-interest in academics' calls for further research, but there was no doubt that all participants in this debate looked to the data. There was no extended discussion of the rights of convicted sex offenders, the obligations of the criminal justice system towards them, the rights of victims and communities, or of the challenge of balancing rights in an adversarial system, all of which might have provided a different vision of what should be done.[103] This was a debate about effectiveness, to be resolved by appeals to science, not by bringing in ethics.[104]

Using the military to combat drug trafficking

In the mid-1990s, the Mexican government opted to use the armed forces to deal with drug trafficking, a strategy which had generated some debate at the time.[105] Following his election to the presidency in 2006 and with violence from and among drug traffickers perceived to be increasing, Felipe Calderón decided to resume this tactic and sent the army to several parts of the country. The renewal of the policy led to the renewal of the debate: should the military be used to counter this and related forms of organized crime?

That something should be done was almost universally agreed. "[It] is unlikely that someone could argue against supporting the combat against organized crime," wrote a former politician.[106] Another saw the state's obligation to "confront these challenges that directly threaten social cohesion, public health and personal safety" as a "truth that should not generate great discussion."[107] But the proposal to militarize parts of the country, and the measures already taken along those lines, elicited contrasting commentaries about its suitability as a means to achieve a universally desired end.

Those in favor drew a stark picture of lawlessness in particular regions, and of a police that had been infiltrated and weakened by threats or payoffs from traffickers.

> I wish you could come and spend a few days in Reynosa [wrote one reader of *El Universal*] so that you see the reality of this city, where there is practically no law ... The police are in the employ of *la maña* [the "Gulf Cartel"], there are swarms of unlicensed taxis paid by the bands of criminals to keep them informed about the movements of the Army for example, with the approval of the authorities.[108]

Militarization was argued to be a necessary response, perhaps not without problems, but better than anything else. "[T]he underlying problem is that the other options seem worse," wrote a political analyst: "For years, the use of the police has proved to be totally ineffective for controlling drug trafficking and has contributed to the growth of this phenomenon."[109] "We should get used to seeing the Mexican Army patrolling the streets, so that we citizens of

88   *Moral agency*

Monterrey can go out again at night," said the Director of the local Chamber of Commerce.[110]

Those against the use of the military rehearsed a number of arguments: that the armed forces would be corrupted by drug money;[111] that the army could achieve only a temporary interruption of the drug business;[112] that the only outcome would be a spiral of increasing violence;[113] and that the army was unsuited for police work.[114] Alternative proposals were made to use "more intelligence, less military force,"[115] and to attack the social problems which, it was argued, pushed people into organized crime.[116]

Most of the arguments involved empirical claims about organized crime or the efforts to control it, but they did not incorporate systematically collected data. "For years the use of the police forces has proved to be totally useless for controlling drug trafficking and has contributed to its growth," wrote a supporter of military responses.[117] "Once the special operation of the Army has finished ... everything apparently returns to normal," wrote an opponent.[118] "[T]he fact is that violence is one of those phenomena which, once unleashed, multiply with increasing severity," wrote another.[119] Whether or not data gathered by researchers or the police was available, its omission (and the seeming lack of interest in whether or not data might be available[120]) helped to cement the certainties that were necessary for prescription.

But in a rhetorical arena such as this, characterized by a low density of empirical information, persuasion was also sought through recourse to practical considerations, through commentary about how things function (or do not function). "Everything indicates that the option of only using the police would serve to boost the corruption which is generated by drug trafficking and to encourage the growth of this business," wrote a supporter of military responses.[121] "One cannot pretend to eliminate that monster of a thousand heads without the prior commitment of the three levels of government and of the three powers of the Republic to seal all the cracks through which crime has penetrated the State," wrote an opponent.[122] These comments were not offered as descriptions or predictions, but as abstract assertions about the workings of particular institutional arrangements, assertions which implied general, rather than specific, prescriptions that could be derived from them ("do not use the police," and "bring together all levels of government," respectively). Using a similar type of commentary, one opponent wrote that:

> Undoubtedly, it is difficult to compete with the high profits which attach to organized crime as a life choice, but it will be more difficult if the alternatives continue to close themselves off for the young people who try to get into the legal and formal labor market.[123]

And, with more attention to practical detail, another opponent concluded:

> If the idea was to halt the infiltration of politics into drug trafficking, perhaps the most convenient thing would be to increase the operations of Cisen [an

intelligence agency] and mobilize groups of investigators from the Secretariat of Public Affairs, the Secretariat of Public Safety and the Attorney General. Without the deployment of this intelligence capability, the mobilization of soldiers will be nothing more than a mere show of military force.[124]

As with the debate over sex offenders in the United States, this collective deliberation in Mexico about responses to drug trafficking largely eschewed matters of principle. Three commentators mentioned abuses and the violation of human rights by the military, one of them devoting a brief paragraph to the uncomfortable proximity of soldiers and civilians.[125] But there was no extended consideration of the potential problems for civilians, bystanders, and those involved in organized crime that flow from military security measures, no attempt to weigh up the competing interests of collective security and individual rights, no argument for or against military involvement that was based entirely on this kind of consideration. Instead, the debate looked to empirical claims and procedural considerations rather than to ethics. One commentator concluded with a rhetorical question that nicely captured the preferred mode of discussion:

> Has not the time arrived for convening a plural and open debate which, with seriousness and responsibility, from a perspective that is both multidisciplinary and global, allows us to build a wide consensus on the most effective ways to approach a challenge of these proportions for society, democracy and its institutions?[126]

Here, as in the deliberations about sex offenders to the north, the debate was primarily about the "effectiveness" rather than the "fairness" of military intervention. But in contrast to the North, that effectiveness was debated as much in practical as in empirical terms.[127]

The limits to effectiveness

While most of those making prescriptions operated in a world of certainty that was of their own making, there was some recognition by others that intervention was a challenging task. For example, Harvey Rosenthal, the Executive Director of the New York Association of Psychiatric Rehabilitation Services, had the following to say about the debate on sex offenders:

> We seem to be making these decisions on fear rather than fact.... We don't have a clear idea of what treatment works, and what doesn't. We don't know what kind of real solution this will bring. We're moving feverishly in a way that will require all kinds of revisions later.[128]

In a discursive domain characterized by a focus on effectiveness rather than fairness, Rosenthal saw the lack of knowledge as a fundamental weakness. In its absence, in the absence of certainty, action would be emotive, "feverish," and counterproductive.

Interestingly, practical comment (which dealt with what can or cannot be achieved) quite often provided some sense of the limits to effectiveness. A social worker in Caracas lamented the number of children killed in the lines of fire between rival gangs: "This is repeated year after year and there is no permanent effective policy which can reduce this type of incident."[129] "[A] writer and professor who helped ... organize [an anti-crime] rally [in New Orleans] scoffed at the idea of officers walking the beat. "This is nothing.... What difference will it make?'"[130] "Breaking the cycle of recidivism and violence [among drug offenders] will continue to be a challenge," wrote a lawyer in New York.[131] "It is not easy to rebuild the structures of public authority in the places where they have disintegrated," editorialized *La Nación*.[132] In these and numerous other comments, doubts surfaced about the capacity to produce change.

Paralysis could have been the corollary to such thoughts.[133] In the continued absence of promising responses, or at least of the knowledge that they were effective, the only course of action might have been inaction, to "throw our hands up in the air and say we can't do anything about this problem."[134] But just as Carnell Cooper refused to do this, so did everyone else. The compulsion to "solve social problems"[135] was everywhere felt. Apart from those who did not doubt the effectiveness of their own prescriptions, some urged that action could be effective, even if only modestly so. "It is said to be easy although it requires a lot of effort, but it can be done," wrote a government functionary in Mexico. "So, when we want to—and in 2006 there is the opportunity—governments will adopt a security agenda and the control of violence, before the latter takes over our lives."[136] A black community leader in Philadelphia, who was involved in an initiative to put 10,000 volunteers on the streets to try to prevent violence in problematic neighborhoods, acknowledged:

> that the plan did not address underlying problems like unemployment, poverty, poor education and the easy availability of guns.... But he said that getting men to take responsibility for their own communities was a step in the right direction.... [Another participant] expressed hope that the plan would work.[137]

Other commentators took up the language of stirring morality, urging that something—anything—be done. Police chiefs in California wrote to the governor declaring an "'urgent need to act now' to keep students from dropping out;"[138] in the Californian city of San Bernardino, "stemming crime—and reassuring residents—[were] difficult propositions.... 'But there's also a culture of faith and a culture of learning—so you have competing forces, and we just refuse to give up,'" said a middle school principal;[139] "We cannot accept living in an insecure and disordered city," wrote a Mexican senator, "we have to demand results."[140] For some there was, as the *Globe and Mail* put it, "a desire to throw everything at crime and hope that something sticks."[141]

In a later editorial, on proposals to increase mandatory minimum sentences in Canada, the *Globe and Mail* argued that such a move would have "no significant effect."[142] In particular, it suggested that prosecutors would continue to manipulate the charges they put forward in order to avoid any unjust imposition of a mandatory minimum sentence. "[I]t is an abdication of responsibility," decried the paper, "for a politician to be swept along with the latest wave of public outrage, without evidence that a harsher response would do any good." Of course, if pressed on evidence, it is very likely that the politicians would have found something to suit their purposes. But the *Globe and Mail* also noted the symbolic significance of these calls for reform: in the words of the justice minister, "the minimums should be increased to 'send a strong message of denunciation.'"

Like the Canadian justice minister, a few of those who called for action in response to crime were not unaware of the symbolic dimension to their words. The Lieutenant Governor of Texas argued that the death penalty for child rape "sends a message to those monsters who want to hurt our children: 'Not in Texas;'"[143] outlining a multi-agency "attack" on gangs, the Mayor of Los Angeles declared that "We have a message for these gang leaders: We are coming with everything we have. We are coming with services and suppression, and we are putting you out of business;"[144] and a Mexican columnist saw in the decision to use the military "a message of governmental determination directed at the groups of drug traffickers."[145] An Argentine congressional politician not only saw the significance of the message, but also brought herself face-to-face with the unthinkable consequences of inaction:

> We cannot keep going from meeting to meeting, from doctrine to doctrine, without ever announcing laws that at least make crime perceive that it has its enemy in the State ... the State should show crime that it is its enemy and that it is going to defeat it. If it were not thus, the battle would already be lost and we would have to tell our voters openly, that we will not take charge of this, that they should learn to live with robberies, death and rape until we have finished discussing which is the best theory.[146]

If effectiveness was lacking or in doubt, action could at least send a message. And surely it was not only a message to criminals and crime but also to civil society, a message that the moral community was alive, well, and determined. However seriously proponents took their recommendations, however certain they felt about the consequences of planned intervention, the mere existence of this kind of talk was testimony that forces for good were at work. This brand of moral engineering was helpful in engineering collective morality.

Drawing back

Both specialist and expository treatments of moral philosophy coincide in identifying three basic approaches to their subject matter: aretaic (relating to virtues), consequentialist, and deontological.[147] The precise content (and significance) of each approach, and the possible overlaps between them, are matters for extensive and thorough discussion, but they have also been seen as descriptors of the moral orientations of individuals[148] or organizations.[149] In a somewhat similar fashion, they can usefully serve as resources for illuminating the character of contemporary collective morality in the Americas.

In the set of texts compiled for the present study, the broad framework for moral agency was aretaic. A single virtue seemed to motivate commentators on crime across the Americas, and it is best described as activeness—a disposition (indeed, a determination) to do something about crime, to intervene in the history of the present, to work to keep criminality contained (in Anglo-America) or to lend aid to a beleaguered civil society (in Latin America). Its corresponding vice was the paralysis cited by an Argentine lawyer; its excess the feverishness warned against by a US psychiatrist. Its importance was underlined by the way in which charges of inaction could be deployed as moral censure against political opponents and by the latter's counterclaims about what they were doing, recited in defense of their moral face. It was the importance of activeness that lay behind the multiple, routine, fragmented, cross-cutting, and often unanswered calls for specific measures to deal with crime, and behind the stirring, idealist, injunctions to do something (anything) in answer to its threats and ravages. The call to action was as important as any specific results that might ensue. And it was the inevitable link between virtue and identity that made activeness a tool for fashioning images of individual and collective morality, a device for sending messages about moral character to "others" and to "ourselves."

Yet for many commentators, the effectiveness of action was also an important consideration, revealing a consequentialist dimension to moral agency that was summed up in the widespread reference (at least in English) to "what works." If activeness was a virtue, effective action was particularly prized. Thus, many prescriptive responses to crime were advanced within a framework which held goals to be universally shared (dealing with sex offenders, confronting drug traffickers, and so on) while means were to be judged on their effectiveness. Morality took on an instrumental hue, and debates occasionally emerged about which measures were the best for achieving a particular objective. Effectiveness was mainly dissected in empirical terms, giving moral significance to whatever research findings could be mustered. In the research-active North, researchers were in a privileged position to contribute to these debates, to some extent taking over the "ownership" of the latter, along the lines described by Gusfield in relation to a variety of social problems.[150] In the South, where there was less research and less interest in research, commentators often appealed to the potential for efficacy that materializes through abstract considerations about procedure and technique. While their arguments in this vein were brief and largely superficial, they were testimony to the possibility that effectiveness can also be considered as an art of engineering,[151] and they provided an implicit counterpoint to the powerful hold of science in the North.

Moral agency 93

These preoccupations with effective action, however conceived and justified, left little room for consideration of principles, rules or duty—the province of deontology. "Nationally, we're up against individual rights versus the health and safety of our citizens.... We need to somehow come to a compromise," had said Dr. Cooper, in Baltimore. But he did not outline what that compromise might be, preferring instead to appeal to the virtue of action. That measures for dealing with sex offenders had been debated in terms of their fairness was acknowledged by the *New York Times*, but its own pages did not carry that debate, nor did any of the other newspapers in this set of texts. The debate between *mano dura* and *garantismo* was recognized in Argentina, but no one wanted to argue things out in newsprint (or, perhaps more accurately, journalists and editors did not orient newsprint in that direction). Moral agency was not envisaged as a matter of formulating and following rules, as a matter of principles to be applied in given situations.

Previous research on social problems, social movements or public policy has naturally included some attention to prescriptive statements, for calls to do something figure frequently in their subject matter. For example, aging drivers should be mandatorily retested;[152] the incineration of waste should be halted;[153] the "abortion pill" should be classed as an abortion service option;[154] and the government should promote lifelong marriage.[155] Yet these and other proposals (or demands) are revealed only by carefully sifting through the texts produced by the researchers who wrote them. Calls for action are an acknowledged component of framing, which provides the conceptual and methodological underpinnings for much of this line of work, but they have not merited separate consideration. They are marshaled, along with other components of framing, into particular construals of social issues and the potential disagreements that therein may be found. While recognizing that the link between frames and policy decisions is neither simple[156] nor guaranteed,[157] much research on framing seems to operate with a notion of soft determinism, seeing prescriptions (and the frames that they are embedded in) as discursive elements which "shape" the "solutions" that are adopted.[158] When prescriptions have come into a slightly sharper focus, some case studies reveal instrumental underpinnings to their justifications, which is similar to findings reported here.[159] In other case studies, principles are also brought into the debate.[160]

But none of these studies has looked at moral agency, at the way(s) in which moral behavior is talked into being. Their interest in discourse has been confined to matters of rhetoric and persuasion.[161] They have not been attentive to the salience of instrumental perspectives within the research community, to the probability that empirically oriented work will focus on effects, therefore aligning itself very easily with a consequentialist version of morality. Indeed, while the constructionist orientation of their inquiry potentially sets it at one remove from the arena of policy debate and creates the opportunity to reflect on its nature rather than join in, many scholars have remained firmly within a paradigm that sees prescriptions as capable of producing effects and which are, therefore, to be judged in terms of effectiveness. And they have sought to warn against the perniciousness of urban myths, exaggerated empirical claims, and distorted research findings, rather than to examine the nature of the prescriptions and proposals that fall within their purview. Where, how, and by whom are aretaic and deontological approaches to crime articulated, and with what consequences for moral agency? The present study does not answer this question, but merely allows it to be asked.

6 American melodramas

The *New York Times*
December 2, 2007 Sunday
Homicide in New York: When the Victims Are Women
To the Editor:
Re "City Homicides Still Dropping, to Under 500" (front page, Nov. 23):
As the total number of homicides has dropped dramatically since the early 1990s, women make up an increasing portion of these homicides.

The proportion of homicide victims who are women has grown by more than a quarter between the early 1990s to the middle of this decade. New York City data show that intimate partners perpetrate about a third of all homicides of women.

The Police Department has adapted to changing homicide patterns and trends throughout its history.

To suggest that it cannot work with communities using innovative techniques to address domestic and other acquaintance homicides ignores a growing body of violence prevention research and practice.

Worse, though, is that this attitude harkens back to the days when what happened behind closed doors stayed there, with tragic results.
Victoria Frye New York, Nov. 26, 2007
The writer is a sociomedical scientist and research investigator for the New York Academy of Medicine's Center for Urban Epidemiologic Studies.

La Nación
Tuesday, October 30 2007
Readers' Letters
Violence in Dominico
Señor Director:
We, the pupils of class 1° D of the basic secondary school No. 6 in Villa Dominico, Avellaneda Municipality, are tired of the violence that we experience in our neighborhood. We feel unprotected by the police, because they do not act swiftly when called.

The lack of street lighting, the lack of police control and the growing increase in crime make us feel helpless in this situation.

We want to live in peace and study, walk safely in the streets and enjoy the things that should be a right for all but which, in fact, are not.

In the course on "Constructing Citizenship," we learn that we are all legal subjects, but we all ask ourselves if we can effectively be citizens in a country which seems to have forgotten us, we who are the future.
Santiago Cantero
Valeria Fosco
Nadir Zugueb
(More signatures follow)

96   *American melodramas*

These letters to the editor do not illustrate all of the differences between commentaries on crime in Anglo-America and Latin America that have been noted in previous chapters. The very nature of collective discourse means that its total characteristics are unlikely to be displayed in a single text. When individual commentators make their respective contributions to public discourse they usually focus on one topic and employ one rhetorical style, and this is nowhere more evident than in letters to the editor of a newspaper. Nevertheless, whether conscious of it or not, commentators draw from, and contribute to, a common repertoire of discursive resources that are, in effect, maintained by civil society, resources which reflect its characteristic modes of thought and self-understanding. These letters do not exemplify every difference between North and South, but they capture a good number of them.

Victoria Frye wrote with the detachment of a researcher. Although her focus was on female victims of homicide, especially in domestic disputes, there was nothing to indicate that she felt herself to be particularly at risk of attack. Rather, she was concerned with a trend that was revealed through an analysis of crime statistics. In particular, she sought to qualify the paper's earlier optimistic report on a decrease in homicides by pointing out that closer study showed women to be an increasing proportion of the victims. Her call was for the police to adapt to this new development and apply innovative prevention techniques that were being suggested by recent research. Her moral approach to the topic, always unostentatious, was signaled by her final reference to the "tragic results" from keeping intimate violence "behind closed doors."

Santiago Cantero and his fellow pupils wrote with the immediacy of witnesses to criminality. Their concern was for themselves as inhabitants of a violent neighborhood, presumably as possible future victims. There were no crime statistics to fuel their plea, merely the mention of personal experience. Theirs was a situation of helplessness, for which the failings of the police were particularly to blame. They made no specific call for measures to be taken; they simply sketched an idyllic image of the urban life they aspired to ("We want to live in peace and study, walk safely in the streets…"). Their moral perspective was not wrought with specific words, but with the dramatic image of the innocent young (future citizens) daily running the gauntlet of crime, forgotten by their country, and unprotected by the police.

In their self-portrayal as civic orphans these pupils not only invoked a theme which is common among Latin American commentators on crime; they also laid bare the melodramatic character of their moralizing, for melodrama often deals in the threat to innocence. But it would be a mistake to conclude that melodrama was a uniquely Latin American rendering of morality, for it was to be found in commentary on crime across the hemisphere. What is visible in these letters to the editor is a difference in the style in which the melodrama played out—more dramatic in the South, less dramatic in the North—but not in the overall mode within which discursive morality moved. With this difference in style were associated differences in staging, props, and characters between the two regions, but the fundamental characteristics of the form were everywhere the same. Melodrama provides a useful conceptual tool for simultaneously examining the commonalities in discursive morality across the hemisphere and the differences that were found between North and South, which form the particular focus of the present chapter.

Melodramatic morality

Melodrama does not have a good reputation in some circles. It evokes visions of emotiveness, excessive theatricality, and lowbrow culture—all of which are frowned on by practitioners of reason, realism, and refinement. It smacks of sobs and superficiality.[1] Yet scholars who have looked carefully at melodrama find in it a noteworthy capacity for survival, adaptation, and reproduction, narrative structures and psychosocial explorations that inform some of the best work in the arts, and a surprising diversity of social and cultural habitats.[2] Melodrama is not simply a literary or artistic genre; it is a pervasive resource for making sense of lived experience.[3]

James Smith's perceptive discussion of the essence of melodrama usefully highlighted its morally significant qualities. Following Heilman,[4] he argued that the melodramatic person is "essentially whole ... undivided, free from the agony of choosing between conflicting imperatives and desires."[5] Such wholeness is also morally uncommitted: "the evil man who is wholly evil is prevented by his wholeness from the self-understanding that might curb his villainy, and the wholly good man who looks inward has nothing to contemplate but his own virtuous perfection."[6] As many who have written about melodrama indicate, this mode of personifying morality leads to a Manichean world peopled by two starkly distinguished groups of inhabitants: the good and the bad. The scene is thus set for epic conflicts since, as Smith notes, "the undivided protagonist of melodrama has only external pressures to fight against: an evil man, a social group, a hostile ideology..." and the result can only ever be "stalemate, victory or defeat."[7]

The depiction of melodrama in these terms allows the easy identification of some of its constitutive elements in the commentaries on crime examined in this book. Most notably, the visions of alterity and identity which emerged in relation to crime were emphatically Manichean, uncomplicated by any doubts about the moral qualities of the speakers or the moral failings of those who purportedly commit crimes. The moral outlook was structured as short narratives—histories of the present—in which civil society was pitted against crime. Moral agency was fundamentally anchored in virtue (a key object of attention in melodrama), and its most valuable quality was a determination to act[8]—always in the hope of victory, never in the search for compromise. Collective morality both imagined and conducted itself as the principal actor in a melodramatic production.[9]

Recognition of the melodramatic conception of identity, outlook, and agency in commentaries on crime in the Americas is of considerable aid when it comes to reflecting on the nature of moral discourse—something which will be taken up in the conclusion to this study. But it is also useful for drawing out some differences between Anglo-America and Latin America in the staging, props, and characters that made up their particular moral discourses, differences that reflected broader social and cultural characteristics.

Staging: the city's defenses

Aquatic metaphors, so common across the hemisphere, offered a portrayal of crime that was more spatial than hydrological. True to the melodramatic mode, concern was with the location, level, and movement of "dirty water"[10] rather than its composition and transformation. There was no complication here, no desire to look deeper. And with this sort of moral geography, attention focused on the defenses against the floods, storms, and overspills in crime that could occur. This was a drama that affected the city, the preferred imaginary habitat for civil society, and its primary defenses against the malevolent flood were the state.

Anglo-American commentators revealed themselves to be largely secure, but ever vigilant. Overall crime rates were generally declining, and had been for some time. But there was always the possibility that particular types of crime, notably violence, might surge again. Most of the city was safe, but there were neighborhoods that looked like some encapsulated version of the American frontier, where crime was rife. Switching metaphors, a number of commentators summarized the prevalent view very well: crime was confined to "isolated pockets" that required special attention.[11] Crime was largely contained—in the eyes of many commentators at least partly because of successful policing—and where it threatened to leak out or overflow, the talk invariably looked to responses that were implemented or orchestrated by government. References to "our" police, "our" courts or "our" prisons were in a tone that revealed both a sense of ownership and a fairly easy coexistence between civil society and the state.

By contrast, in Latin America crime was seen to be out of control. It had reached unprecedented levels and could be found everywhere, even in sacrosanct spaces. It went to school, walked in the parks, attended weddings, and visited churches. It could victimize anyone, anywhere. Its ubiquity and artful insinuation into urban life meant that no one was secure: thus, insecurity was the personal and collective result. Its constant accompaniment was an acute dissatisfaction with the state: government was deaf, indolent, inefficient or deviant. The defenses against crime were weak and fragmented, or dangerously porous to criminal infiltration. There was a general situation of impunity, and commentators felt themselves beleaguered. Like the Argentine students who wrote to *La Nación*, civil society was a civic orphan.

Critical and pessimistic visions of the state, as seen from the perspective of civil society, are a common finding in studies of Latin America. Many observers summarize their own and others' general experiences in forceful indictments of the state's institutional weakness,[12] ineffectiveness,[13] low credibility,[14] and corruption.[15] More systematic work has looked at levels of trust in government and found Latin America to be towards the bottom of the global scales. As Manning and Wetzel put it, there seems to be "structured distrust" in the region, which distinguishes it from other parts of the world, including Africa and East Asia.[16] In the most thorough study conducted to date, using data from the World Values Surveys, Segovia Arancibia found that there were significant variations between Latin American countries in confidence in parliament and the civil service but that, in general, Latin American citizens were less trusting of government than their counterparts in the industrialized countries, although not (it should be added) as far below them on these quantitative scales as the widespread anecdotally-driven criticisms would suggest. In a statistical analysis of 50 countries, including Latin American nations, Segovia Arancibia found that higher perceived levels of corruption and adherence to "postmaterialist"[17] values were the variables most strongly associated with lower levels of trust in government.[18]

As other researchers on trust in government have done, Segovia Arancibia also looked at the results for specific public institutions and found that in Latin America the police were at the bottom of the heap. This is of a piece with the results of studies that focus on crime and criminal justice in the region. For example, Hinton referred to "the perception that the police (and thus the state) are not trusted allies in providing protection or redress from crime,"[19] an observation borne out by other studies, conducted with various methods and at various sites, throughout the region.[20] One researcher, purportedly summing up public feeling but also aligning himself with it, noted that:

> This "social" violence which predominates in our region has its own character which makes it different to other types of violence. It can appear anywhere and victimize anyone, in other words, it is unpredictable and diffuse. This causes feelings of uncertainty and insecurity, especially when the problem becomes endemic and when the state shows itself to be incapable of dealing with violence, where it does not tacitly tolerate it.[21]

The deteriorated image of the Latin American police contrasts quite strongly with that of its counterpart in Anglo-America, where a recent introductory text proclaims the police to be "intricately intertwined in the social fabric of American democracy," and "perform[ing] the critical role of protecting individual rights and ensuring social order."[22] Anglo-American research on public perceptions of the police notes short-term and often issue-specific decreases in approval ratings but, overall, "the general public views the police favorably."[23] If appearances in the media are also indicative of social position and status, then the sample of texts compiled for the present study confirms the different images fashioned for, and by, the police in the two regions. Thus, the Anglo-American police were three times more likely than the Latin American police to feature as sources in articles, and they offered opinions on a wide range of topics, including policy matters that are not directly connected with policing.[24] Latin American police, often represented by their political bosses, had much less to say, confining themselves mainly to chronicling the crime they were supposed to deal with.[25] They had a marginal role in commentary on crime, compared to the more central position taken up by the Anglo-American police.

More broadly, while researchers in Anglo-America note declining levels of trust in public institutions over the last 30 years,[26] the comparative studies already referred to indicate that perceptions of government are still more positive there than they are in the South. Anglo-American citizens clearly see the state as a bulwark against disorder and disaster, while Latin Americans seriously doubt its protective capacity. These markedly different visions of the political and institutional world represent deep-seated differences in moral outlook which color the commentary on crime, just as they are likely to tinge discourses on other sources of social concern.

Props: facts and evidence

Moral discourse about crime tends, inevitably, to orient itself to the world of lived experience, and commentaries about crime and the measures taken in response to it were replete with observations about things that were happening, or things that were being done. Most of these observations were set forth as certainties, or rendered provisionally certain for the purposes of comment, certainty being an apparent prerequisite for moralizing. To the limited extent that disagreements about moral outlook or agency emerged, they largely concerned empirical claims. Thus, trends in crime numbers or crime rates could be questioned, or the results of actions to deal with crime cast in doubt. This kind of challenge was mainly confined to Anglo-American commentators, and was almost always accompanied by a particular use of vocabulary: information was not merely treated as factual but presented as "evidence." Therein lay a cultural and intellectual stance that reflected the societal importance of research.

Facts, of course, were cited by many across the hemisphere as unchallenged (and, when hyperbolic, unchallengeable) assertions: crime was increasing, violence was a "gathering storm," crime was decreasing, gangs caused crime, organized crime caused violence, poverty caused crime, more policing reduced crime, corrupt police increased crime, and so on. They were part of the standard fare of commentary, purveyed in different quantities and forms, and dealing with different topics or concerns. But on the relatively rare occasions when they were challenged, recourse was made to evidence. Thus, Mike Males, featured in Chapter 4, criticized "officials [who] find it so pathetically easy to incite and re-incite visceral fears of the young even as solid evidence shows violent offenders are getting older."[27] And the *New York Times* reporters, featured in Chapter 5, noted that while residence restrictions for sex offenders "are politically appealing, there is little empirical evidence to suggest a connection between recidivism and proximity to schools."[28] Elsewhere, a researcher sought to convince readers of the *New York Times* that "evidence points to increased immigration as a major factor associated with the lower crime rate,"[29] while in the *Los Angeles Times* a law professor "found no evidence for the proposition that disorder causes crime,"[30] and a columnist for the *Globe and Mail* sardonically noted that "Crime sells newspapers and drives TV ratings ('if it bleeds, it leads') ... despite the statistical evidence that serious crime is declining."[31]

This kind of rhetorical stance was largely absent in Latin America, where most empirical information, whether collected systematically, institutionally or anecdotally, was presented as fact. In the rare disputes about crime rates, evidence could be brought into play, for example, when *La Nación* argued that "the evidence" contradicted the claim by the Argentine Minister of the Interior that crime had not run wild.[32] And one article in *El Universal* went into a detailed examination of crime rates, showing how the "evidence" revealed that, contrary to public perceptions, Mexico's murder rate had been declining since 1993 and that violent crime more generally may also have been declining, at least in Mexico City.[33] But it is a telling detail that this article was written by an Anglo-American professor and its translation very faithfully reproduced the vocabulary and approach that are typical among Anglo-American researchers.

"[T]he stuff of the world only becomes 'evidence' when 'it' is constituted and inserted into a research practice and then deployed in the framework of an argument," wrote Marston and Watts.[34] Their phrasing nicely captures the nature of the subject they were critiquing (evidence-based policy-making) and, more generally, the way in which empirical evidence comes to be conceived and deployed in certain cultural settings. Argument can be prosecuted by a variety of strategies, but when it involves evidence (of the non-legal kind) research is not far behind. More than the production of facts and information, research is a framework for evaluating the validity of knowledge claims and for assessing the significance of data as evidence, assessments which will vary according to the particular epistemological and methodological framework adopted. When making recourse to "evidence," commentators on crime were invoking one of those frameworks to bolster their own claims or diminish the claims of others. If there were debates about moral outlook or moral agency, they were seemingly best resolved by adopting some form of scientific perspective.

The recourse to "evidence" arguably reflected the more highly embedded nature of research in Anglo-American culture, compared to Latin America. Thus, according to one historian, the United States has for long been "permeated by the culture of science."[35] Recent quantitative estimates indicate that there are at least five times more researchers per million inhabitants in Anglo-America than there are in the Latin American countries that feature in the present study, and at least five times as much investment in research and development.[36] The President of the US Social Science Research Council estimates that there are more than 100,000 social scientists engaged in academic research in Anglo-America, while many other researchers work in government, business, and non-profit organizations.[37] Accompanying the disparities in numerical indicators, Latin American observers have routinely noted the comparative dearth of science and research in the region,[38] although there are undoubted signs of greater levels of activity over the last 20 years.[39]

The situation for science and the social sciences is reproduced for criminology, the specialist area of study that is nominally most relevant to commentary on crime. Haen-Marshall observes that the "American [i.e., US] criminological enterprise is the largest in the world," with sustained investment in academic and governmental research on crime and justice,[40] while Simon notes a commitment to science which has "continued unabated and has become ever more integrated into policing, corrections, and the administration of justice."[41] By contrast, several Latin American scholars comment on the comparative scarcities of data, research and sophisticated analysis in the region.[42] Although there are clear signs of increased research activity over the last two decades,[43] Elbert claims that conditions have recently become increasingly restrictive for some Latin American criminologists.[44]

Interestingly, these regional contrasts do not translate into marked differences in the frequency with which those labeled as researchers, or the results of apparently systematic data collection exercises (such as opinion surveys, research projects, and official statistics), were featured in the commentaries on crime compiled for the present study.[45] Data, facts, and those who produced them were a staple source of information for newspapers across the hemisphere, and of considerable moral significance. Nevertheless, in the relatively infrequent debates concerning the moral outlook or moral agency it was the appeal to evidence that revealed the particular significance of research and the key role assigned to it as moral arbiter. It is noteworthy that a recent study of the sources cited by editorials in the *New York Times* and various Spanish language newspapers (including *El Universal* from Mexico) found that the most frequently attributed source type in the former were "specialists/experts/reports," whereas in Mexico it was political figures, businessmen, lawyers, and high-ranking religious figures.[46] While most research activity does not make it into newspapers, research provides a particularly important prop for collective moral discourse on crime in Anglo-America, and thereby acquires considerable moral significance in its own right.

Characters: moralists and experts

Some work by Canadian researcher Anne-Marie Ambert (mentioned in Chapter 4) was critically reviewed by the *Globe and Mail*. She had published a report, which had been copied to the press, on "the rise in the number of children and adolescents with problematic behaviours."[47] The newspaper took aim at some of the claims advanced in the report, suggesting that they lacked empirical foundation—a critical stance that was a further reflection of the embeddedness of research in Anglo-American culture and of its status as a discursive resource for the media. But the editors were also unhappy with the multiplicity and nature of the causes cited by Ambert for the purported increase in problematic behaviors. If, as they felt, Ambert had included "everyone" as part of those causes, and found "societal villains hiding in every corner," "modern society might just as well pull the covers over its head and give up." Ambert had, in their view, gone too far and had given her report an "overlay of moral lecture."

She had apparently been too judgmental and insufficiently practical in her opinions.

What is striking about this final criticism is the content of the claim, not its validity. Indeed, the newspaper was in almost all respects incorrect to cast Ambert's report as a moral lecture. It was written as a summary of research, filled with factual claims and almost 200 supporting references, and rounded off with a number of recommendations about "what can be done."[48] There was no discussion of the moral significance of the behaviors in question; no dramatic language employed to characterize their purported increase; no overt chiding of parents, teachers, society, and government for either intentional or thoughtless contributions to the problem. This report was morally significant—the reference to "problematic behaviours" was sufficient to indicate that—but it is difficult to see it as a "moral lecture." It is the dismissal of Ambert's work as a moral text that is more important here. The "overlay of moral lecture" was seen to make the report empirically questionable and practically unhelpful. It was as if the putative moral content had devalued the whole exercise.

Certain sorts of morality get a bad press in Anglo-America. What has been called "moralism," and understood as "the public judgment of others' actions as morally wrong,"[49] has itself been judged as "the *vice* of overdoing morality."[50] It conflicts with the "modest virtues" of "middle class morality," which are demanding on the self while nonjudgmental in relation to others.[51] Lovett comments that "indictments of moralism are frequent, both in moral philosophy and in the general media."[52] For example, one US philosopher wrote of "morally hyperactive individuals" who "go about trying to impose their moral will on others too much," likening them to "a broken air conditioner—constantly running, making a lot of noise, but helping nobody and indeed probably spouting a lot of hot air."[53] Away from the strictly personal and interpersonal domain of moralism, "moralization" (understood as normative social commentary) has similarly been targeted for critical attention by a group of social psychologists, who define it as "the use of morality, and specifically ... the over-use of morality, and one's self-certainty in applying it."[54] Much earlier, and much more generally, Baier simply observed that "moral talk is often repugnant."[55]

In a revealing passage on "de-moralized society" (afflicted, among other things, by crime and deviance), Gertrude Himmelfarb wrote that:

> Moral principles, still more moral judgments, are thought to be at best an intellectual embarrassment, at worst evidence of an illiberal and repressive disposition. It is this reluctance to speak the language of morality, far more than any specific values, that separates us from the Victorians.[56]

This reference to the Victorians harks back to the age of what Collini (a historian of British Victorian cultural life) has called "public moralists," when members of the educated classes consciously pursued a "highly developed sense of being, and having to be seen to be, ... a moral coach, keeping the national conscience in trim."[57] These intellectuals did not shy away from explicit moral commentary, even as they combined it with their particular political, economic or philosophical leaning. Yet even nineteenth century Anglo-America did not appear to look with unfailing kindness on contemporary moral commentators, labelling them in a somewhat derogatory manner as "Mugwumps"[58] or "populist social critics."[59] Moreover, as a recognized cultural category, the social critic seemed to disappear in Anglo-America after 1918.[60] In a similar manner, a recent reflection on the fortunes of a closely related cultural type, the "public intellectual," notes that "the position of the social critic has been unjustifiably disempowered in the contemporary public domain of discourse."[61] What all of this indicates is a distaste, and to some extent a disdain, for conspicuous moralizing in Anglo-America. The prominent use of moral vocabulary in relation to the subject at hand, or specific appeals to the relevance of morality in addressing it, are likely to attract criticism, even ridicule. Yet, whether or not Anglo-Americans are aware of it, their commentaries on crime (and presumably on many other social problems) often include moral utterances, albeit as a prosaic and "suitably" inconspicuous dimension of their content. Anglo-Americans have not lost their moral voice, merely changed its tenor and tone.

The situation in Latin America is rather different, and best approached by examining the distinctive fortunes across the hemisphere of the essay (understood as a literary product rather than an educational output). Some time ago, Earle commented on the decline of the essay in Anglo culture (a trend which may parallel the decline in importance of the social critic, for essays were one of the principle instruments for communicating their ideas).[62] "In Hispanic America," wrote Earle, "it's a different story,"[63] for much critical attention was still being given to essays and essay-like writings (which, presumably, reflected a continuing healthy output). More recent studies confirm the enduring place of essays in Latin American cultural life, if not the level of social attention that they seemed to attract in the late nineteenth and early twentieth centuries.[64] And all observers remark on the importance of the essay as a form of social criticism. In the words of Skirius: "By revealing the ills of the epoch through instant X-rays, the essayist takes on the role of the committed intellectual."[65] Thus, the continued production of essays reflects the ongoing importance of moralizing in Latin American public life; and the critical appreciations concerning those who write them are largely laudatory. In this respect, the role of the public moralist still seems assured.[66]

Skirius, who was much interested in style, commented that "the essay is ... nonfictional prose, which frequently approximates poetical techniques, the elements of fiction and, more rarely, dramatic effects."[67] He sought to separate the essay as literary form from the essay as "ancillary literature" in which literary elements are employed for non-literary purposes. Such ancillary literature can appear in a variety of guises, but newsprint is a common form; indeed, the mutual interactions of journalism and essay writing appear to have marked both types of cultural production in Latin America.[68] Among other things, the literary pretensions of the essayist sometimes carry over into the opinion columnist's style, a process that is ultimately anchored in a broader cultural commitment to intricate and imaginative communication. Scholars working in, and sometimes largely on, English are often disparaging in their comments concerning Spanish written text, seeing "ornate phrases,"[69] "flowery language,"[70] or "windy argumentation, and ... high flown rhetoric,"[71] where Latin Americans would see eloquence and articulacy. These are best considered as differences in aesthetic appreciation, but it is interesting to speculate that "ornate phrases" and "high flown rhetoric" may well exhibit a greater density of moral utterances than the plain language evidently preferred in the North, raising morality to a level of conspicuousness that is unattractive to the Anglo-American eye but which confirms its standing in the South.

The eminent Spanish philosopher and writer Ortega y Gasset once defined the essay as "science without explicit proof;"[72] a phrase that has been widely cited in commentary on this genre in Latin America.[73] Although his particular "science" was philosophy, he defended the essay as a vehicle for the communication of any scientific ideas in a form where "as far as possible footnotes are left out, and the rigid mechanical apparatus of proof is dissolved into a more organic, lively and personal elocution."[74] While Ortega y Gasset insisted that proof should be available, indeed subtly woven into the text so that interested readers could unearth it, critical commentators in Latin America have largely chosen to emphasize the literary pretensions of the essay, and either leave the question of proof aside, or actively discount it. If Ortega y Gasset's was a rather idiosyncratic view of the essay, he at least seemed to subscribe, in some way or other, to the evidentiary culture that pervades contemporary science and research. In Latin America, the popular and particular interpretation of his definition of the essay not only underlines the more marginal role of science in that region, but also reflects the greater discursive freedom claimed by those who would write some kind of social commentary or criticism. Therein lies cultural support for lawyers, politicians, and others to express themselves in conspicuously moral terms, as exemplified in Chapter 3.

That some version of the public moralist is occasionally to be found in the pages of Latin American newspapers represents a notable contrast with commentary on crime in Anglo-America. There, the voice of expertise is preferred to that of morality, even as morality tinges the very commentary being made.[75] The expert has specialized knowledge and a putative ability to use it in ways that are deemed to be socially beneficial.[76] Experts are granted authority to talk about what has happened, or will happen, and about what can, or might be, done. In so doing, they invariably focus on questions of knowledge and technique, but they often add some low-key moral talk: for example, a reference to the "tragic results" of domestic violence (as seen in Victoria Frye's letter to the *New York Times*) or to the "worrying" nature of recent crime trends and to other causes of "concern" (as seen in previous chapters). Criminologists and police chiefs represent different types of expert on crime and criminal justice—the one drawing specialist knowledge and skills from research, the other from practice—and they are often joined by other researchers and criminal justice practitioners in collective commentary on crime.[77] Indeed, journalists and politicians who aspire to expertise in their own right must spend time reading the research or watching the practitioners at work. Directly or indirectly, researchers and practitioners must be heard, or read.

Expertise, of course, is also a very common ingredient in commentary about crime in Latin America, as evidenced in preceding pages. Researchers and other purveyors of data were routinely cited as sources of knowledge; bureaucrats, entrepreneurs, and NGOs were consulted on matters of procedure and practice.[78] Compared to Anglo-America, there were some differences, already noted, in the frequency with which one or other type of source appeared and in the content of their statements. Nevertheless, there was much that was similar in the style and tone of many articles, reflecting basic congruities, and perhaps increasing concordance,[79] in the use of expertise as a journalistic resource. It was the presence, alongside expertise, of conspicuous moralizing that was a distinctive feature of the Latin American press and which gave its output a more heterogeneous character.

Context and collective moral discourse

The contextual understanding of contrasts in the melodramas of crime in the Americas must be fashioned by recourse to preexisting studies that are either explicitly comparative or can be worked into a comparative framework. It is the nature and results of those studies that determine the type of reflection that can be developed in relation to the findings presented here. Thus, the first difference discussed, a difference in moral outlook, is also a difference that has been explored by other researchers. The cynical attitude towards the state which was found in the South and the more trusting attitude expressed in the North can be seen as one more example of similar contrasts in the level of trust in government established by other types of study. Possible explanations for this difference can be found in the extensive literature on the determinants of trust, which has thrown up a variety of factors ranging from macro-level conditions, such as a nation's wealth and type of political system, to micro-level characteristics, such as perceptions of governmental corruption and the degree of interpersonal trust.[80] One implication of these studies is that the frequent criticisms of government that are found in Latin American commentary on crime would not be a new phenomenon, and may well pre-date the recent rapid increases in crime seen in the region.[81] High crime rates may not be the explanation for the gloomy assessment of government.

In the second case, the differing significance of scientific research (greater in the North, lesser in the South) in the discourse directed at crime and criminal justice cannot be cited as one more example of a tendency revealed by other studies, because such studies do not exist. There are no hemispheric comparisons or broader cross-cultural projects that focus on the rhetorical treatment of social problems.[82] Instead, this finding must be assessed in relation to studies that focus on the quantity of scientific research in different societies and which indicate its relative abundance in Anglo-America and scarcity in Latin America. As such, those studies offer a potential explanation for the more central role of research in depictions of moral outlook and moral agency in the North which, if valid, would predict a similar pattern for the differential salience of science in other arenas of social commentary.

Similar to this second case, the third contrast between the two regions—in the conspicuousness with which moralizing is sometimes expressed—cannot be placed alongside similar findings from other studies because, once again, comparative work of this kind does not exist. Nevertheless, it can be related to studies on social criticism, essay writing and moralizing, which suggest that the social critic is still a recognizable and accepted figure in Latin America, but viewed with misgivings, and even antipathy, in Anglo-America. The greater conspicuousness of moralizing about crime in the South can, therefore, be understood as an instance of a broader culturally sanctioned practice.

It is difficult to put these three contrasts together as indicators of some more basic social, political or cultural difference between the two regions. It is not at all clear how perceptions of government and levels of trust might relate to levels of investment in research or to the cultural status of social criticism. The political and socio-cultural dimensions seem to be quite separate here. More plausible could be an inverse relationship between research and conspicuous moralizing, the rise of the former perhaps contributing to the demise of the latter, suggesting a contrast between empirical preoccupations in the North and normative preoccupations in the South. But this can only be speculative. There is, as yet, no discernible meta-narrative to the different melodramatic productions discussed in this chapter.

One of the implications of the foregoing analysis is that the differences in collective morality noted between the two regions appear to be fairly stable and do not represent short-term divergences. Not only do they look to have existed for some time; they also relate to social, economic or cultural phenomena that are unlikely to change rapidly. Thus, they can also be expected to remain for some time. One of the contributions of this kind of analysis is the ready acknowledgement that collective moral discourse is shaped by the context in which it is produced, even though that process is not the primary focus of attention in the present study.

7 The artifacts of talk

As purveyed by the newsprint studied here, public discourse on crime accomplishes a number of interesting things in relation to morality. Most basically, its monophonic production and reproduction of the voices of rectitude provides a continual demonstration, and perhaps reassurance, that the moral project exists. The relatively frequent, if often perfunctory and stylistically varied, materializations of censure and prescription are evidence that morality is at work. That, in the segment of the public sphere constituted by newspapers, these utterances are pitched in collective terms reflects and reinforces the idea of civil society as a moral community. Their Manichean conception of the moral world represents a simple template for affirming aggregate and individual virtue against a constant threat from the unexplored and voiceless world of criminality. The moral outlook demands a narrative clothed in certainty. It banishes doubt by permitting multiple histories of the present and eschewing nearly all confrontation between them. Moral agency is fundamentally conceived as the virtue of action, tempered frequently by a drive to effectiveness. Collective moralizing about crime is a permanently unfinished melodramatic production in which the narrators are always in danger of being surprised or overwhelmed, but steadfastly committed to victory.

Six newspapers, five countries, two years

The set of texts compiled for this study were drawn from what are often called "newspapers of record," publications that are generally seen to be careful about sources and veracity (hence the term "record"), but which are also written by, and for, the better educated and better connected segments of society. That the moral talk in this type of press was overwhelmingly uncomplicated, pervasively melodramatic, frequently clichéd, and occasionally dramatic is, perhaps, surprising. These might be characteristics more frequently associated with the tabloid press, which is typically assumed to deal with most subject matter in superficial and dramatic ways. Some researchers who have looked at newspapers and other mass media have asked whether there is a trend towards "tabloidization," in which all outlets are increasingly oriented towards sensational cases, if not sensational language, in their copy on crime and justice.[1] While this is a possibility, there is also plenty of evidence that differences can be found between the quality and popular press in relation to the types of crime that are the preferred objects of attention, the sources that are consulted, and the style of writing.[2] Similar types of difference can also be found when newspapers are compared with TV broadcasts or other media.[3] Additionally, "medium theory" has argued that representations of the collective self—of "us" and "them"—are contingent on the physical, psychological and social particularities of each kind of medium.[4] Thus, there is an obvious possibility that actual or potential differences of these kinds are associated with variations in the character and content of collective moral talk about crime.

Nevertheless, it must also be remembered that the present study is not an inquiry into the journalistic production of morality; it simply takes newspaper articles as one type of text in which the collective discourse on crime materializes. Indeed, given journalism's particular orientation to reporting, it is inevitable that some newspaper content is drawn from other domains where public commentary on crime can be found: academic lectures and reports; political speeches, meetings and debates; neighborhood gatherings, lobbying, marches and protests; and so on. Hence, newsprint is likely to reproduce, at least in part, the characteristic modes of expression of its constituent sources. Moreover, while each domain is likely to impart some specific characteristics to what is said or written,[5] the multiple overlaps among them mean that there will also be many commonalities.

Collective morality is also likely to vary by geography and culture. Even assuming that the six newspapers used as sources in this study are in some way representative of the five countries in which they are published, there are 30 other countries in the Americas, from the Caribbean to Tierra del Fuego, each with its own press and its own crime. While the sampling frame was designed to straddle the major cultural, economic, and political difference in the hemisphere, between Anglo-America and Latin America, there is also the possibility that news items drawn from a different set of countries might have led to somewhat different results. And, whether or not this would have been the case, the findings from the present study must be permanently tagged with their geographical and cultural origin in the Americas. For example, comparative studies which examine cultural phenomena of relevance to moral discourse, such as "repertoires of evaluation,"[6] the "quality of public discourse,"[7] or the journalistic construction of social problems,[8] indicate intriguing and important differences between the United States and continental European countries. Widening the geographical focus, studies of more abstract expressions of morality (or adjuncts to morality), notably those dealing with values and beliefs, find considerable diversity around the world.[9] Differences in the language, style, and content of collective moral discourse on crime (and differences in moral identity, outlook, and agency) are, therefore, to be expected, even as some features of this discourse prove to be widely distributed. If the present study has managed to tap into broader patterns of variation and constancy, its findings suggest that differences will be observed in, among other things, the specific objects of attention (the types of crime, the legal and institutional responses to crime, etc.), the primary focus of concern ("ourselves" or others), the salience of moral utterances in commentary on crime, and the significance of science. More pervasive characteristics in moral discourse on crime may be the melodramatic structuring of the social universe and the suspension of empirical doubt.

Just as geography maps relevant cultural differences, history also charts them. Thus, Peter Brooks located the rise of literary melodrama "within the context of the French Revolution," a time when the traditional notions of the sacred (as embodied in church and monarchy) were thrown aside and "the traditional imperatives of truth and ethics [had] been violently thrown into question."[10] With it came the melodramatic perspective on politics and society that has persisted to this day. Gertrude Himmelfarb lamented the contemporary unwillingness (in Anglo-America, at least) to "speak the language of morality"[11] that was so conspicuously employed by the Victorians (those avid consumers of the theatrical genre publicly advertized as "melodrama"). These are but two examples of how a relatively long view of history would uncover differences in the style and orientation of moral discourse, along with the obvious changes in the topics that drew the attention of the day, the journalistic practices that wrought them into newspaper text, and the facts that were cited in commentary. A shorter historical view is likely to discover more muted changes, even as the developments in mass media, the changes in political systems, and the growth in research activity exert their effects. For example, in a study of items about crime published in Costa Rica since 1940, Huhn found that "crime has always been a topic that has generated pervasive feelings of insecurity and social pessimism."[12] Indeed, in relation to one text he commented that "Like several articles already cited, [the newspaper] could reprint this column in its issue for tomorrow and nobody would guess that it was written 33 years ago."[13] Some things may change only relatively slowly.

Crime, of course, is merely one among numerous objects of social concern. Moralizing can emerge in relation to anything in the field of human activity that catches the individual or collective eye: child labor and sweat shops, poverty, unemployment, homelessness, education, environmental issues, nuclear power, man-made disasters and the responses to natural disasters, diet, smoking, drinking, healthcare, abortion, pornography, prostitution, gender relations, war, slavery, race and ethnicity, the treatment of animals, social etiquette, and so on.[14] The social and ecological dynamics and consequences attributed to these phenomena obviously vary, and with that it is possible that not merely the objects of moral discourse but conceptions of moral outlook and agency will also vary. Yet there may also be underlying similarities. Some cultural sociologists, for example, have argued for the existence of deeply rooted categories in collective thinking which would predict considerable similarities in the construction of morality and identity across topically varied discourses.[15]

Political opinion researchers often distinguish between "valence issues" and "position issues," the former characterized by high levels of agreement (they "do not have an adversarial quality"), but the latter by "alternative and highly conflictual responses."[16] Thus, matters such as crime could be seen as valence issues, about which there is a great deal of moral consensus, while matters such as abortion, nuclear power, and seal hunting could be seen as position issues, about which there is much disagreement. The character of moral discourse that materializes in relation to one or other type of issue may, therefore, be quite distinctive. Alternatively, agreement and disagreement may attach to particular levels in a hierarchy of values,[17] such that a "progressive stripping away of layers of meaning in an attempt to lay bare the physiology of a moral system ... [a]t the deeper levels ... might unearth understandings which are so universally taken for granted that they are not even noticed by those who maintain them."[18]

What if...?

Considerations regarding stability and variation underline a view of collective moral discourses as particular configurations of textual style, collective identity, moral outlook, and moral agency. One very natural sociological perspective on these potentially variable characteristics is to seek to identify the processes that produce them, treating collective morality something like—in common scientific parlance—a dependent variable.[19] This is an interesting line of approach, but it has not been pursued here.[20] A different perspective is to speculate on other possible configurations of collective morality, which is useful both for posing normative questions about its quality and content and for understanding its social significance. These are the subjects of the remaining paragraphs.

That collective moral discourse on crime in the Americas looks to be melodramatic and Manichean, that it is fuelled by multiple and often competing empirical claims, that it insists on action and judges action almost exclusively in terms of consequences, suggests an exercise in moralizing that is both narrow and superficial. Other ways of structuring the social universe and other conceptions of moral agency would broaden it; other visions of criminality and of knowledge would deepen it.

Something of this latter point was made by Silvio Waisbord in his study of exposé journalism in Latin America. Investigative stories, he argued, "contribute little to a public examination of the moral order" and involve only a "narrow discussion of morality."[21] He felt that the superficial treatment of scandals, in a medium addicted to instant and ephemeral news, militated against any detailed consideration of the causes of corruption and the possible remedies for abuses of power. Tipping his hat (unwittingly or not) to the deliberative caucus, he charged that exposés "fail to serve as a forum for a wider public discussion on the moral dimensions of democracy."[22]

This is one way to push for a different kind of moral commentary, especially given interest in the "communicative action" and "discourse ethics" so influentially proposed by Habermas, which offer a model by which to fashion and judge discourse in the public sphere.[23] But it is worth noting that the newsprint examined by Waisbord seems no different to other sorts of public issue discourse which, when assessed from a Habermasian perspective, fairly clearly fail to approximate the ideal.[24] It is not as if journalists, or Latin Americans, are particularly deficient in this regard; simply that the quality of public deliberation is not as inclusive, structured or reasoned as it apparently needs to be if it is to meet democratic aspirations. Moreover, studies informed by discourse ethics have largely focused on the structural properties of deliberation (for example, the extent to which it is inclusive or exclusive) and its formal characteristics (for example, the degree of dialogue).[25] They have yet to look at the width and depth of the ideas put forward.[26]

In an earlier study on newsmaking in the United States, Herbert Gans rather memorably described the adherence to convention among journalists and those whom they consult:

> sources and other people try to be on their best behavior because they are exposed, at least potentially, to public visibility. Consequently, journalists guard not only the moral order embodied in enduring values but a wide range of ideals, mores and customs as well. When sources are interviewed by journalists, they demonstrate their adherence to national and societal ideals, and they refrain from picking their noses while on camera.[27]

This striking, but inelegant, nasal metaphor hints at melodrama. It points to the absence of any meaningful self-examination on the part of a community that talks itself into being through the words of journalists and their sources. It implies an unwillingness to look inwards, or to air in public the less attractive attributes; it criticizes the keeping up of appearances. And, if the findings of the present study are brought into play, it must be said that the same—melodramatic—community also fails to cast a discerning eye on the criminality that preoccupies it.

The rise of melodrama as a literary form is generally seen to have displaced tragedy as a mode of narrative and reflection, and it may well be sustained in its contemporary prominence by enduring cultural conditions.[28] But what if a tragic vision of criminality were to prevail? The tragic person is, in the words of Heilman, a "divided" person, largely "good" but also "flawed."[29] Where melodrama eschews the dissection of moral identity and works with solid and cemented oppositions of (we the) good and (they the) bad, tragedy explores inner complications, turbulences, and failings. While melodrama is concerned with "the reordering of one's relations with others, with the world of people or things," tragedy is concerned with "the reordering of the self,"[30] and with the knowledge, self-awareness, and growth that, hopefully, accompany it. In the theater, the ostensible dramatic project invites contemplation of a fictional rendering of the tragic persona; yet the best tragedies "envisage the malfunctionings of human life, not as stemming from the eccentricities and barbarisms of 'others' but as rooted in the characteristic longings and temptations of Everyman," and they "force us into identity with that Everyman,"[31] with inevitable consequences for moral knowledge and moral judgment.

Melodramatic commentary on crime is a discursive production in which criminality and virtue are personified. Morality and immorality are depicted as antagonistic groups of actors rather than coexisting potentials of individual behavior. There is no attempt to explore their sources, interrelations, conflicts, and complementarities; no re-visioning of the social world to endow everyone with the capability of doing right and doing wrong. Perhaps the rigidity of this conception betrays anxiety, a deep uncertainty about what would happen if criminal behavior were placed under an inquiring lens. The residents of Toronto's Regent Park (see Chapter 3) began every "peace circle" with a ritual quote from Longfellow: "If we could read the secret history of our enemies, we should find in each man's life sorrow and suffering enough to disarm all hostility."[32] Yet even their actions were cast in melodramatic terms, as they "fought back" against the "heroin dealers" in their building and the housing managers brought in a private security firm that finally drove the dealers out. There was no reading of the latter's "secret history," no lessening of hostility, no attempt to contextualize, understand, and critically assess the complex, ambiguous, and ambivalent circumstances crudely captured by the term "heroin dealing." Moral disarmament might have been the result of such an exercise, perhaps accompanied by misplaced fears of an ensuing moral vacuum, which probably diminished any appetite for examining the "heroin dealers" more closely.

Of course, if secret histories are to be read, they must first be told; and this can only be done by giving a voice to those who have lived them. Just as the heroin dealers in Regent Park were left voiceless by the newspaper (and were probably content, perhaps relieved, that things were thus), so more generally the individuals and groups that symbolize criminality are not heard in the public sphere. The adherence to conventionality that powerfully marks the mass media works strongly in favor of silence, or requires some kind of contrition as a prologue to any statement from those who would acknowledge, and must not celebrate, their criminal behavior. Putting aside the superficial and dramatized images offered by much that is purveyed as "true crime,"[33] it falls to a few novelists, playwrights, and ethnographers to give a voice to criminality, and at the same time chart a sensitive course between sensationalism and sympathy (that "dangerously unstable emotion"[34]). But, so great is the discomfort with crime that, even here, readers or viewers often must be prepared for the assault on the moral senses. Thus, Katz, in his preface to *Seductions of Crime*, writes:

> Morally as well as sensually, it is likely that some readers will feel personally victimized by my effort to convey the offender's experience. But if guided by empathy, this text does not compel sympathy. The adage "To understand is to forgive" was false when touted by George Herbert Mead and has misguided generations of social researchers on deviance. A trip "to the other side" does not have to be a permanent change in spiritual address.[35]

Nevertheless, a "trip to the other side" dispels the comfort offered by melodrama and, if successfully accomplished, provokes self-examination. Indeed, the tragic vision suggests that the "other side" is not some alien terrain inhabited by outlaws, but a moral (or, more precisely, immoral) space within. Lawrence Durrell once imagined "a detective story in which the reader at the end discovers that he is the criminal."[36] In the non-fictional domain of commentary on crime this kind of artifice can be achieved only by the social critic, but—as the preceding chapters show—social critics are few and far between. Even critical criminology, for which Durrell's epigram could well serve as its motto, finds itself on the margins of the public sphere.[37] As a result, there is little "tragic awareness in the community soul,"[38] no real consciousness of the possibility that morality may spill over—especially through indignation—into immorality, no alertness to the ways in which the moralities of pity or self-pity may exacerbate the very problems that brought them into existence.

In Heilman's conception of tragedy, the individual is torn between imperatives and impulses (passions). For Hegel, a tragedy was a collision between two imperatives.[39] For Aristotle, it was, more enigmatically, "an imitation of an action."[40] These and other visions of the tragic encompass, or allow for, more than one perspective on moral agency, notably the deontology implied by imperatives or the various virtues (stoicism, courage, magnanimity, etc.) that might flourish in heroic encounters with unreason and fate. They also suggest that melodrama might have its own inventory of preferred moralities—the virtue of determined action and the language of consequentialism, if the present study is any indication—and they insinuate the potential for different conceptions of moral agency in the approach to crime. That potential is evident in specialist forums on what is often called "criminal justice ethics,"[41] and in texts for students and practitioners,[42] but it does not overflow to other parts of the public domain. This is not to argue that it should, for it is clear that many people find it hard to make their moralizing ethical;[43] it is simply to recognize that ethics has inventoried and developed considerably more visions of moral agency than those found in contemporary newsprint commentary on crime. Melodrama is often dismissed as trivial, but its persistence and pervasiveness suggest that there are strong social and cultural determinants working against alternative views of moral agency. Even so, it is interesting to ask what collective moral discourse on crime might look like if it could extricate itself from the melodramatic lens. Can civil societies with "tragic awareness" be found? Are there alternative non-ethical conceptions of moral agency to be uncovered in public or private commentary on crime? How would alternative ethical conceptions of moral agency, perhaps purveyed through some sort of "newsmaking criminology,"[44] fare in the non-academic domain? These are matters for further exploration.

A final source of potential variation in the character of moralizing derives from the possibility of empirical perplexity. "Ethics demands certain foreknowledge," wrote Dupuy and Grinbaum in a recent article; indeed, they considered this requirement to be one of the "foundations" of the ethical project.[45] Their reference to "foreknowledge" (which broadly refers to forecasting) is explained by their particular field of interest (climate change), but the axiomatic tone of their claim reflects a general principle that moralizing can proceed only on the basis of certain knowledge. This same principle was observed in Chapters 4 and 5, where commentators on crime fashioned confident factual claims into portraits of the moral outlook, or worked them into defenses or critiques of measures to deal with crime. Even uncertainties about the future course of events were granted conditional certainty for the purpose of expressing concern.[46] Competing or conflicting factual claims were sometimes acknowledged but then put aside in order to get on with the business of censure or prescription. That certainty is considered crucial to morally driven action is reflected in the extensive literature on the meanings of uncertainty[47] (with particular attention to the notion of risk[48]), and on the ways in which certainty and uncertainty are constructed, affirmed, negotiated or denied in the scientific and policy domains.[49]

Thus, if ethics demands certain knowledge there is a strong possibility that it will manufacture certainty. But, what if empirical doubt reigns? What if there is felt to be insufficient knowledge, or plural and potentially irreconcilable empirical claims? What if researchers insist on uncertainty, and everyone confesses to ignorance? What if commentators (people with something to say) become more like spectators (who can only watch because they know that they do not know)? What would this aporia[50] imply for moralizing? Paralysis; inaction; or something different? Such a condition would undoubtedly make it more difficult to construct the histories of the present that inform the moral outlook, perhaps forcing commentators to rely more explicitly on personal experience as a supposedly solid source of knowledge—more explicitly, because there is always the possibility that personal experience influences the choice of empirical claims about the collectivity; supposedly solid, because there is always the possibility that individuals may be puzzled by the particularities of their own experience. And if histories of the present are harder to construct, so—also—is the idea of a moral community. Aporia, as puzzlement, could lead to collective existential doubt.

But it does not imply moral paralysis. Uncertainty may subvert a consequentialist approach to moral agency, precisely because there is considerable perplexity about the consequences of any course of action, but it may insinuate the propriety of particular imperatives (such as justice) or virtues (such as patience) in the face of the unknown.[51] The form that collective moral discourse might take in these conditions can be explored only by searching for potential aporia (puzzles) and examining the responses to them; in the case of crime, by looking for "new" or disturbing events—a schoolroom massacre, a "9/11," a rash of kidnappings, a decapitated corpse, or an outbreak of lynching—and examining the commentary they generate.[52]

What consequence?

That the character and content of collective moral discourse about crime could vary really acquires significance only if those variations are of some consequence. But what might the consequences of such variations be?

Chapter 5 noted that much of the research on framing social issues seems to require a perspective of soft determinism in order to establish its raison d'être. There is an assumption that talk about a social issue somehow influences decisions that are taken in relation to it; and there is a further assumption that decisions which are taken will somehow influence organizational and individual behavior. Couched in such tentative terms, neither of these assumptions is particularly problematic; but, of course, the "somehow" makes them very bland because it glosses over the very demanding task of establishing a clear line of sight between talk, decisions, and outcomes.[53] The whole approach can also be cast into doubt by treating talk as a narrative or account; that is, as an attempt to make sense of events rather than influence them.[54] Thus, while there is an inevitable curiosity about the ways in which particular moral discourses might be—loosely or tightly—connected with the criminality and control that occupy their attention, there are no simple or linear answers; and none have been essayed here, although undoubtedly the search for them would be interesting.

Instead, the present study has focused on some artifacts of talk, the intangible objects that are created through words. The particular artifacts described here concern the interrelated subjects of identity and experience. Chief among them is the moral community—a virtuous civil society—which is routinely and repeatedly invoked in commentary on crime and which seems to provide a necessary demonstration that the forces for good not only exist but are on constant alert. Whether or not there is a collective conscience of the non-discursive type, as conceptualized by Durkheim or explored by contemporary inquiries into values, the present study suggests that talk of a moral community at least provides some legible and audible reassurances that morality exists, that any existential anxieties about creeping amorality can be put on temporary hold.

The imagined moral community not only provides reassurance that the world is not lost; it also serves as a vehicle for fashioning individual identity. In the arena of conventionality that is largely coterminous with the public sphere, and which includes the mass media, moral talk about crime confers a positive identity on the speakers. To talk in moral terms is, obviously, to assert a moral identity; but the standing of the speakers also depends on the extent to which they align themselves, through their words, with the moral community. The present study offers numerous examples of the conventional, and repetitive, moral language that does this work. But it also suggests that social approval will diminish when moralizing becomes unconventional or attacks conventionality itself.

Moral outlook and moral agency are also artifacts of talk. While oriented towards, although not necessarily determinants of, the business of living, they are also bound up with conceptions of moral order and identity. In the innumerable histories that are told of the present, and the multiple prescriptions for action "in response," a moral universe is depicted, its future drafted, and commentators placed on the stage. Outlook and agency incorporate knowledge claims of diverse types, which can also be considered as artifacts of talk. The present study suggests that one such artifact—research—is a particularly important constituent of contemporary moral outlook and agency. It provides a vital ingredient for much consequentialist thinking and, at least in the Americas, seems to drown out the art of engineering, except for broadly technical considerations occasionally advanced in the South.

Morality, identity, and the business of living represent large and undeniably important slices of human experience. Although none of them is entirely, or perhaps even predominantly, constituted by words, they are obviously too important to be consigned to silence. But how to talk about them is a permanent challenge. Take, as one example, Boltanski's extended analysis of the ways of talking about "distant suffering," suffering which may be at great social and spatial remove from the observer.

> When confronted with suffering all moral demands converge on the single imperative of action ... [Boltanski wrote].... But what form can this [action] take when those called upon to act are thousands of miles away from the person suffering? The answer we propose ... is that one can commit oneself through speech; by adopting the stance, even when alone in front of the television, of someone who speaks to somebody else about what they have seen.[55]

Yet there are many challenges to achieving a morally adequate response through speech: talk may be criticized as an empty substitute for action; emotions may look sham; "tender-heartedness [may be] no more than selfish enjoyment unaware of itself."[56] Most generally, "there is also speech that is derisively described as *merely verbal*, as just words, precisely in order to indicate the fact that these words in no way commit the person who uttered them."[57] Here, the singular importance and the immense difficulty of talking are combined and revealed, with all that they imply, in this case, for personal identity. Talking may be seen as obligatory, yet, at best, performed (or perceived) as a social chore, at worst, as a piece of hypocrisy. It is, always, consequential.

Boltanski argued that, in relation to distant suffering, talk "must at the same time report to the other both what was seen and how this personally affected and involved the spectator."[58] He felt that there are only a finite number of ways of achieving this. One is through denunciation, in which observers transform pity into indignation and seek to identify the persecutors who are responsible for the suffering that is observed. Another is through sentiment, in which sympathy gestures towards benefactors and acts of charity. A third way is to adopt an "aesthetic" perspective and "look evil in the face without immediately turning away towards imaginary benefactors or persecutors."[59] The spectator must possess:

> the faculty required to make something of this suffering, that is to say to examine it, take it into himself and get it to work like an operator so as to apprehend and display an internal evil. Moral capacity is assigned solely to the person who, in amazement, takes the other person's suffering by surprise and grasps hold of it.[60]

Denunciation and sentiment represent melodramatic conceptions of experience in which the discursive gaze is directed at the suffering of others, and at those who might cause or ameliorate it. The aesthetic perspective is much closer to a tragic conception, in that the discursive gaze looks inward. Crucially, each perspective is bound by conventions regarding what can be said and by whom; and, it might be added, convention papers over the difficulties that inhere in talking.

Distant Suffering: Morality, Media and Politics illustrates the more general point that the way in which morality is conceived orients the preferences for particular kinds of talk. For example, a morality that is concerned with imperatives might give a much greater voice to ethicists, while one concerned with virtue might look mainly to "spiritual" leaders. By contrast, the present study suggests that a utilitarian approach, in the contemporary era at least, draws increasingly on research and is in turn buttressed by it. If the moral lens were changed, the artifacts of talk would look different (as would their constitutive voices) and so, to some extent, would identity and experience.

Appendix
Notes on method and sources

Preliminaries

The present study grew out of a curiosity regarding "talked" or, more precisely, "written" morality: What does it look like? What might its social significance be? How edifying is it? These questions were explored through a study of commentary about crime—a topic of inherently moral significance.

At least two proposals for studying public moral discourse have been made in the past. In the first, Lee and Ungar[1] developed a complex set of categories for coding moral discourse, focusing on such things as sides in the debate, voice (i.e., who is doing the moral talking), key words, metaphors, and rhetorical strategies. In the second, Ibarra and Kitsuse[2] developed a framework for classifying and studying moral arguments as a key part of their proposal to refine the definition of social problems as "claims-making discourse." For example, they suggested that there are "rhetorical idioms" in social problems discourse (texts which invoke clusters of images designed to mobilize the sentiments of others in ways favorable to the claims-maker), and also "counterrhetorics" (the answering arguments to these idioms). They also drew attention to "motifs" (shorthand characterizations of an issue) and claims-making styles.[3]

Neither of these proposals generated much, if any, take-up. Lee and Ungar's work met with silence, possibly because their coding categories were very numerous and not well systematized.[4] Ibarra and Kitsuse's essay generated a lot of debate concerning its argument that social problems should be treated as "condition-categories,"[5] but the largely critical response to their proposal was accompanied by a general lack of interest in the "ethnography of moral discourse" (as they called their approach).[6]

Beyond any methodological difficulties that might have arisen in trying to adopt and adapt either of these approaches for the present study, they have the added inconvenience that they were developed with a focus on moral discourse as rhetoric. Treating it as such is to highlight, and partly contribute to, the emergence of social "issues," understood as disagreements—often quite heated—about selected aspects of the social world. Social issues are the specialized objects of study in the social problems and social movements literatures, and their scholars have devoted a great deal of attention to the argumentative strategies used to advance a particular side of the issue or attack alternative positions.[7] From that perspective, moral discourse (which is undeniably a component of social issues[8]) becomes a form of argument or persuasion; in other words, rhetoric.

There are three difficulties here. The first, already alluded to in Chapter 1, is that social issues may depend for their existence on the process of framing—the selective compilation of fragments of discourse to construct one or more "sides" to a debate. Such framing may make issues look much neater in appearance than their fuzzier, less systematic, manifestations in naturally occurring text. The second problem is that the focus on disagreement may overlook equally important signs of agreement or consensus about at least *some* aspects of the matter under discussion. And a third, more significant, problem is that framing tends to assume (perhaps even encourage) debate where none may exist. Different opinions about the nature, causes, and consequences of particular social conditions, and the best measures for addressing them, may simply materialize in natural text as disconnected comments that have no explicit dialogic role. They are not necessarily oriented to debate. Thus, treating moral discourse exclusively as rhetoric did not seem particularly helpful. The analysis reported in this book employed an alternative, and more general, set of discursive categories than those developed by Lee and Ungar or Ibarra and Kitsuse, from which the outlines of a collective and shared morality began to emerge and assume considerable significance.

The set of texts

"Commentary," as used throughout this book, refers to statements about the totality of incidents of one, several, or all types of crime, rather than statements which give details of a single incident. In newspapers, commentary on crime is found in a number of different commonly recognized types of text. Most obviously, editorials, opinion columns, and letters to the paper represent formats for making statements about the totality of crime (although sometimes these types of text may focus exclusively on the details of a crime incident, in which case they were not of interest for the present study[9]). Numerically more important than editorials/opinions/letters are "news features," which deal with one or more types of crime, or crime in general. A single feature may include commentaries from a number of different sources: for example, a report by a public agency, a speech by a political figure, and an interview with a community representative. While there is no absolute difference between editorials/opinions/letters and news features, the former tend to have an explicit argument structure, to include fewer (or no) sources, and to be shorter; the latter tend to purvey "information" rather than argument, to include more sources, and to be longer. Texts giving information about single incidents, often called "spot, hard, or straight news,"[10] are by far the most frequent type of item published about crime. However, they rarely contain commentary about crime in general.[11] Thus, in contrast to many studies of crime[12] or other topics in the news, the present study did not examine "spot reporting."

Texts with commentary on crime were drawn from three newspapers in Anglo-America (the *Globe and Mail* from Canada; the *Los Angeles Times* and the *New York Times* from the United States) and three in Latin America (*El Universal* from Mexico, *El Nacional* from Venezuela, and *La Nación* from Argentina). All of these are considered "papers of record," and their readership is found primarily in the higher socioeconomic strata. Circulation figures are among the highest for broadsheet newspapers in each country: The *Globe and Mail*—321,000; the *New York Times*—nearly 1.1 million; *Los Angeles Times*—739,000; *El Universal*—153,000; *El Nacional*—144,000; *La Nación*—195,000.[13] All are based in major cities (Toronto, New York, Los Angeles, Mexico City, Caracas and Buenos Aires, respectively), and offer local, national, and international news. Distribution of the print edition tends to be concentrated in the home city but, in addition, each is accessible electronically. Their locations in research-active countries also mean that the Anglo-American newspapers have been used with some frequency as sources for studying crime in the media.[14] The same cannot be said of the Latin American newspapers used in this study.[15]

While their professional ethos stresses independence, and their targeted readership is centrist rather than radical, each paper has recognizable political sympathies, which can vary over time. For example, the *Globe and Mail* supported Liberal political candidates during the 1990s and early 2000s, but endorsed the Conservatives in 2006.[16] An analysis of articles published in the *New York Times* between 1946 and 1997 concluded that it showed some partisanship for the Democrats, but that its watchdog function was exercised more symmetrically over Democrats and Republicans after the 1960s.[17] Meanwhile, the *Los Angeles Times* recently broke with a fairly lengthy tradition of non-involvement in politics by endorsing Barack Obama for the 2008 presidential election.[18] In Latin America, *El Nacional* declares itself to be politically independent and began to publish full-length editorials only in the late 1990s, although it has included opinion articles since its earliest days.[19] In recent years it has been a strong critic of the Chávez government. *El Universal* has had longstanding (although recently weakened) links with the Partido Revolucionario Institucional;[20] while *La Nación* was openly critical of Néstor Kirchner's left-leaning government that was in power in 2006–2007.[21]

For the present study, commentary on crime was compiled from material published during the calendar years 2006 and 2007. Potential items for inclusion were retrieved electronically, using "crime" as the key word for the Anglo-American press and *delincuencia*, *criminalidad*, and *inseguridad* as the three most relevant terms in Latin America. These were then scanned rapidly to exclude any "spot news" that focused entirely on the details of a single incident and offered no commentary about crime in general. Items focusing entirely on the criminal justice system, with no mention of crime, were similarly excluded. For example, an item reporting on a new police patrol strategy in response to increasing levels of crime would be included in the analysis, but an article about new police uniforms would not (unless those uniforms were portrayed as being significant for responses to crime). An article on the use of DNA technology to solve crimes would be included, but an article about a new criminal court facility would not.

An additional criterion in selection was to exclude items referring to crime in other countries, unless the item also gave some consideration to the significance or implications of that crime for the country in which the item was published. This is because collective morality is still tied strongly to that other "imagined community" of importance—the nation. Indeed, in relation to crime this situation could hardly be otherwise, because newspapers themselves select items on the basis of their perceived interest to readers. High-profile incidents from other countries may make it into the national press because of the curiosity they typically arouse, but they offer no commentary on crime in general. Items about general crime in other countries will be prepared and published only if that crime is linked in some way to things happening "at home."

Following the initial selection process, items were set up in files on NVivo (a software package for qualitative text analysis), through which coding and analysis were conducted. On detailed reading, a few additional items did not meet the selection criteria and were excluded from the study. The final set of texts consisted of 853 items published in the six newspapers during the two years selected for study[22] (see the complete listing in the final section of this Appendix). These were judged to be sufficient for the purposes of analysis and, indeed, allowed the identification both of the general characteristics of public moral discourse across the region and some specific differences between Anglo-America and Latin America.

Coding

Coding proceeded by identifying and classifying segments of text in terms of a set of categories that was provisionally developed, tested with a few articles, subsequently refined, and then used for the complete set of items.

The category of primary and initial interest was obviously that of moral discourse. In line with the definition given in Chapter 1, a segment of text was considered to be morally significant if it communicated or implied a putative obligation or prohibition, or desirability and undesirability, in relation to behavior. These directions of normativity can be usefully labelled as "prescription" and "censure," respectively.

Prescriptive text specifies things which ought to be done, should be done, or which are desirable. Consequently, the words "ought," "should," and "desirable" were obviously ones to look for in commentary on crime. For example, "social problems should be addressed through education, more employment and rescuing children who have been abandoned,"[23] is a clearly prescriptive statement, as is the following: "...minimum [...sentences] should be increased to 'send a strong message of denunciation...'"[24] However, an automated search-and-retrieval of words like these would not have been sufficient to identify the relevant segments of text. One problem is that words which look to be prescriptive may not be used in that way. For example, when cities are told that "they should not count on increased federal assistance [to deal with crime],"[25] they are simply being given the information that federal funding is not a certainty. Here, there is no statement of principle, no claim that city administrations would be doing something wrong if they took federal funds. Similarly, to say that "the Risk [crime] Prevention Program should be accompanied by other specific measures in order to be more efficient,"[26] is to speak to matters of method or procedure, not to obligations.

Another problem with an automated text search is that prescriptive statements can be expressed in a multiplicity of ways, which defies their meaningful reduction to a convenient short list of words. For example, a teenage curfew can be "called for" by community leaders[27] (meaning a curfew ought to be put in place), just as a columnist can write that "it is time to face the pressures [from insecurity] by means of actions that go beyond the here and now,"[28] (meaning that the pressures must be faced). Similarly, doing everything possible to get criminals with guns off the street might be "owed" to "the families that lost loved ones;"[29] while trying to stop people taking the law into their own hands may be a matter of "urgency."[30]

Inevitably, there were also segments of texts that were ambiguous—open to interpretation as morally significant or not. For example, when a citizen opines that "The only way we're going to get this [gang] violence to stop is to make the penalties tougher ... [the] laws are too soft,"[31] is he simply giving advice about the best method for dealing with gangs, or is he demanding that something be done? When an editorial states that "The [gun amnesty] campaign is well inspired and it is to be hoped that it achieves encouraging results,"[32] is this simply a nod to the fact that it might work, or a plaudit that underlines its desirability? Doubts such as these could be resolved only by looking at the particular segment in relation to the surrounding text. The latter may have contained other, more explicit, morally significant statements which were congruent with the meaning that seemed to inhere in the segment under consideration and which allowed it to be categorized, also, as morally significant.[33] If doubts persisted about meaning, even after this contextual analysis had been undertaken, a segment was simply left uncoded: the present study was not concerned to develop a structural analysis of the total text in each newspaper item, but to identify moral discourse as it materialized across a set of items. In that regard, there were plenty of unambiguous segments of moral discourse on which analysis could focus.

A second type of moral discourse, censorious text, refers to things which ought not to happen, or that should not be done. Here, semantic variation was even more evident, ranging from the simple and straightforward ("ominous" trends, the "problem" of crime, "the forces of evil," and so on) to the wordy or indirect: "half a dozen victims-rights advocates who told heart-wrenching stories of how their loved ones were killed by violent criminals or drunk drivers;"[34] or "the overflow of crime puts national security at risk."[35] As with prescription, the censorious intent of some segments was unclear and, when not resolved by contextual analysis, these were left uncoded. Censorious text, of which there was a great deal, also subdivided itself into comments about crime and comments about responses to crime (or, just as frequently, the lack of responses to crime), which was useful when it came to charting the history of the imagined moral community that is set out in Chapters 4 and 5.

Apart from the identification of segments of moral discourse, text was also coded in terms of two other important intellective dimensions: the empirical and the practical. The empirical dimension refers to what is known (or thought to be known) about the world; the practical dimension refers to action. The potential significance of these dimensions for understanding public moral discourse was suggested by their implications for moral outlook and moral agency, and by the way in which they might be intertwined with them.[36]

Empirical discourse was considered to be any descriptive, explanatory or predictive segment of text referring to crime or the responses to it, varying from the qualitative (e.g., "I think that, irrespective of the number of incidents, people are afraid"[37]) to the quantitative (e.g., "the number of homicides is lower than its peak in the early 90's"[38]), from the scientific (e.g., "Many reputable social scientists have suggested that there is no reliable evidence of a 'broken windows' effect whatsoever"[39]) to the lay (e.g., "'Spider Man.' This type [of burglary in apartments] has become famous and is practiced with frequency"[40]), from the plodding (e.g., "Most [organized crime] groups continue to use legitimate businesses to hide their activities and launder their cash"[41]) to the dramatic (e.g., "the crime crisis ... has become a daily blight which has permeated all of the urban fabric of the nation"[42]).

Practical discourse deals either with resolutions or procedure. Resolutions are understood as declarations of intent regarding what will be done, and are therefore different to an empirical prediction about what will happen. Typical examples were: "Bratton said he plans to announce a new strategy for reducing crime in the coming weeks;"[43] or "I am going to go on the offensive against crime and criminals."[44] Procedure deals with how things work in an abstract sense, not with how things are working (or not working) in an empirical sense. It is an exercise in engineering, broadly conceived. For example, "Banishment is a punishment, but there are no cells, no bars. A person is sent away to think about what they've done and whether they can change their ways."[45] Procedural discourse also materialized in statements about what can possibly be done in relation to crime, for example: "money alone won't solve the problem;"[46] or "by ... limiting the number of firearms in circulation it is hoped that their acquisition in the black market will be more difficult."[47] Such discourse also appeared as "recipes" for action, as in:

> [T]he best way to ensure that young people achieve full development as adults, even when their surrounding environment is violent, is to encourage their participation in any kind of sport or other activity which keeps them occupied and removes them from crime and vice.[48]

Often these recipes came close to being prescriptions for action, marking the shortest distance between procedural and moral discourse.

The resulting set of coding categories was as follows:

A   MORAL DISCOURSE

    a   Censorious statements about crime or responses to crime
    b   Prescriptive statements about responses to crime

B   EMPIRICAL DISCOURSE

    a   Descriptive statements about crime or responses to crime
    b   Explanations offered for crime
    c   Predictions about crime

C   PRACTICAL DISCOURSE

    a   Resolutions—statements about what will be done in relation to crime
    b   Procedural text

        i   Statements about how anti-crime measures work
        ii   Statements concerning what might be done about crime
        iii   Recipes for action

To aid analysis, segments of text were also classified simultaneously by three additional characteristics (where present):

D   TYPE(S) OF CRIME MENTIONED IN THE COMMENTARY

    a   Drugs
    b   Gangs
    c   Guns
    d   Murder
    Etc.

E   PERSON(S) FEATURED (directly quoted or paraphrased in the item)

    a   Bureaucrat
    b   Businessperson
    c   Citizen
    d   Defense lawyer
    Etc.

F   COMPONENT OF THE CRIMINAL JUSTICE SYSTEM MENTIONED

    a   Law
    b   Police work
    c   Prosecutorial work
    d   Prisons

Categories D, E, and F were not primary objects of analysis but additional dimensions on which text could be retrieved as an aid to analysis. For example, text on gangs was useful when analyzing the history of the imagined moral

126   *Appendix*

community because it contained a vision of the spatial and social relations between "gangs" and civil society. Similarly, comments made by politicians were particularly useful for studying the links between moral discourse and identity.

The basic unit of coding was the sentence, but even at this level of measurement some sentences contained more than one type of discourse. For example, the following sentence combines empirical and moral discourse and was, therefore, coded simultaneously to both dimensions: "On a daily basis, the inhabitants of the capital are victims of thefts from their vehicles, homes, businesses, wallets and handbags, which makes this crime the principal scourge of those who live in the Federal District."[49] Similarly, the verb "has to" in the following comment mixes prescriptive and procedural meanings, which were both coded: "Th[e] message [that gang crime will be prosecuted aggressively] has to be sent, to achieve the deterrent goal."[50] While individual sentences could carry more than one type of discourse, a single type of discourse could also stretch across several sentences or, occasionally, paragraphs. Single or consecutive sentences were therefore coded to the relevant discursive categories for subsequent retrieval and analysis.

Analysis

Analytical attention focused primarily on Categories A to C above. Each contained all segments of text coded to the category and subcategory, and these could be linked back to the items from which they came and across to other subcategories to which they were simultaneously coded. The text in each category was treated as a type of discourse which materialized across the items in which it appeared.[51]

Analysis began with Category A (moral discourse), and the first task was to discover which types of moral utterance suggested themselves as being relatively frequent or relatively interesting. Initial readings led to the identification of three types:

- dramatic expressions of censure regarding crime[52]
- criticism of inaction or of previous actions taken in relation to crime[53]
- proposals for doing something about crime[54]

Each of these types of utterance suggested potentially fruitful lines of inquiry and reflection. Thus, the dramatic expressions of censure involved or implied categorical empirical statements about the prevalence or nature of crime. Meanwhile, proposals for doing something about crime often seemed to arise without due consideration for the challenges to doing it—they seemed to give a discursive closure, rather than any assured factual closure to the question of crime. In addition, the critical comments about inaction, or purportedly faulty prior actions, sometimes appeared to bolster the identity of the person making the criticism.

As these lines of inquiry were being explored, it became apparent that they were not always restricted to the type of utterance that had initially suggested them. Thus, categorical empirical statements were linked both to censure and prescription; the avoidance of practical complexities in relation to procedure was found in both critical and prescriptive statements about anti-crime actions; and personal identity construction occasionally appeared to be at work in all three types of utterance. The preliminary identification of different types of utterance, each suggesting a particular kind of discursive stance, therefore seemed to have been successful in highlighting those stances; but they were stances that could be seen to characterize moral discourse in general, not merely the types of utterance that initially suggested them.

This initial exercise was followed by a more detailed re-consideration of the first type of utterance mentioned above (dramatic statements of censure about crime) and then widened to include all statements that involved censure of crime. Attention focused on the type of statements made about crime and criminals, and the way in which they were depicted in morally relevant terms. Particularly striking was the way in which crime and criminals were often treated in a very superficial and simplistic manner. Most notably, criminality was a largely unexamined and poorly comprehended activity, and criminals never had a voice in the commentary (unless they had already shown some kind of repentance, or could present themselves as "former" criminals, and so on). This was a discourse monopolized by putatively law-abiding individuals, who placed themselves at a moral and physical distance from crime. Their commentary was less interesting for what it revealed about criminality than for what it revealed about conformity.

Use of the phrase "we the good" in one of the Latin American news items seemed to confirm this fundamental insight. "We the good" implied the existence of an imagined moral community which, as subsequent study revealed, was called up by frequent use of the first person plural and its equivalents. It was rarely labelled explicitly as the community of "the good," but did not need to be because censorious statements about crime were testimony enough to its existence and moral worth. It was from this discovery of the imagined moral community that the central questions of this study were developed. How does this moral community come into being? What is its conception of itself? How does it imagine its relationship with crime and criminals, and how does it see its recent history and immediate future?

Exploring each of those questions required a rereading, and sometimes additional coding, of the material. Thus, for an examination of how the imagined moral community comes into existence, it was necessary to reread not only moral discourse but also empirical and practical discourse, to look for instances in which the first person plural, or its equivalents, were used. This revealed, for example, that many segments with a largely empirical content relating to crime or responses to it (and coded as empirical discourse) also contained references to the collective dimension.[55] Similarly, when examining the immediate "future" of the moral community, it was important to look not only at proposals being made (prescriptive statements) but also at statements about what will be done (resolutions), both of which affirmed a vocation to influence the course of developments.

For each question about the imagined moral community, analysis proceeded through the identification and grouping of types of statement that appeared relevant to the construction of an answer. For example, in relation to the way in which the moral community comes into being (or is sustained), it became evident that there were several different objects of collective concern mentioned by different commentators (others, ourselves, society, and the criminal justice system—see Chapter 2) and coding subcategories were set up for each of these, allowing organization and retrieval of statements of each type. In relation to the moral collective's conception of itself, a decision was made to distinguish between statements about criminals and crime (the relevant alterity in this study) and statements which more directly revealed personal or collective identity. The first type of statement was largely located in the subcategories of censure about crime, while the second was mainly found in the subcategories of proposals and resolutions. Thus, the material already coded in these subcategories was sufficient for the purposes of analysis, and additional coding was not deemed to be necessary.

In exploring each research question, analysis sought to synthesize the meaning of groups of statements and assess their intrinsic and extrinsic significance. For example, statements about "criminals" frequently characterized them as less than human, or confined them to the one-dimensional status encapsulated in their label. What was striking in this was not the occasional metaphoric portrayal of offenders as animals or insects, but the consistent omission of any hint that someone who commits a crime has a more complex moral character than that of being monotonically bad. This depiction could survive only by keeping a distance from crime, skirting around its complex dynamics, and leaving its individual histories and moral complications unexamined. The intrinsic significance of this discursive technique lay in the simple and routine creation of the criminal as an "Other," in relation to whom many strong things might be said and done. Its extrinsic significance lay not merely in the possibility of creating an identity in symmetrical opposition to criminality, but mainly in the parallel possibility that this identity could be as uncomplicated as the alterity of the criminal. Thus, statements about "criminals" also directed attention to the general manner in which commentators presented both themselves and the moral collective that they invoked. Here, the one-dimensional characterization of "the good" was as evident as the one-dimensional references to "the bad."

Without attempting to develop precise counts, attention also focused on the relative frequency with which particular kinds of statement appeared. This was partly designed to give a sense of the types of statement that were most common and thereby ensure that the analysis reported the typical features found in this particular set of items. It also permitted comparisons between Anglo-America and Latin America. For example, the much greater frequency in Latin America of statements critical of governmental responses to crime was noted and discussed in Chapter 3, just as the greater frequency with which the police appear as sources in Anglo-America was noted in Chapter 6. However, the most common, or typical, statements were not the only focus of attention. In some cases, it was the *infrequency* of particular types of statement that was as important as the *frequency* of other types of statement in confirming a finding. For example, the occasional call for the collective to show a concern for crime stood in significant contrast to the routine invocation of terms and phrases that displayed this concern. The infrequency of the former was congruent with the frequency of the latter.

Reporting

Given that the study presented in this book is based on textual analysis, some thought needed to be given to the way in which segments of text were incorporated into the final report. One challenge was posed by the number of segments of text in a given coding category: for example, there were nearly 1,000 segments with censorious comments about crime and nearly 600 with prescriptive statements about what should be done in response to it. Obviously, to attempt to include all of these in the report of findings would have been to overload the reader with information and relegate the analysis to second place. In addition, many segments of text only became intelligible in context, and the provision of that context would have made data reporting even more unwieldy.

In light of this, three strategies were employed to illustrate the depth and breadth of the materials. First, single items were selected as primary exemplars for the theme of each substantive chapter. These items were transcribed substantially, or fully, and analyzed in some detail in order to present the theme being discussed. Second, a few additional cases were selected for inclusion based on the possibilities that they offered, along with the exemplars, for exploring and illustrating the relevant themes at several points in the chapter. A "case" comprised one or more items relating to a particular topic, such as the various items mentioning the death of Jane Creba in Toronto (which appear in Chapters 2 and 3) and the single item describing attempts to deal with drug selling and crime in a Toronto apartment complex (which is also to be found in Chapter 3). By concentrating analysis on the exemplar and cases, less background information was required once they had been introduced and greater continuity in the analysis could be provided for the reader. Third, several brief examples were also provided of additional segments of text that illustrated each theme or idea being developed. The objective in including them was to demonstrate that particular types of statement had a broader distribution than that represented by the exemplars and cases. Where individual themes were found across the Americas, examples were provided from both the Anglo-American and Latin American papers. Where the theme was more prevalent in one region than the other, or restricted to one of them, the examples also reflected this.

List of items—organized by newspaper and date of publication

Globe and Mail

Date	Title
January 2, 2006	Targeting gun offenses is quagmire
January 3, 2006	Handling gun violence
January 3, 2006	Opposition parties toughen messages
January 4, 2006	Gun bill may be toughened
January 4, 2006	Read my lips: no crime epidemic
January 5, 2006	A knife registry
January 6, 2006	Harper trumpets tough plan
January 6, 2006	Ontario to spend millions on gun crime
January 7, 2006	Crime and punishment editorial
January 7, 2006	Democrats talk tough on crime
January 7, 2006	Reaching out to quell gun violence
January 7, 2006	The building that fought back
January 7, 2006	Tough love
January 12, 2006	More women needed
January 12, 2006	Stop the soft talk on drugs
January 12, 2006	The Rivers message
January 13, 2006	Sentenced by politics
January 17, 2006	Politicians urged to get tough on crime
February 8, 2006	Natives try banishment to fight crime
March 3, 2006	Blowing the whistle on gun murder
April 4, 2006	Harper wrong on crime
April 5, 2006	Criminal errors
April 6, 2006	Expedient crackdown
April 7, 2006	Our streets are safe
April 7, 2006	Punishment feeds the crime
April 12, 2006	Take on the biker gangs
April 19, 2006	Gang prevention 101
May 5, 2006	Crackdown takes aim at guns
May 5, 2006	The new crime bills
May 5, 2006	Tories take on sentencing is a crime
May 6, 2006	Crime and punishment letter
May 6, 2006	Crime and punishment letter 2
May 8, 2006	Toews weighs in
May 9, 2006	RCMP can't probe all organized crime
May 11, 2006	A few unnerving words
May 26, 2006	Provinces co-ordinate organized crime fight
May 27, 2006	Vancouver too soft on crime
June 7, 2006	Natives and crime sadly linked
June 9, 2006	Bait car program reduces thefts
June 19, 2006	They attacked computer system
June 24, 2006	Youth jail terms less common
June 29, 2006	Violent crime up 5 percent
July 15, 2006	Can these angels fly?
July 21, 2006	Homicide rate hits high
July 21, 2006	Province's crime rates fell
July 22, 2006	Safer but that's not how we feel
August 12, 2006	Blair's working it like Fantino

Date	Title
August 19, 2006	Organized crime groups number 800
August 26, 2006	The rougher end of Danforth
August 28, 2006	Drug arrests up in Vancouver
September 16, 2006	Rush to remedy violent crime
September 18, 2006	Crime causes gun laws
September 21, 2006	Violent offenders in legislation
September 27, 2006	Looking to Europe for answers
October 9, 2006	A surfeit of cameras
October 26, 2006	Tories playing politics of justice
October 31, 2006	Assault rate triples for northerners
November 8, 2006	Gun bill would cost 246 million
November 16, 2006	Police numbers growing
November 17, 2006	Consider legalizing drug use
November 24, 2006	Harper touts tougher bail
December 18, 2006	Alberta fights dark side
December 26, 2006	Police focus on domestic violence
January 13, 2007	Wave of crackdowns on gangs
January 13, 2007	The new market high
January 25, 2007	Gangsterism ruling
February 14, 2007	RCMP finds violent crime on rise
February 22, 2007	So, how are the kids?
February 27, 2007	Shootings need more officers
March 6, 2007	Dion losing law and order votes
March 14, 2007	Dion gets tough on crime
March 15, 2007	Stephane Dion's crime fighting day
March 15, 2007	Liberals' plans for crime
March 17, 2007	Crime victims get advocate
April 21, 2007	Politicians and crime
April 28, 2007	Passionate voice for porn victims
April 30, 2007	Does Harper's message match stats?
May 8, 2007	Crimes of perception
May 10, 2007	Skytrain riders
June 9, 2007	Youth crime
June 14, 2007	Quick arrests keep streets safe
June 21, 2007	Gangs, guns and drugs
July 6, 2007	Project to pay for hate-crime security
July 19, 2007	Canada's crime lowest in 25 years
July 19, 2007	The Wild West
July 27, 2007	Adjust our definition of news
August 10, 2007	Wasn't the start and isn't the end
August 18, 2007	Organized crime groups rise
August 25, 2007	Police recruit v property crimes
August 31, 2007	Statistics rebut Halifax crime wave
September 5, 2007	Fairly safe is not enough
September 17, 2007	Judges constitutional guardians
October 1, 2007	Chief must deal with rising crime
October 10, 2007	Tories vow to toughen sentences
October 13, 2007	Homicide tally's relentless rise
October 15, 2007	Girls gone violent

Appendix

Date	Title
October 18, 2007	Crime stats and Tory pledge
October 18, 2007	Hot buttons sizzle
October 19, 2007	Guns and poses
October 19, 2007	Ship offenders home
October 19, 2007	Showdown over Tories' crime bill
October 24, 2007	Gang scene unique to BC
October 29, 2007	The answer lies at home
October 31, 2007	Gangs have foreign links
November 5, 2007	Muggings don't signal epidemic
November 6, 2007	Wanted: a regional police service
November 9, 2007	Alberta gets tough on arrests
November 9, 2007	Slayings highlight need for bill
November 10, 2007	Surge in violence won't dampen Olympics
November 12, 2007	Fog of BC's gang war
November 14, 2007	BC asks for help in gang war
November 17, 2007	Stiffer penalties for gang-related deaths
November 20, 2007	Tories introduce youth crime legislation
November 21, 2007	Tories seek tougher drug penalties
November 22, 2007	Cracking down sparks turf wars
November 22, 2007	Prison population climbs
November 22, 2007	Task force slows gun violence
November 24, 2007	Prevention over enforcement
November 27, 2007	Victoria police's insufficient resources
December 3, 2007	Will 2007 be a record year for murder?
December 7, 2007	Treat gangs as terrorists
December 21, 2007	Gangs cruise in armed vehicles

Los Angeles Times

Date	Title
January 3, 2006	Crime is easing its grip on LA
January 6, 2006	Bratton vows to reduce crime by 8 percent
January 12, 2006	Homicides up 15 percent in sheriff's territory
February 7, 2006	Tracking bad policy
March 8, 2006	Homicides an issue in race for attorney general
March 10, 2006	LAPD's skid row divide
March 10, 2006	Website puts crime tracking on the map
April 20, 2006	Bratton's broken windows
May 8, 2006	LA's busiest crooks do more time
May 19, 2006	Anomaly in hate crime decrease
May 29, 2006	DNA can catch burglars too
June 10, 2006	Killings drop 11 percent as crime totals decline
June 13, 2006	Violent crime rises in some big cities
June 21, 2006	LAPD seeks anti crime features on buildings
July 18, 2006	Angelides backs initiative to boost sex crime penalties
July 22, 2006	DC cracks down during crime lull
August 8, 2006	As LA violent crime drops the desert becomes hotspot
August 15, 2006	Crime rate climbs in first six months

Date	Title
September 3, 2006	Guns, crime and no data
September 6, 2006	Killings up over long weekend
September 9, 2006	California elections: crime a key issue in race
September 11, 2006	Rates of slayings and gun violence are up
September 14, 2006	Massive backlog plagues DNA lab
September 15, 2006	Crime lab conundrum
September 15, 2006	LAPD adds ten cameras to curb skid row crime
September 15, 2006	Law officials decry DNA lab backlog
September 16, 2006	Gang members are fewer but resilient
September 17, 2006	It's a crime how we misjudge the young
September 18, 2006	Arm against Katricians
September 27, 2006	Drug offenders to be banned from skid row
October 7, 2006	Crime is down in skid row
October 19, 2006	City takes aim at illegal guns
October 31, 2006	Anxiety builds as crime increases in Koreatown
November 6, 2006	A city strains to arrest a deadly trend
November 22, 2006	Police, FBI, target Valley gang crimes
December 6, 2006	Crime down for 4th year, Bratton says
December 10, 2006	A prison of our own making
December 13, 2006	Crimes and punishments
December 15, 2006	Hate crimes up, study says
December 19, 2006	Crime data will be shared
December 19, 2006	FBI reports rise in violent crime
December 27, 2006	LA crime decreases for the 5th year
December 29, 2006	Domestic violence found to fall by half over decade
December 30, 2006	Flight from gang violence proved to be futile
January 3, 2007	Mayor backs chief's second term
January 4, 2007	Bill calls for DNA in every arrest
January 9, 2007	Bratton sets goal of 5 percent cut in crime
January 10, 2007	LA shifts tactics against gangs
January 10, 2007	New Orleans announces crackdown amid crime wave
January 13, 2007	Alarm on gangs sounded
January 19, 2007	FBI joins LA effort in war on street gang crime
January 21, 2007	Racial attacks by gangs rising
January 27, 2007	New Orleans gets anti-crime update
January 28, 2007	Latinos and gangs—the hopeful flip side
February 2, 2007	CSI isn't the real world
February 6, 2007	Bratton fine tuning plan to cut gang crime in LA
February 9, 2007	LAPD targets city's worst gangs
February 11, 2007	Will the strategy to battle gangs work?
February 13, 2007	Gang activity factor in 6 percent crime hike in Ventura
February 13, 2007	Ventura County sees 6 percent increase in crime
February 15, 2007	Crime steady in Oxnard, down in Simi
February 16, 2007	Bills target criminals use of guns
February 18, 2007	The decline of rape
March 6, 2007	Gov. seeks coordinated gang effort
March 11, 2007	The new American witch hunt
March 16, 2007	Democrats stake out turf in war on gangs
March 21, 2007	Latino leaders' silence is killing us

Appendix

Date	Title
March 24, 2007	Effects of gang initiative mixed
April 20, 2007	In defense of guns
April 25, 2007	LAPD skid row searches found unconstitutional
April 27, 2007	Crime victims' families rally in Riverside
April 30, 2007	Bratton says there's more work to do
May 8, 2007	Hate crimes need their own category
May 13, 2007	Define the crime
May 17, 2007	Law should cover all acts of hate
May 18, 2007	O.C.'s reported hate crimes inched upward last year
May 24, 2007	Bullets can tell tales
June 1, 2007	L.A. gang killings drop 32 percent
June 6, 2007	The nation; Congress focuses on local crime fighting
June 8, 2007	LA County sees slight drop in hate crimes in 2006
July 18, 2007	Homicide rates decline in the Southland
July 26, 2007	LAPD staffing taking heat as Valley gets a bit meaner
July 29, 2007	Westside task force targets gang crime
July 31, 2007	New Orleans' violent tempest
August 2, 2007	Crime falls in Ventura County
August 10, 2007	Crime rates are mixed
August 15, 2007	Gun ID bill takes a shot at illegal weapons market
August 18, 2007	Violent crime falls in Simi Valley
August 23, 2007	The gospel and hate crimes
August 27, 2007	Hate-crime legislation
September 13, 2007	L.A. officials target crime near 20 schools
September 22, 2007	Study finds no racial crime wave
September 25, 2007	Violent crime is up for 2nd. year in a row
September 26, 2007	Crime off but plan is faulted
September 28, 2007	Big drop in L.A. homicides
October 3, 2007	Massive sweep deports hundreds
October 4, 2007	Bratton admits skid row displacement
October 8, 2007	Parole, the right way
October 10, 2007	Operation targets gang members
October 11, 2007	Gov. to sign five new laws to battle gangs
October 15, 2007	Neighborhood watch, magnified
October 25, 2007	Bratton vows city will be safer
October 29, 2007	Too big a tent
October 30, 2007	Uptick in crime spurs push for more police
November 11, 2007	Violent crime climbs in Bay Area
November 17, 2007	Sharpton leads call for fed investigation of hate
November 18, 2007	Newest police beat: patrolling the internet
November 18, 2007	Skid row in rehab
November 20, 2007	Hate crimes decline in LA
November 25, 2007	Learning to flex their civic muscles
December 2, 2007	States rethink tough penalties for juveniles
December 7, 2007	Shutting door to treatment
December 24, 2007	Killings decline sharply in LA
December 25, 2007	Pasadena gang violence raises fears
December 26, 2007	Cutting dropout rates also fights crime
December 29, 2007	Keeping killers in check

Appendix 135

New York Times

Date	Title
January 8, 2006	Does it work? Campus security
January 8, 2006	Reform the reforms
January 12, 2006	Drugs and racial discrimination
January 13, 2006	A fallen judge rethinks crime and punishment
January 22, 2006	A place for sex offenders
February 5, 2006	False conviction study
February 6, 2006	As Albany weighs confinement of sex offenders
February 12, 2006	Violent crime rising sharply in some cities
February 26, 2006	After prison more debt
March 5, 2006	Amid the glitter, Jersey City's growing pains
March 11, 2006	Washington—sweep of gang members
March 11, 2006	Open doors don't invite criminals
March 15, 2006	Iowa's residency rules drive sex offenders underground
March 17, 2006	Caught up in DNA's growing web
March 21, 2006	Report urges requiring all convicts to give DNA
March 26, 2006	Counting heads along the thin blue line
March 29, 2006	Jersey City ratchets up police efforts against crime
March 31, 2006	Cities that lead the way
April 2, 2006	Redefining juvenile criminals
April 2, 2006	The cost of staying out of jail
April 4, 2006	Schumer seeks funds to protect local witnesses
April 9, 2006	Take DNA when you can
April 16, 2006	Church battles to break gang cycle
April 16, 2006	Pros and cons of DNA collection
April 23, 2006	When fans are rude
May 4, 2006	New York State nearer to collecting DNA in all crimes
May 11, 2006	FBI focus on corruption includes 2,000 investigations
May 12, 2006	Wider use of DNA lists is urged in fighting crime
May 21, 2006	Doing more than their time
June 6, 2006	Albany crime dropping
June 13, 2006	Violent crime rose in 2005 with murders up by 4.8 percent
June 15, 2006	Small cities in region grow more violent, data show
June 20, 2006	Crime rising—New Orleans asks for National Guard
July 13, 2006	Washington officials try to ease crime fear
July 27, 2006	Forensic skills uncover hidden patterns of elder abuse
July 30, 2006	The insanity defense goes back on trial
August 7, 2006	Fifteen states expand right to shoot in self-defense
August 14, 2006	Shoot first—no questions asked
August 31, 2006	Police chiefs want US aid in crime fight
September 11, 2006	Robberies and gun violence up despite crime drop
September 18, 2006	State crime rates continue to fall
September 26, 2006	Where Congress is soft on criminals
September 29, 2006	Despite a decrease in city crime, troubling signs emerge
December 8, 2006	New Haven rethinking tactics on crime
February 15, 2007	School crime up 21 percent in first third of fiscal year
March 13, 2007	Wrong turn on sex offenders
March 22, 2007	Guardian Angels seek out more mean streets

Date	Title
March 29, 2007	Killings in first quarter drop to one a day
April 2, 2007	Crime drops in Newark
April 8, 2007	Little changes, big results
April 15, 2007	New Haven police seek technology to fight crime
April 15, 2007	The crime rate and birth control
April 22, 2007	Poor people and criminality
April 29, 2007	Disarming the merchants
May 3, 2007	Baltimore mayor unveils strategy to attack gun crime
May 4, 2007	House votes to expand hate-crime protection
May 11, 2007	Juvenile injustice
May 20, 2007	Texas weighs death penalty for rapes of children
May 24, 2007	Giving juvenile offenders a chance
May 29, 2007	The crime rate drops
June 2, 2007	Violent crime rose in 2006
June 5, 2007	NY remains safest big city
June 10, 2007	FBI crime report for Bridgeport is mixed
June 16, 2007	Washington's secret gun files
June 17, 2007	Why protect shady gun dealers?
June 22, 2007	Killings surge in Oakland
June 26, 2007	An easy target, but does that mean hatred?
June 28, 2007	Study lauds police effort
July 8, 2007	Access to gun data
July 10, 2007	A precinct of contrasts
July 12, 2007	Juvenile justice
July 19, 2007	The wrong approach to gangs
August 7, 2007	The protection battered spouses don't need
August 10, 2007	Deaths in Newark
August 14, 2007	100,000 gone since 2001
August 17, 2007	In Newark a first step in regulating guns
August 19, 2007	To fight gun violence, a high tech plan
August 21, 2007	Violence in America
August 22, 2007	State names 17 more persistently dangerous schools
August 22, 2007	Thompson brings gun control to the fore
September 24, 2007	An opportunity for Mr Schwarzenegger
September 24, 2007	Crime as a campaign issue
September 25, 2007	Violent crime reported up 2 percent in 2006
September 26, 2007	Albany: a drop in crime
September 28, 2007	Senate votes for expanded Federal authority to prosecute hate crimes
September 29, 2007	A trend grows in policing
September 30, 2007	Blacks mull call for 10,000 to curb violence
September 30, 2007	Ditch these drug laws
September 30, 2007	Jena, OJ and the jailing of black America
October 3, 2007	Enlightened policing
October 7, 2007	Officials report rise in anti-Jewish crimes
October 7, 2007	Who will saddle up for Mt Vernon's police?
October 10, 2007	Trenton state crime strategy
October 20, 2007	A cruel turn for Irvington
October 21, 2007	Criminal element
October 28, 2007	The right model for juvenile justice

Date	Title
November 15, 2007	Caught on a block that conjures up the Wild West
November 16, 2007	In ID theft some victims see opportunity
November 23, 2007	Texas seeks to break prison recidivism cycle
November 29, 2007	Spreading the misery
December 2, 2007	Death to capital punishment
December 2, 2007	Fact and fiction on the campaign trail
December 2, 2007	Homicide in NY: when the victims are women
December 7, 2007	Congressional maneuvring dooms hate crime bill
December 10, 2007	Caving in on hate crimes
December 16, 2007	Crime is low but fear knows no numbers
December 16, 2007	Catch and release and catch again
December 23, 2007	Getting away with murder
December 30, 2007	So many crimes and reasons not to cooperate
December 30, 2007	The police's excellent year

El Universal

Date	Title
January 6, 2006	Cifras: ¿quién miente?
January 7, 2006	Alarma por incidencia delictiva en secundarias
January 10, 2006	Más de 9 mil agentes llegarán a unidades de élite
January 11, 2006	Binoculares
January 11, 2006	Robo: principal delito en el país
January 15, 2006	Radiografía de la impunidad
January 16, 2006	Se siente protegido 60 percent de capitalinos en su barrio
January 17, 2006	Soberanes: la inseguridad compromiso incumplido
January 20, 2006	A diario ingresan 50 'maras', reportan
January 21, 2006	Profundizar los cómos
January 22, 2006	Vecinos trabajando
January 23, 2006	Madrazo y Calderón encaran al narcotráfico
January 26, 2006	En seguridad pública el Estado está fallando
January 28, 2006	Ciudadanía del miedo
January 30, 2006	CNDH llama a cambiar Ley de Readaptación Social
January 30, 2006	Campa acusa a Fox de rehuir responsabilidad
January 31, 2006	Acuerdan más recursos contra el narcomenudeo
January 31, 2006	Fox batalla sin tregua al crimen organizado
January 31, 2006	Mercado propone crear una policía nacional
January 31, 2006	Vuelven a combatir narco y crimen organizado
February 1, 2006	Impulsan crear un centro para investigar narco
February 1, 2006	Incontenible violencia criminal
February 1, 2006	Violencia e inversión
February 2, 2006	Gobierno atacará ola de violencia
February 2, 2006	Inmujeres avala restricciones para prevenir violencia
February 2, 2006	Piden a Fox asumir gravedad de inseguridad
February 3, 2006	Sube temor por inseguridad
February 4, 2006	AMLO: más militares
February 6, 2006	Policía nacional y reformar leyes, plantean contra inseguridad

Date	Title
February 7, 2006	México supera a Estados Unidos en homicidios
February 9, 2006	Mercado promete atacar inseguridad
February 12, 2006	Vecinos trabajando
February 16, 2006	Narcomenudeo y presupuesto
February 18, 2006	Reforzarán operativos en estados que colindan con Michoacán
February 18, 2006	Las muertas que no mueren
February 28, 2006	Conjuntan ataque a delitos y adicciones
March 1, 2006	Tips de protección para altos ejecutivos
March 3, 2006	Preocupación por la seguridad
March 5, 2006	Abusos y drogadicción agravan situación de las niñas
March 10, 2006	Ciudadanía opina que se avanza en seguridad
March 22, 2006	Víctimas y verdugos
March 26, 2006	Por 500 pesos reclutan a jóvenes para robar autos
March 27, 2006	Tamaulipas: narcos de esta frontera no se acercan a Dios
March 27, 2006	Y tú ¿qué tan seguro estás?
March 28, 2006	Critican uso de recursos en materia de seguridad
April 1, 2006	Picaderos plaga mortal en Mexicali
April 9, 2006	Madrazo ofrece dar la batalla al narcotráfico
April 14, 2006	Mexicali víctima de la inseguridad
April 15, 2006	Mejorar combate a ciberdelitos
April 15, 2006	Critican mano dura y sugieren trabajo vecinal
April 21, 2006	Solos ante el crimen
May 1, 2006	El narco busca consolidar mercado interno
May 4, 2006	Plantea aumentar cifra de policías
May 10, 2006	Adicción despenalizada
May 30, 2006	Cometen en Edomex 429 feminicidios cada año
May 31, 2006	Sin resolver 90 de cada 100 delitos en la capital
May 31, 2006	Calderón propone unificar policías
June 2, 2006	Plantean prisión preventiva sólo para inculpados de delito grave
June 4, 2006	Mercado rechaza la pena de muerte
June 8, 2006	Conflictos personales y de pareja motivan ejecuciones
June 14, 2006	Demagogia e inseguridad
June 15, 2006	Quieren sistema nacional para prevenir delitos
June 23, 2006	Caravanas de la muerte
June 24, 2006	Voto anticrimen
July 8, 2006	Aumentan secuestros en Tijuana
July 8, 2006	Surgen nuevos delitos nocturnos en la capital
July 14, 2006	Alcoholismo juvenil
July 23, 2006	México y el mundo
July 25, 2006	Alto ya a la violencia
August 1, 2006	Tentáculos del narco atrapan a más jóvenes
August 7, 2006	Vecinos de Naucalpan se encierran en sus colonias
September 11, 2006	Evitan criminalidad más programas sociales
September 16, 2006	Amenaza a la nación
September 16, 2006	Seguridad pública
September 16, 2006	Inseguridad en la frontera
September 19, 2006	Exponen situación sobre inseguridad a Calderón
September 20, 2006	Criminalidad desbordada
September 23, 2006	Alarma inseguridad en frontera norte
September 23, 2006	Fox: seguridad fronteriza es compartida

Appendix 139

Date	Title
September 23, 2006	Fox: En EU es más aguda la inseguridad
September 30, 2006	Refuerzan vigilancia en calles de Tijuana
October 2, 2006	Entre el deber y el temor
October 2, 2006	Más pobreza puede detonar la violencia
October 6, 2006	Justicia en el DF: el MP
October 7, 2006	Seguridad: el nuevo paradigma
October 12, 2006	Critican plan de seguridad de Calderón
October 13, 2006	El reto de la inseguridad
October 19, 2006	Contrate seguridad, no problemas
October 26, 2006	Al filo de la ingobernabilidad
October 27, 2006	DF: capital de la inseguridad
October 30, 2006	M Contreras prepara plan contra la inseguridad
November 6, 2006	Llama IP a combatir la pobreza y criminalidad
November 6, 2006	Banco seguro en línea
November 6, 2006	Concluye marcha contra la inseguridad
November 7, 2006	Inician operativo para prevenir más feminicidios
November 8, 2006	Alarma en Sinaloa alto índice de inseguridad
November 11, 2006	Padres vigilarán calles de Edomex
November 15, 2006	Inseguridad aniquilante
November 17, 2006	Encrucijada de la inseguridad
November 23, 2006	Delitos bajaron 23 percent en seis años
November 27, 2006	Critican construcción de más cárceles en la ciudad
November 27, 2006	Indolencia sinaloense ante narcoviolencia
November 28, 2006	En 2006 seis ejecutados por día
November 28, 2006	Crimen organizado reta a las autoridades
November 30, 2006	Sociedad mexicana tolera acción de los narcotraficantes
November 30, 2006	Muchos no salen de noche por temor a morir
December 1, 2006	Crear empleos inhibe la delincuencia
December 1, 2006	Ejecuciones, un parte de guerra
December 3, 2006	Pisó la cárcel 10 percent de capitalinos
December 5, 2006	Sí se logró combatir la inseguridad
December 8, 2006	Seguridad y democracia
December 10, 2006	Los sistemas ciudadanos de seguridad
December 10, 2006	Promueven autoridades trabajo vecinal
December 10, 2006	Operativos la nueva estrategia anticrimen
December 13, 2006	Ecatepec solicitará presencia de la PFP
December 13, 2006	Crimen organizado transnacional
December 14, 2006	Poca gente denuncia delitos
December 14, 2006	Sacerdote pide tregua navideña a delincuentes
December 15, 2006	Más violencia en el corto plazo
December 15, 2006	Seguridad pública y la paz, un buen recuerdo
December 18, 2006	Alertan de inseguridad en carreteras del país
December 21, 2006	Guerra al crimen organizado
December 23, 2006	Cerrar filas
December 25, 2006	Hubo 2 crímenes violentos cada día en este sexenio
December 25, 2006	La inseguridad pública
December 28, 2006	Hijos no deseados
December 28, 2006	10 años de propuestas y ninguna política de Estado
January 2, 2007	Critican suspensión de juntas de seguridad
January 2, 2007	Consumo y narcocultura

140 Appendix

Date	Title
January 2, 2007	Michoacán: el estado más violento en el sexenio
January 3, 2007	Narcomenudeo asuela calles de Tijuana
January 5, 2007	La prioridad oficial
January 5, 2007	Rescatando a Tijuana
January 9, 2007	Atacan delitos en operativo conjunto
January 9, 2007	Ven con reservas anuncio de operativo en NL
January 15, 2007	Concentra colonia muertes violentas
January 15, 2007	Viene Guerrero
January 18, 2007	Zona reconocida por su peligrosidad
January 23, 2007	Alto el costo de la violencia
January 26, 2007	Lecciones colombianas
January 26, 2007	DF: procurador a prueba
January 27, 2007	Garrote y zanahoria
February 8, 2007	Narco y crimen organizados rebasaron el Estado
February 8, 2007	Sin resolver problema de inseguridad en BC
February 10, 2007	Despolicializar la seguridad
February 11, 2007	Cada acto de violencia será respondido
February 23, 2007	La estrategia anticrimen
February 25, 2007	En Sinaloa refuerzan seguridad
March 10, 2007	Cadena perpetua
March 12, 2007	Roban 70 vehículos al día en la ciudad de México
March 13, 2007	Pulso Político critica iniciativas penales de Calderón
March 13, 2007	Avalan acciones antinarco en Tepito
March 16, 2007	Vivir en la frontera olvidada
March 21, 2007	Operativo en Sinaloa solo para abatir cultivos
March 23, 2007	Hay víctimas de delincuencia en 1 de cada 4 hogares
March 27, 2007	Arranca en Tepito el canje de armas por computador
March 27, 2007	Menos soldados, mejores policías
March 29, 2007	Por 4 años les negaron más seguridad
April 1, 2007	Refuerzan vigilancia afuera de escuelas
April 8, 2007	En Iztapalapa operan 30 bandas delictivas
April 18, 2007	Estamos en guerra contra el narco
April 18, 2007	Los policías y las víctimas
April 22, 2007	Actuarán contra quien se coluda con la delincuencia
April 22, 2007	Coludirse con el crimen es una traición
April 22, 2007	Necesario reforzar leyes contra el crimen
April 23, 2007	Percepciones y realidades
April 25, 2007	No estamos dispuestos a vivir en la violencia
April 30, 2007	Reforma penal
May 9, 2007	Debilidad nacional
May 9, 2007	Estado de excepción
May 13, 2007	Calderón pide apoyo para combatir a delincuencia
May 14, 2007	El dilema de Calderón
May 14, 2007	Percepción de inseguridad a su menor nivel desde 2005
May 14, 2007	Seguridad: ¿cuál estrategia?
May 16, 2007	Crimen organizado recrudece acciones
May 16, 2007	Enfrentar al narcotráfico
May 17, 2007	Ejército vs. el narco
May 22, 2007	Entre narcos y policías
May 22, 2007	Preocupa a IP que la delincuencia se infiltre en el gobierno

Date	Title
May 23, 2007	Ejército refuerza patrullaje en Monterrey
May 23, 2007	Ortega admite que van al alza narcoejecuciones
May 26, 2007	Redefinir la estrategia
May 27, 2007	Denuncian falta de información para prevenir delito
May 28, 2007	Sistema político y delincuencia
May 29, 2007	El cuarto de pánico
May 30, 2007	Inicia Ebrard plan de vigilancia en escuelas
June 3, 2007	La escuela ya no evita delitos de jóvenes
June 4, 2007	Coordinación: clave anticrimen
June 6, 2007	Gobernación prende focos amarillos en la capital
June 8, 2007	Desde la web víctimas pueden denunciar robo
June 11, 2007	Sin opción, tijuanenses conviven con el crimen
June 12, 2007	Inseguridad afecta al sector turismo
June 20, 2007	Pega la violencia al sector de la construcción
June 20, 2007	Preocupa a abanderados violencia en Gómez Palacio
June 21, 2007	Hay 200 escuelas de alto riesgo por delincuencia
June 21, 2007	Refuerzan seguridad en Comarca Lagunera
June 25, 2007	Ocasionará narco más inseguridad
June 25, 2007	Combaten inseguridad en taxis y microbuses
June 27, 2007	Denuncian promesas sin cumplir en seguridad
June 28, 2007	El riesgo de la impunidad
June 29, 2007	ONG llaman a enfrentar inseguridad
June 30, 2007	Evalúan inseguridad con criterios distintos
June 30, 2007	Medir en el DF la peligrosidad
July 10, 2007	Ortega llama a refundar las instituciones de seguridad
July 18, 2007	Atizapán arranca plan para detectar vehículos robados
July 19, 2007	Preocupa inseguridad en el estado
July 26, 2007	Tepito: zona insegura pese a operativos
July 27, 2007	Osuna apuesta por un sistema de inteligencia anticrimen
August 2, 2007	Aconsejan usar brazaletes en lugar de prisión preventiva
August 7, 2007	Ocurren 60 percent de delitos en STC en las líneas 1, 2 y 3
August 20, 2007	Edomex pondrá 'botones de pánico' en colegios
August 27, 2007	IP denuncia avance de la inseguridad
August 28, 2007	Olvidan atacar venta y consumo de droga
September 1, 2007	Informe: ¿qué para seguridad?
September 19, 2007	Violencia en el sur prende focos rojos
September 24, 2007	Jóvenes víctimas y victimarios
September 26, 2007	Critican mecanismos para atacar delincuencia
September 26, 2007	Detectan 20 zonas donde hay más robos
September 27, 2007	Comerciantes de Toluca se unen contra robos
October 1, 2007	Abatiremos crimen con trabajo de inteligencia
October 1, 2007	La traición de los servicios de inteligencia
October 1, 2007	Piden mayor capacitación policiaca
October 4, 2007	Imperan en Pantitlán desorden y delitos
October 6, 2007	Delincuencia más joven y violenta
October 7, 2007	Se agudiza la delincuencia e indigencia en La Merced
October 8, 2007	Enfrentan a ladrones con piedras y palos
October 8, 2007	Plan México al Senado
October 8, 2007	Queremos vivir tranquilos y que nos cuiden

142 Appendix

Date	Title
October 12, 2007	Orden del día
October 16, 2007	Anuncian acciones contra la inseguridad
October 17, 2007	Botellita de jerez
October 18, 2007	Aumentó 200 percent en 2 años cifra de presos por plagio
October 19, 2007	Jueces y MP frenan castigo a plagiarios
October 21, 2007	'Piratería', un delito "socialmente aceptado"
October 22, 2007	Hasta dónde tolerar el crimen
October 24, 2007	Convierten debate en exposición de ideas
October 29, 2007	Tijuanenses marchan contra la violencia
October 31, 2007	Tierra de ciegos
November 12, 2007	Alerta ante el narcotráfico
November 13, 2007	La SSP de Tijuana admite rezago en lucha anticrimen
November 16, 2007	Intentan al día 360 extorsiones
November 19, 2007	Lanzan ofensiva policiaca contra narcos en Yucatán
November 21, 2007	Refuerzan seguridad en la colonia Morelos
November 26, 2007	Edomex, segundo lugar en homicidios contra mujeres
November 29, 2007	Capella Ibarra seguirá su lucha
November 29, 2007	Feminicidios sin solución
December 1, 2007	En Aguascalientes exigen frenar ola de inseguridad
December 5, 2007	Hechos contra palabras
December 6, 2007	IP exige seguridad para no ahuyentar inversionistas
December 7, 2007	Mas inteligencia, menos fuerza militar
December 8, 2007	Perseguiremos a policías corruptos
December 10, 2007	Por los policías caídos
December 12, 2007	Año de violencia
December 13, 2007	Creen que aumentará inseguridad
December 14, 2007	Atienden al GDF en reforma judicial
December 14, 2007	Lucha anticrimen no justifica reducir gastos
December 18, 2007	Implementa A Obregón medidas por alta violencia
December 18, 2007	Lanzan en 15 municipios operativos de seguridad
December 18, 2007	Molinar reforma judicial
December 19, 2007	Nuevo eslabón del narco
December 20, 2007	Estado de sitio permanente
December 21, 2007	Calderón: no habrá tregua contra crimen
December 21, 2007	DF será la ciudad más vigilada
December 21, 2007	Edil de BC reconoce corrupción policiaca
December 21, 2007	La sensación efímera de seguridad
December 28, 2007	Enviarán a 2,500 militares y policías a Sinaloa
December 28, 2007	Inocentes
December 28, 2007	Timadores pueden acceder a bases de datos
December 29, 2007	Persisten delitos en que participan taxistas
December 30, 2007	Sinaloa tiene cifra record de ejecuciones
December 30, 2007	Zacatecas pide ayuda contra violencia
December 31, 2007	Seguridad y empleo principales reclamos

El Nacional

Date	Title
January 26, 2006	En una semana han robado 11 locales de Petare
February 27, 2006	Los códigos de la violencia en América Latina
March 12, 2006	Inseguridad acompaña a choferes como un pasajero más
March 19, 2006	Vecinos de Santa Mónica aprendieron a convivir con la delincuencia
March 26, 2006	Zulianos están preocupados por la inseguridad
April 4, 2006	Delincuencia uniformada
April 7, 2006	Frustración por la inseguridad llegó a 75 percent
April 8, 2006	Asamblea elaborará plan integral para combatir el crimen
April 9, 2006	Chávez oficia un culto contradictorio por lo ilegal
April 12, 2006	Jóvenes manifestarán por las 67.000 muertes
April 17, 2006	Políticas de seguridad están raspadas
April 22, 2006	Tiempo de reflexión
April 24, 2006	85% rechaza labor del gobierno frente a la inseguridad
May 12, 2006	Inseguridad (II)
May 13, 2006	Insensibilidad e ineptitud
May 23, 2006	La prevención del delito
May 23, 2006	Más de 2000 choferes paralizaron Ciudad Guayana
May 26, 2006	Inseguridad (III)
May 27, 2006	Responsabilizan a la oposición por inseguridad táchirense
May 28, 2006	Monseñor Moronta: en Caracas ¡no prestan atención!
June 11, 2006	Expendedores de gasolina asumen costo de seguridad
June 16, 2006	Altos índices delictivos preocupan a los industriales
June 16, 2006	Asamblea creó sala situacional para combatir la inseguridad
June 19, 2006	Copei: delincuencia está matando a los jóvencs
June 21, 2006	Ganaderos denuncian negligencia del gobierno
June 22, 2006	44 muertes violentas se registraron en Alto Apure
June 24, 2006	82.6% desaprueba gestión en materia de seguridad
June 26, 2006	Por la presidencia
August 13, 2006	Venezuela es el país más violento de América Latina
August 19, 2006	López pide a Mundaraín atender la inseguridad
September 2, 2006	Alcalde de Maturín declaró emergencia en materia de seguridad
September 2, 2006	Ciudadanos deben participar en políticas de seguridad
September 2, 2006	Consejo Nacional de Prevención coordinará actividades sociales
September 2, 2006	Ganaderos analizarán medidas contra inseguridad
September 9, 2006	Transportistas en protesta por homicidios y robos
September 21, 2006	Incrementa la violencia infantil
September 24, 2006	Presidente planteó nacionalizar el Proyecto Alcatraz
October 6, 2006	Contra la inseguridad
October 11, 2006	Chávez atribuye inseguridad a venta ilegal de cerveza
October 13, 2006	Venezuela está pintada de rojo por la guerrilla
October 14, 2006	La reforma del COPP genera objeciones y apoyos
October 21, 2006	La vida no vale nada
October 21, 2006	Nos hemos llenado de policías
October 30, 2006	A los que vienen de afuera

Date	Title
October 30, 2006	En Miranda hay 60.000 delincuentes
November 20, 2006	Lolita: discurso del Presidente genera la delincuencia
November 21, 2006	30 taxistas han sido asesinados durante 2006 en Guayana
November 26, 2006	Las exigencias siguen en la calle
November 29, 2006	Varías veces víctima
March 13, 2007	Delincuencia y violencia a granel
March 18, 2007	La muerte usa calibre 9 mm
March 29, 2007	¿Qué está pasando señor Presidente?
April 7, 2007	Copei acusa al gobierno por la inseguridad
May 3, 2007	Habla lo que no ha ocurrido
May 5, 2007	Harán un paro contra el secuestro
May 7, 2007	Me van a matar
May 8, 2007	Para Marcos Chávez la delincuencia disminuyó
May 9, 2007	Cuestionan criterios del Cicpc para definir el homicidio
May 12, 2007	Los robos han disminuido 40 percent en Ciudad Universitaria
May 13, 2007	La violencia también asiste a clases
May 13, 2007	Metro inseguro
May 13, 2007	Territorios de inseguridad
May 14, 2007	Alta cifra en atracos a conductores
May 15, 2007	Arrancar y estacionar son críticos para un conductor
May 15, 2007	Carreño niega aumento de cifras de delitos
May 16, 2007	Cambian hábitos nocturnos para eludir la delincuencia
May 17, 2007	Al robarme el apartamento perdí la sensación de seguridad
May 18, 2007	Ser asaltado en la calle o el Metro
May 19, 2007	Médicos temen ser interceptados
May 29, 2007	Vecinos se atrincheran en las zonas residenciales
May 21, 2007	Me quité el permiso de morir
May 22, 2007	Creció número de venezolanos con miedo a la inseguridad
May 23, 2007	Entre el bien y el mal
May 24, 2007	Policía Nacional compete a la AN
June 6, 2007	Con 170 cámaras vigilarán a transeúntes caraqueños
June 18, 2007	Delincuencia sin freno en Caracas
June 24, 2007	Transporte público
June 28, 2007	Ejecutan plan desarme para reducir inseguridad
June 29, 2007	Afirman que en 2007 hubo 12.157 homicidios
July 1, 2007	Delincuencia diabólica
July 12, 2007	Reserva bancaria dificulta combate contra lavado del dinero
July 15, 2007	Delincuencia juvenil
July 28, 2007	Comerciantes piden medidas contra el secuestro
August 9, 2007	La labor sigue en las zonas populares
August 19, 2007	Reforma deja a un lado corrupción e inseguridad
September 3, 2007	77% de los motorizados han sido asaltados
September 3, 2007	La inseguridad incrementa el blindaje de vehículos
September 30, 2007	La cruz de la inseguridad
October 10, 2007	Videos e impunidad
October 23, 2007	Revolucionario triste
October 27, 2007	La inseguridad: una amenaza que ocupa a pocos
October 28, 2007	La delincuencia continúa reinando en San Bernardino
November 14, 2007	Un total de 44 operadores controlarán el 171
November 26, 2007	Arremetida mortal

Date	Title
December 11, 2007	El que es pobre de mente, es pobre de todo
December 16, 2007	La delincuencia se traslada en vehículos robados
December 23, 2007	Liquidar la inseguridad
December 27, 2007	8% bajó el delito en el municipio Chacao en 2007
December 31, 2007	En Sucre, homicidios aumentaron 11%

La Nación

Date	Title
January 16, 2006	Osadía e impunidad
May 9, 2006	Prostitución: un debate inconcluso
May 23, 2006	El escenario de la violencia joven
June 13, 2006	Cada vez hay más víctimas de delitos
June 13, 2006	Combatir la criminalidad
June 13, 2006	La criminalidad: el mal mayor
June 14, 2006	Datos que no sólo sirven a los políticos
June 14, 2006	La justicia rosarina ordenó más vigilancia
June 15, 2006	Envían 1.000 policías a Rosario
June 15, 2006	Editorial I—inquietante sensación de inseguridad
June 16, 2006	Grave retroceso frente al delito
June 19, 2006	Crece la explotación de personas
June 25, 2006	Delitos en la capital
June 25, 2006	Inseguridad: el carro delante el caballo
June 25, 2006	La inseguridad y el Código Penal
June 29, 2006	La creciente violencia social
June 30, 2006	Cartas de lectores: inseguridad
July 9, 2006	Inseguridad: hay funcionarios que parecen de otro país
July 14, 2006	Miles de vecinos exigieron seguridad
July 16, 2006	Cartas de lectores—inseguridad
July 16, 2006	Desgobierno sobre la seguridad
July 23, 2006	Proyecto País: ideas para crecer
July 26, 2006	Fernández se disculpó por lo dicho sobre la inseguridad
July 30, 2006	Los hábitos cambiaron por la inseguridad
July 31, 2006	Seguridad: la calle o la academia
August 3, 2006	Ocultar la inseguridad sólo logrará acrecentarla
August 9, 2006	Kirchner rechazó aumento de penas
August 11, 2006	Inseguridad—problema que Kirchner teme
August 12, 2006	La inseguridad: principal problema para los porteños
August 14, 2006	Lanzan un plan para prevenir el delito
August 20, 2006	Inseguridad II
August 23, 2006	El desarme: apenas una ilusión
August 26, 2006	En una década el delito aumentó 70%
August 27, 2006	Inseguridad: mucho más que cifras
August 31, 2006	La marcha de hoy
September 2, 2006	El mensaje de la marcha
September 3, 2006	Fernández respondió a Blumberg
September 3, 2006	Las propuestas de Blumberg

Date	Title
September 4, 2006	Un reclamo popular sin respuesta
September 18, 2006	Las nuevas amenazas y la defensa nacional
September 22, 2006	Optimismo para crecer
September 24, 2006	Reconstruir la seguridad
October 3, 2006	Vecinos en defensa propia
October 9, 2006	Herramientas tecnológicas que ayudan a reducir los crímenes
October 29, 2006	Inseguridad: vigencia de un reclamo
November 4, 2006	Maldita inseguridad
November 7, 2006	Una epidemia de inseguridad
November 9, 2006	Pagarán incentivos por entregar armas
November 20, 2006	Las sociedades del miedo
November 21, 2006	La ola de inseguridad
November 28, 2006	Seguridad: hechos y no promesas
November 30, 2006	La seguridad empobrecida
November 30, 2006	Medidas para vivir más seguros
December 1, 2006	Documento de consenso sobre la inseguridad
December 27, 2006	Los políticos nos quieren hacer creer que disminuye la delincuencia
January 9, 2007	Delincuencia
January 17, 2007	Siete de cada diez vecinos temen ser víctimas de un delito
January 26, 2007	Alarma en la ciudad
January 30, 2007	Darán $450 por armas cedidas
February 12, 2007	Las causas de la inseguridad
February 13, 2007	La inseguridad según el ministro
March 7, 2007	Un plan que apuesta a desarmar la violencia
March 29, 2007	Impunidad criminal
April 12, 2007	Sensación de inseguridad tan dañina como la inseguridad
April 21, 2007	Editorial I—delito y sensación de inseguridad
April 22, 2007	Editorial—crisis del principio de autoridad
April 25, 2007	Solá admitió que aumentó el delito
April 29, 2007	En Pilar intentan reducir hechos delictivos
May 4, 2007	Editorial I—delincuencia en moto
May 7, 2007	Cartas de lectores—violencia escolar
June 2, 2007	Vecinos preocupados por la creciente inseguridad
June 3, 2007	Editorial II—cifras de la delincuencia
June 5, 2007	Un millón de armas para defenderse
June 8, 2007	Editorial II—el drama de la delincuencia precoz
June 9, 2007	Macri mostró su receta contra la inseguridad
June 11, 2007	La errónea idea de que las altas penas disuaden
June 16, 2007	Se mantiene la inseguridad
July 1, 2007	Hay más traumas por la inseguridad
July 8, 2007	Seguridad interior
July 16, 2007	Inseguridad: nuevos retrocesos
July 26, 2007	Editorial II—la entrega voluntaria de armas
August 4, 2007	Mendocinos movilizados por una ola de inseguridad
August 9, 2007	Jujuy es la provincia con mayor inseguridad
August 11, 2007	Polémica en Mar del Plata por zonas liberadas
August 12, 2007	Un porteño de cada cuatro fue víctima de la inseguridad
August 14, 2007	Editorial I—la inseguridad nos sigue acosando
August 23, 2007	Editorial II—robos de autos al por mayor

Date	Title
August 23, 2007	Lavagna quiere más policías
August 27, 2007	Editorial II—identidades hurtadas
August 27, 2007	El combate contra la inseguridad
September 7, 2007	Kirchner promulgó reforma de Ley Cafiero
September 8, 2007	Creció la sensación de inseguridad
September 17, 2007	GBA—9 de cada 10 víctimas de delitos
September 24, 2007	Nos acostumbramos a vivir en una sociedad insegura
September 29, 2007	Editorial II—countries blancos de la delincuencia
October 1, 2007	Editorial II—vandalismo e inseguridad
October 4, 2007	La inseguridad preocupa al campo
October 6, 2007	Eje de la campaña bonaerense
October 6, 2007	Ni mano dura ni garantismo ingenuo
October 9, 2007	Solá admitió que no logró su objetivo en seguridad
October 10, 2007	Autocrítica de Solá por la inseguridad
October 10, 2007	El miedo al delito provoca trastornos psíquicos y físicos
October 14, 2007	La inseguridad bonaerense
October 14, 2007	La seguridad: eje de la pelea bonaerense
October 14, 2007	Preocupa la influencia de la droga en los chicos
October 15, 2007	Un plan para combatir las drogas y la inseguridad
October 20, 2007	El crimen roza la campaña
October 20, 2007	La inseguridad—una evidencia concreta
October 21, 2007	Creció la sensación de inseguridad
October 21, 2007	Las palabras que parecen prohibidas
October 21, 2007	Reclama la oposición medidas urgentes
October 22, 2007	Como Aznar con Atocha
October 23, 2007	Editorial I—inseguridad un problema de todos
October 24, 2007	Cartas de lectores—inseguridad
October 24, 2007	Cristina evitó definiciones
October 24, 2007	Inseguridad—la culpa es de otro
October 30, 2007	Cartas de lectores
November 5, 2007	Cartas de lectores—la inseguridad
November 11, 2007	Panic rooms
November 12, 2007	Editorial I—los desafíos bonaerenses
November 16, 2007	Una sensación confirmada
November 20, 2007	Stornelli criticó gestión de Arslanian
November 23, 2007	Cartas de lectores—plan antidrogas
November 24, 2007	Cartas de lectores—inseguridad y policía
December 5, 2007	Kirchner hizo un balance de su gestión
December 6, 2007	Seguridad se ubica al tope de reclamos vecinales
December 6, 2007	Un problema de difícil resolución
December 10, 2007	Editorial I—desafíos del nuevo gobierno porteño
December 10, 2007	Jaque se comprometió a combatir el delito
December 10, 2007	Macri prometió eficacia
December 13, 2007	Editorial I—la dura tarea que le espera a Scioli
December 14, 2007	Cartas de lectores—inseguridad social
December 14, 2007	Mejoraremos la potencia de fuego
December 15, 2007	Inseguridad en la provincia de Buenos Aires

Notes

1 Collective moral discourse

1 *Los Angeles Times*, "FBI reports rise in violent crime," December 19, 2006.
2 *El Nacional*, "La prevención del delito," May 23, 2006.
3 *Globe and Mail*, "Crime and punishment," January 7, 2006.
4 *Globe and Mail*, "Fairly safe is not safe enough," September 5, 2007.
5 *El Universal*, "Alcoholismo juvenil," July 14, 2006.
6 *New York Times*, "Metro briefing. New York: state crime rates continued to fall in 2005," September 18, 2006.
7 *La Nación*, "Tecnología para empresas. Herramientas tecnológicas que ayudan a reducir los crímenes," October 9, 2006.
8 Luhmann, N. *The Reality of the Mass Media*, Stanford, CA: Stanford University Press, 2000.
9 Anderson, E. *Code of the Street: Decency, Violence and the Moral Life of the Inner City*, New York: W.W. Norton and Company, 1999.
10 Linger, D.T. *Dangerous Encounters: Meanings of Violence in a Brazilian City*, Stanford, CA: Stanford University Press, 1992.
11 See, for example, Alexander, J.C. *The Meanings of Social Life: A Cultural Sociology*, New York: Oxford University Press, 2003.
12 Cohen, S. *Folk Devils and Moral Panics*, London: Routledge, third edition, 2002.
13 See, for example, Gusfield, J. *The Culture of Public Problems*, Chicago: University of Chicago Press, 1981.
14 Entman, R.M. "Framing: toward clarification of a fractured paradigm," *Journal of Communication*, vol. 43, no. 4, 1993, p. 52 (emphasis in the original).
15 See, for example, Best, J. *Images of Issues: Typifying Contemporary Social Problems*, New Brunswick, NJ: Transaction Publishers, 2009.
16 Gamson, W.A. and A. Modigliani, "Media discourse and public opinion on nuclear power. A constructionist approach," *The American Journal of Sociology*, vol. 95, no. 1, 1989, pp. 1–37.
17 Benford, R.D. and D.A. Snow, "Framing processes and social movements: an overview and assessment," *Annual Review of Sociology*, vol. 26, 2000, pp. 611–639.
18 Benford, R.D. "'You could be the hundredth monkey': collective action frames and vocabularies of motive within the nuclear disarmament movement," *The Sociological Quarterly*, vol. 34, no. 2, 1993, pp. 195–216.
19 Benford, R.D. "'You could be the hundredth monkey': collective action frames and vocabularies of motive within the nuclear disarmament movement," *The Sociological Quarterly*, vol. 34, no. 2, 1993, p. 202.
20 Benford, R.D. "'You could be the hundredth monkey': collective action frames and vocabularies of motive within the nuclear disarmament movement," *The Sociological Quarterly*, vol. 34, no. 2, 1993, p. 207.

21 Cohen, S. *Folk Devils and Moral Panics*, London: Routledge, third edition, 2002.
22 Cohen, S. *Folk Devils and Moral Panics*, London: Routledge, third edition, 2002, p. 40.
23 Cohen, S. *Folk Devils and Moral Panics*, London: Routledge, third edition, 2002, p. 106.
24 On moral panics as collective behavior, see Watney, S. *Policing Desire: Pornography, Aids and the Media*, London: Methuen, 1987; and Young, J. "Moral panic: its origins in resistance, ressentiment and the translation of fantasy into reality," *British Journal of Criminology*, vol. 49, no. 1, 2009, pp. 4–16. On moral panics and the workings of the media, see Hall, S., C. Crichter, T. Jefferson, J. Clarke, and B. Roberts, *Policing the Crisis: Mugging, the State, and Law and Order*, London: Palgrave Macmillan, 1978; and Critcher, C. *Moral Panics and the Media*, Buckingham, UK: Open University Press, 2003. On moral panics as outbreaks of emotiveness and unreason see Goode, E. and N. Ben-Yehuda, *Moral Panics: The Social Construction of Deviance*, New York: Wiley-Blackwell, 2009.
25 "Text" here refers to both written and spoken language. See Halliday, M.A.K. *Language as Social Semiotic*, London: Edward Arnold, 1978; and Fairclough, N. *Discourse and Social Change*, Cambridge, UK: Polity Press, 1993.
26 Abend, G. "Two main problems in the sociology of morality," *Theory and Society*, vol. 37, no. 2, 2008, pp. 87–125; Hitlin, S. and S. Vaisey (eds.), *Handbook of the Sociology of Morality*, New York: Springer, 2010; Stivers, R. "Towards a sociology of morality," *International Journal of Sociology and Social Policy*, vol. 16, nos.1–2, 1996, pp. 1–14.
27 For example, Lakoff, G. *Moral Politics: What Conservatives Know That Liberals Don't*, Chicago: University of Chicago Press, 1996a; Weber, M. *The Protestant Ethic and the Spirit of Capitalism*, Roxbury, CA: Blackwell, 2002.
28 For example, Abramson, P.R. and R. Inglehart, *Value Change in Global Perspective*, Ann Arbor, MI: University of Michigan Press, 1995; Hitlin, S. and J.A. Piliavin, "Values: reviving a dormant concept," *Annual Review of Sociology*, vol. 30, 2004, pp. 359–393; Rokeach, M. *Understanding Human Values*, New York: Simon and Schuster, 1979.
29 On the relation of discourse to texts, see Fairclough, N. *Discourse and Social Change*, Cambridge: Polity Press, 1993; Parker, I. *Discourse Dynamics: Critical Analysis for Individual and Social Psychology*, London: Routledge, 1992; Phillips, N., T.B. Lawrence, and C. Hardy, "Discourse and institutions," *Academy of Management Review* vol. 29, no. 4, 2004, pp. 635–652.
30 Borrowing from Anderson, B. (*Imagined Communities. Reflections on the Origin and Spread of Nationalism*, London: Verso, 2006), this imagined social world might be thought of as an "imagined moral community."
31 Cohen, S. *Folk Devils and Moral Panics*, London: Routledge, third edition, 2002, p. 1.
32 See Lakoff, G. "The metaphor system for morality," in Goldberg, A. (ed.), *Conceptual Structure, Discourse and Language*, San Diego, CA: University of California, Center for the Study of Language and Information, 1996b.
33 On moral crusaders, and moral entrepreneurs more generally, see Becker, H. *Outsiders: Studies in the Sociology of Deviance*, New York: The Free Press, 1963.
34 Heritage, J. *Garfinkel and Ethnomethodology*, Cambridge, UK: Polity Press, 1984, p. 290.
35 A description of the newspapers and the procedures for selecting and analyzing the texts is provided in the Appendix.
36 As with the word "text," "talk" is used throughout this book to refer to spoken or written utterances.

2 Making crime "our" concern

1. *La Nación*, "Cartas de lectores—inseguridad," June 30, 2006 (emphasis in the original).
2. Gutman, Y. *Encyclopedia of the Holocaust, Volume 3*, New York: Macmillan, 1990, p. 1061.
3. In this sense, the echoes of Niemöller at the beginning of the letter set the scene for a moral reflection that incorporated his own: concern about the fate of others is ultimately in one's own best interests.
4. *El Universal*, "Preocupa a IP que delincuencia se infiltre en gobierno y sociedad," May 2, 2007.
5. *New York Times*, "Guardian Angels seek out more mean streets," March 22, 2007.
6. *El Universal*, "Calderón pide apoyo a ediles para combatir a delincuencia," May 13, 2007.
7. *Los Angeles Times*, "Gov. seeks coordinated gang effort," March 6, 2007.
8. *El Nacional*, "Para Marcos Chávez la delincuencia disminuyó," May 8, 2007.
9. *New York Times*, "Guardian Angels seek out more mean streets," March 22, 2007.
10. *New York Times*, "As Albany weighs confinement of sex offenders, some fear a threat to civil liberties," February 6, 2006.
11. *Los Angeles Times*, "In defense of guns," September 17, 2006.
12. *El Universal*, "ONG llaman a enfrentar inseguridad," June 29, 2007.
13. The variety of these generic terms was wider in Latin America, including references to, for example, "the whole population," "all social sectors," and "families and institutions."
14. In Mexico, one NGO made direct reference to the collective dimension by calling itself *México Unido Contra la Delincuencia* [Mexico United Against Crime]. See, for example, *El Universal*, "Delincuencia más joven y violenta," October 6, 2007.
15. Other semantic tactics for invoking the collectivity were occasionally used, for example, in references to "everybody," "everyone," or "no one," and (in North America mainly) to "you," in the sense of anyone (and therefore everyone).
16. *El Universal*, "Actuarán contra quien se coluda con la delincuencia," April 22, 2007.
17. *Globe and Mail*, "Tories hope youth-crime legislation will shift focus from Schreiber saga," November 20, 2007.
18. *La Nación*, "Cartas de lectores—inseguridad y policía," November 24, 2007.
19. *New York Times*, "New York: state crime rates continued to fall in 2005," September 18, 2006.
20. *New York Times*, "Doing more than their time," May 21, 2006.
21. *El Nacional*, "Creció número de venezolanos con miedo a la inseguridad," May 22, 2007.
22. *New York Times*, "The police's excellent year," December 30, 2007.
23. *New York Times*, "Little changes, big results," April 8, 2007 (emphasis added).
24. *New York Times*, "Despite a decrease in city crime, troubling signs emerge," September 29, 2006 (emphasis added).
25. *Los Angeles Times*, "Bills target criminals' use of guns," February 16, 2007.
26. *El Universal*, "Quieren sistema nacional para prevenir los delitos," June 15, 2006.
27. *New York Times*, "The insanity defense goes back on trial," July 30, 2006.
28. *Globe and Mail*, "The Rivers message," January 12, 2006.
29. *El Nacional*, "Monseñor Moronta: en Caracas, ¡no prestan atención!," May 28, 2006.
30. *La Nación*, "Cartas de lectores. Plan antidrogas," November 23, 2007.
31. *Globe and Mail*, "Blowing the whistle on gun murder," January 3, 2006.
32. *Globe and Mail*, "Reaching out is the only way to quell gun violence, youth worker says," January 7, 2006.

33 *Globe and Mail*, "Blair's working it like Fantino never could," August 12, 2006.
34 *El Universal*, "Edomex pondrá 'botones de pánico' en 50% de colegios," August 20, 2007.
35 *El Universal*, "Alcoholismo juvenil," July 14, 2006.
36 *New York Times*, "Texas weighs death penalty for rapes of children," May 20, 2007.
37 *New York Times*, "Violence in America (2 letters)," August 21, 2007.
38 "In recent months, the country has been very worried about what is happening in some of the states on the northern border of the Republic, given the high rates of violence, which have reached unheard of levels and which must be checked immediately" (*El Universal*, "Caravanas de la muerte," June 23, 2006).
39 *El Universal*, "Vivir en la frontera olvidada," March 16, 2007.
40 *Globe and Mail*, "The new market high," January 13, 2007.
41 *Globe and Mail*, "Assault rates triple for Northerners, Justice study finds," October 31, 2006.
42 *Los Angeles Times*, "Hate crimes need their own category," May 8, 2007.
43 *El Nacional*, "ONG's y comunidades: contralores sociales de quienes administran justicia," September 2, 2006.
44 *El Nacional*, "Delincuencia sin freno en Caracas," June 18, 2007.
45 *El Nacional*, "Incrementa la violencia infantil," September 24, 2006.
46 *Globe and Mail*, "Blowing the whistle on gun murder," January 3, 2006.
47 *Globe and Mail*, "Politicians urged to get tough on gun crime," January 17, 2006.
48 *El Nacional*, "Harán un paro contra el secuestro," May 5, 2007.
49 *La Nación*, "Indignación por una seguidilla de homicidios y asaltos," August 4, 2007.
50 *El Universal*, "Aumentan secuestros en Tijuana, alerta la IP," July 8, 2006.
51 *Globe and Mail*, "Blowing the whistle on gun murder," January 3, 2006.
52 *El Universal*, "Ciudadanía del miedo," January 28, 2006.
53 See, for example, Altamirano Molina, X. "urban insecurity [is] the sensation of individual vulnerability to the threat of crime and violence in cities, which tends to be included under the term crime;" ("Discursos y encuadres de la prensa escrita chilena sobre la inseguridad urbana: atribución de responsabilidades y agenda política," in Rey, G. (ed.), *Los Relatos Periodísticos del Crimen*, Bogotá: Centro de Competencia en Comunicación para América Latina, 2007, p. 95). On the concept of ontological insecurity, see, for example, Young, J. *The Exclusive Society: Social Exclusion, Crime and Difference in Late Modernity*, London: Sage, 1999.
54 The frequency count for some terms commonly used to refer to crime in the Latin American set of texts is as follows: *criminalidad* (130); *delincuencia* (646); *inseguridad* (984); *violencia* (502).
55 *El Nacional*, "Territorios de inseguridad," May 13, 2007.
56 *La Nación*, "Editorial I. Inseguridad: mucho más que cifras," August 27, 2006.
57 *La Nación*, "Rigurosamente incierto. Maldita inseguridad," November 4, 2006.
58 *Globe and Mail*, "If we adjusted our definition of 'news,' we'd be better informed," July 27, 2007.
59 *Los Angeles Times*, "Tracking bad policy," February 7, 2006.
60 *Los Angeles Times*, "It's a crime how we misjudge the young," September 17, 2006.
61 *New York Times*, "Police chiefs want U.S. aid in crime fight," August 31, 2006.
62 *El Universal*, "Ciudadanía del miedo," January 28, 2006.
63 *New York Times*, "Deaths in Newark," August 10, 2007.
64 *Globe and Mail*, "'Stop the soft talk on drugs,' pastor says," January 12, 2006.
65 *Los Angeles Times*, "A city strains to arrest a deadly trend," November 6, 2006.
66 *El Universal*, "Tijuanenses marchan contra la violencia," October 29, 2007.
67 *Globe and Mail*, "Harper trumpets get-tough crime plan," January 6, 2006.
68 *El Nacional*, "Rosales: Venezuela está pintada de rojo por la guerrilla," October 13, 2006.

69 *El Universal*, "Jóvenes: víctimas y victimarios," September 24, 2007.
70 *Los Angeles Times*, "It's a crime how we misjudge the young," September 17, 2006.
71 *El Universal*, "Aumentan secuestros en Tijuana," July 8, 2006.
72 *La Nación*, "Inseguridad: el carro delante del caballo," June 25, 2006.
73 *Los Angeles Times*, "A prison of our own making," December 10, 2006.
74 *Los Angeles Times*, "Crimes and punishments," December 13, 2006.
75 *Los Angeles Times*, "LAPD targets city's worst gangs," February 9, 2007.
76 *New York Times*, "As Albany weighs confinement of sex offenders, some fear a threat to civil liberties," February 6, 2006.
77 *El Universal*, "Fox: seguridad fronteriza es compartida," September 23, 2006.
78 *El Nacional*, "ONG's y comunidades: contralores sociales de quienes administran justicia," September 2, 2006.
79 *New York Times*, "Police chiefs want U.S. aid in crime fight," August 31, 2006.
80 *New York Times*, "Deaths in Newark," August 10, 2007.
81 See, for example, an article in *El Universal* which criticized Sinaloan "indolence" in the face of violent crime: "From time to time, society wakes from its lethargy and goes onto the streets to show its discontent with the climate of insecurity and violence that it lives in. Afterwards, the nightmare is forgotten again as people come to see it as something that does not concern them" (*El Universal*, "Indolencia sinaolense ante narcoviolencia," November 27, 2006).
82 Best, J. "Rhetoric in claims-making: constructing the missing children problem," *Social Problems*, vol. 34, no. 2, 1987, p. 105 (emphasis added).
83 Hopkins, N. and S. Reicher, "Social movement rhetoric and the social psychology of collective action: a case study of anti-abortion mobilization," *Human Relations*, vol. 50, no. 3, 1997, p. 270 (emphasis added).
84 Best, J. *Random Violence: How We Talk about New Crimes and New Victims*, Berkeley, CA: University of California Press, 1999.
85 For example, Fowler, R. *Language in the News: Discourse and Ideology in the Press*, London: Routledge, 1991.
86 For example, Grimshaw, A.D. "Referential ambiguity in pronominal inclusion: social and linguistic boundary marking," in Grimshaw, A.D. (ed.), *What's Going on Here? Complementary Studies of Professional Talk*, Norwood, NJ: Ablex, 1994.
87 Scheppele, K.L. "Telling stories," *Michigan Law Review*, vol. 87, no. 8, 1989, pp. 2073–2098.
88 Spiegelberg, H. "On the right to say 'we': a linguistic and phenomenological analysis," in Psathas, G. (ed.), *Phenomenological Sociology: Issues and Applications*, New York: John Wiley, 1973.
89 J.L. Dunn speaks of "sympathy entrepreneurs" ("Accounting for victimization: social constructionist perspectives," *Sociology Compass*, vol. 2, no. 5, 2008, p. 1613).
90 Best, J. "Rhetoric in claims-making: constructing the missing children problem," *Social Problems*, vol. 34, no. 2, 1987, p. 105.
91 Coltrane, S. and M. Adams, "The social construction of the divorce 'problem': morality, child victims and the politics of gender," *Family Relations*, vol. 52, no. 4, 2003, p. 368; DeYoung, M. "Speak of the devil: rhetoric in claims-making about the satanic ritual abuse problem," *Journal of Sociology and Social Welfare*, vol. 23, no. 2, 1996, pp. 55–74.; Furedi, F. *Culture of Fear*, New York: Cassell, 1997, p. 5.
92 Titus, J.J. "Boy trouble: rhetorical framing of boys' underachievement," *Discourse: Studies in the Cultural Politics of Education*, vol. 25, no. 2, 2004, p. 149.
93 Abdullah, N. "Exploring constructions of the 'drug problem' in historical and contemporary Singapore," *New Zealand Journal of Asian Studies*, vol. 7, no. 2, 2005, p. 53.
94 Hunt, A. *Governing Morals. A Social History of Moral Regulation*, Cambridge, UK: Cambridge University Press, 1999, p. 147.

95 Berns, N. "My problem and how I solved it," *The Sociological Quarterly*, vol. 40, 1999, pp. 85–108.
96 Baumann, E.A. "Research rhetoric and the social construction of elder abuse," in Best, J. (ed.), *Images of Issues: Typifying Contemporary Social Problems*, New York: Aldine de Gruyter, 1989, p. 63; Harbison, J. "The changing career of 'elder abuse and neglect' as a social problem in Canada," *Journal of Elder Abuse and Neglect*, vol. 11, no. 4, 1999, p. 65.
97 Lowe, B.M. "*Hearts and Minds* and morality: analyzing moral vocabularies in qualitative studies," *Qualitative Sociology*, vol. 25, no. 1, 2002, p. 110; Maurer, D. "Meat as a social problem: rhetorical strategies in the contemporary vegetarian literature," in Maurer, D. and J. Sobal (eds.), *Eating Agendas: Food and Nutrition as Social Problems*, Hawthorne, NY: Aldine de Gruyter, 1995.
98 Loseke, D. *Thinking about Social Problems*, New York: Transaction Books, second edition, 2003.
99 Clark, C. *Misery and Company. Sympathy in Everyday Life*, Chicago, IL: University of Chicago Press, 1997, p. 22.
100 See, for example, Johnson, T.C. "Child perpetrators—children who molest other children: preliminary findings," *Child Abuse and Neglect*, vol. 12, 1988, p. 226; Baumann, E.A. "Research rhetoric and the social construction of elder abuse," in Best, J. (ed.), *Images of Issues: Typifying Contemporary Social Problems*, New York: Aldine de Gruyter, 1989, p. 63; Furedi, F. "Coping with adversity: the turn to the rhetoric of vulnerability," *Security Journal*, vol. 20, 2007, pp. 171–184.
101 Abdullah, N. "Exploring constructions of the 'drug problem' in historical and contemporary Singapore," *New Zealand Journal of Asian Studies*, vol. 7, no. 2, 2005, p. 53.; Lowe, B.M. "*Hearts and Minds* and morality: analyzing moral vocabularies in qualitative studies," *Qualitative Sociology*, vol. 25, no. 1, 2002, pp. 110–111; Harbison, J. "The changing career of 'elder abuse and neglect' as a social problem in Canada," *Journal of Elder Abuse and Neglect*, vol. 11, no. 4, 1999, p. 65.
102 For example, "What brings us together is our concern for children" (anti-divorce activist cited by Coltrane, S. and M. Adams, "The social construction of the divorce 'problem': morality, child victims and the politics of gender," *Family Relations*, vol. 52, no. 4, 2003, p. 368).
103 Cf. Hunt, A. "Risk and moralization in everyday life," in Ericson, R.V. and A. Doyle (eds.), *Risk and Morality*, Toronto: University of Toronto Press, 2003, p. 173.
104 Best, J. *Random Violence: How We Talk about New Crimes and New Victims*, Berkeley, CA: University of California Press, 1999.
105 Jenness, V. "Social movement growth, domain expansion, and framing processes: the gay/lesbian movement and violence against gays and lesbians as a social problem," *Social Problems*, vol. 42, no. 1, 1995, p. 157; Williams, R. "Constructing the public good: social movements and cultural resources," *Social Problems*, vol. 42, no. 1, 1995, p. 136. Additionally, the idea that a troubling condition could happen to anyone is sometimes used when concern is directed at others. For example, it is sometimes claimed that abduction or sexual abuse could happen to "any child" (see Best, J. *Threatened Children: Rhetoric and Concern about Child Victims*, Chicago, IL: University of Chicago Press, 1990; Johnson, J.M. "Horror stories and the construction of child abuse," in Best, J. (ed.), *Images of Issues: Typifying Contemporary Social Problems*, Hawthorne, NY: Aldine de Gruyter, 1989).
106 Armstrong, E.M. and E.L. Abel, "Fetal alcohol syndrome: the origins of a moral panic," *Alcohol and Alcoholism*, vol. 35, no. 3, 2000, p. 277.
107 Wagner, D. "The universalization of social problems: some radical explanations," *Critical Sociology*, vol. 23, no. 1, 1997, pp. 3–23.
108 Cromer, G. "Analogies to terror: the construction of social problems in Israel during the Intifada Al Aqsa," *Terrorism and Political Violence*, vol. 18, no. 3, 2006, p. 391.
109 Albert, E. "AIDS and the press: the creation and transformation of a social problem,"

154 *Notes*

in Best, J. (ed.), *Images of Issues: Typifying Contemporary Social Problems*, New York: Aldine de Gruyter, 1989, p. 45 (emphasis added).
110 Lakoff, G. *Moral Politics: How Liberals and Conservatives Think*, Chicago, IL: University of Chicago Press, 2002, p. 86.
111 DeYoung, M. "Speak of the devil: rhetoric in claims-making about the satanic ritual abuse problem," *Journal of Sociology and Social Welfare*, vol. XXIII, no. 2, 1996, p. 64.
112 Miceli, M.S. "Morality politics vs. identity politics: framing processes and competition among Christian right and gay social movement organizations," *Sociological Forum*, vol. 20, no. 4, 2005, p. 597.
113 Rainham, D. "Risk communication and public response to industrial chemical contamination in Sydney, Nova Scotia: a case study," *Journal of Environmental Health*, vol. 65, no. 5, 2002, p. 30.
114 Williams, R. "Constructing the public good: social movements and cultural resources," *Social Problems*, vol. 42, no. 1, 1995, p. 131.
115 Abdullah, N. "Exploring constructions of the 'drug problem' in historical and contemporary Singapore," *New Zealand Journal of Asian Studies*, vol. 7, no. 2, 2005, p. 53.
116 Girling, E., I. Loader and R. Sparks, *Crime and Social Change in Middle England: Questions of Order in an English Town*, London: Routledge, 2000, p. 11.
117 Smith, D.E. "'Literacy' and business: 'social problems' as social organization," in Holstein J.A. and G. Miller (eds.), *Reconsidering Social Constructionism: Debates in Social Problems Theory*, New York: Aldine de Gruyter, 1993, pp. 340–341. Smith comments: "'Our' and 'we' of the first sentence in the last quotation do not [sic] longer refer to the company, but are spoken as what might be described as the 'societal we,' locating a generalized subject external to the particular local context" (Ibid. p. 341).
118 Johnson, T.C. "Child perpetrators—children who molest other children: preliminary findings," *Child Abuse and Neglect*, vol. 12, 1988, p. 219.
119 Johnson, T.C. "Child perpetrators—children who molest other children: preliminary findings," *Child Abuse and Neglect*, vol. 12, 1988, p. 222.
120 Jenness, V. "Social movement growth, domain expansion, and framing processes: the gay/lesbian movement and violence against gays and lesbians as a social problem," *Social Problems*, vol. 42, no. 1, 1995; Ulrich, C.L. "Hate crime legislation: a policy analysis," *Houston Law Review*, vol. 36, no. 4, 1999, p. 1467–1529.
121 de Sousa Santos, B. "*Nuestra America*: reinventing a subaltern paradigm of recognition and redistribution," *Theory, Culture and Society*, vol. 18, 2001, p. 197.
122 See, for example, Young, J. *The Exclusive Society: Social Exclusion, Crime and Difference in Late Modernity*, London: Sage, 1999, p. 69.

3 "We the good"

1 See www.usembassy-mexico.gov/PDH/sGertzBio.html, (accessed April 26, 2011).
2 The origin of the term *notables* appears to lie in pre-revolutionary France (e.g., Gruder, V.R. "'No taxation without representation': The Assembly of Notables of 1787 and political ideology in France," *Legislative Studies Quarterly*, vol. VII, no. 2, 1982, pp. 263–279).
3 See, for example, "Carta de Los Notables" (Letter from the Notables [to the President of Venezuela]), on August 10, 1990, reproduced at www.analitica.com/Bitblio/notables/default.asp, (accessed April 21, 2011).
4 See http://es.wikipedia.org/wiki/Alejandro_Gertz_Manero, (accessed April 21, 2011).
5 The ISSSTE is a social security organization for public sector employees.
6 *El Universal*, "Víctimas y verdugos," March 22, 2006, (commas, inverted commas, and emphasis as in the original; a few sentences have been omitted for brevity).
7 *El Universal*, "Concluye marcha contra la inseguridad," November 6, 2006.

Notes 155

8 *El Universal*, "Denuncian promesas sin cumplir en seguridad," June 27, 2007.
9 *La Nación*, "Rigurosamente incierto. Maldita inseguridad," November 4, 2006.
10 *La Nación*, "Editorial I. La inseguridad nos sigue acosando," August 14, 2007.
11 *Globe and Mail*, "'Stop the soft talk on drugs,' pastor says," January 12, 2006.
12 *Los Angeles Times*, "Arm against Katricians," September 18, 2006.
13 *Globe and Mail*, "Reaching out is the only way to quell gun violence, youth worker says," January 7, 2006.
14 *Globe and Mail*, "New Democrats talk tough on crime," January 7, 2006, (emphasis added).
15 *Los Angeles Times*, "Skid row in rehab," November 18, 2007.
16 *New York Times*, "Deaths in Newark," August 10, 2007. See also, for example, "Mr. Royster's brutal eight-day rampage..." (*New York Times*, "Take DNA when you can," April 9, 2006); "brutality [in Los Angeles] yielded some particularly horrendous results" (*New York Times*, "A trend grows in policing," September 9, 2007); "several brutal attacks ... [in Halifax, Nova Scotia]" (*Globe and Mail*, "Statistics rebut claims Halifax has crime-wave, experts say," August 31, 2007).
17 *New York Times*, "100,000 gone since 2001," August 14, 2007.
18 *El Universal*, "Piden a Fox que asuma gravedad de inseguridad," February 2, 2006.
19 *La Nación*, "Inseguridad: la culpa es de otro," October 24, 2007.
20 *El Nacional*, "La frustración por la inseguridad llegó a 75% después de 7 años," April 7, 2006.
21 *El Universal*, "Atizapán arranca plan para detectar vehículos robados," July 18, 2007. Another Mexican commentator wrote of "the cockroach effect" in relation to the government's actions against drug trafficking: "A frequent criticism is that these operations only produce a cockroach effect and that is true, but what the government has to do is to continue chasing the cockroaches wherever they go..." (*El Universal*, "La estrategia anticrimen," February 23, 2007).
22 *La Nación*, "El combate contra la inseguridad," August 27, 2007; *El Universal*, "Redefinir la estrategia," May 26, 2007; *El Nacional*, "Delincuencia uniformada," April 4, 2006; *El Universal*, "Inseguridad aniquilante," November 15, 2006.
23 *Los Angeles Times*, "Skid row in rehab," November 18, 2007 (emphasis added).
24 *New York Times*, "Deaths in Newark," August 10, 2007.
25 *Los Angeles Times*, "Alarm on gangs sounded," January 13, 2007; *Los Angeles Times*, "Small cities in region grow more violent, data show," June 15, 2006.
26 *Globe and Mail*, "Judges are constitutional guardians, not cheerleaders for the police," September 17, 2007; *Globe and Mail*, "Statistics rebut claims Halifax has crime-wave, experts say," August 31, 2007.
27 For example, "vicious and cold-blooded ... waves of crime" (*New York Times*, "100,000 gone since 2001," August 14, 2007); a "vicious biker gang" (*Globe and Mail*, "Take on the biker gangs," April 12, 2006).
28 For example, "the ruthless violence unleashed by Venezuelan criminals" (*El Nacional*, "Delincuencia diabólica," July 1, 2007); "audacious and ruthless crime" (*La Nación*, "Editorial II: la entrega voluntaria de armas," July 26, 2007).
29 *El Universal*, "Refuerzan seguridad en la Colonia Morelos," November 21, 2007.
30 *La Nación*, "Editorial I: delincuencia en moto," May 4, 2007).
31 *La Nación*, "Alarma en la ciudad," January 26, 2007.
32 Sarmiento, D.F. *Facundo. Civilización y Barbarie*, Madrid: Alianza, [1845]1988.
33 *Globe and Mail*, "Crimes of perception," May 8, 2007 (emphasis added).
34 *El Nacional*, "Metro inseguro," May 13, 2007 (emphasis added).
35 *Los Angeles Times*, "Racial attacks by gangs rising, LA officials fear," January 21, 2007 (emphasis added).
36 *El Nacional*, "Jóvenes manifestarán por las 67.000 muertes a manos del hampa registradas en el país," April 12, 2006 (emphasis added).
37 *New York Times*, "Ditch these drug laws," September 30, 2007 (emphasis added).

156 Notes

38 *El Universal*, "Tamaulipas: narcos de esta frontera no se acercan a Dios," March 27, 2006 (emphasis added).
39 The most commonly used terms (and frequencies) in the whole sample were as follows. North America: "criminals" (152); "gang(s)" (1,112); "offender(s)" (323). Latin America: "*bandas*" or "*pandillas*" [gangs] (120); "*criminales*" or "*delincuente(s)*" [criminals] (403); "*el hampa*" [the underworld] (59).
40 Foucault, M. *Madness and Civilization: A History of Insanity in the Age of Reason*, London: Routledge, 1989, p. 201.
41 Cf. Rock, P. "The sociology of deviance and conceptions of moral order," *British Journal of Criminology*, vol. 14, no. 2, 1974, p. 147.
42 *Los Angeles Times*, "A city strains to arrest a deadly trend," November 6, 2006.
43 *New York Times*, "A precinct of contrasts, where violence still lurks," July 10, 2007.
44 *El Nacional*, "Vecinos de Santa Mónica aprendieron a convivir con la delincuencia," March 19, 2006.
45 *Globe and Mail*, "The building that fought back," January 7, 2006.
46 *Globe and Mail*, "Reaching out is the only way to quell gun violence, youth worker says," January 7, 2006.
47 *Los Angeles Times*, "Big drop in L.A. homicides," September 28, 2007.
48 *New York Times*, "States rethink tough penalties for juveniles," December 2, 2007.
49 *New York Times*, "A fallen judge rethinks crime and punishment," January 13, 2006.
50 *La Nación*, "Preocupa la influencia de la droga en los chicos," October 14, 2007 (emphasis added).
51 *Los Angeles Times*, "Skid row in rehab," November 18, 2007 (emphasis added).
52 *New York Times*, "15 states expand the right to shoot in self-defense," August 7, 2006.
53 *Oxford English Dictionary*, 1989 (emphasis added).
54 Corbey, R. and J. Leerssen, "Studying alterity: backgrounds and perspectives," in Corbey, R. and J. Leerssen (eds.) *Alterity, Identity and Image: Selves and Others in Society and Scholarship*, Amsterdam: Rodopi, 1991; Gingrich, A. "Conceptualising identities: anthropological alternatives to essentialising difference and moralising about the other," in Baumann, G. and A. Gingrich (eds.), *Grammars of Identity/Alterity: A Structural Approach*, Oxford: Berghahn Books, 2004; Voestermans, P. "Alterity/identity: a deficient image of culture," in Corbey, R. and J. Leerssen (eds.), *Alterity, Identity, Image: Selves and Others in Society and Scholarship*, Amsterdam: Editions Rodopi, 1991.
55 Corbey, R. and J. Leerssen, "Studying alterity: backgrounds and perspectives," in Corbey, R. and J. Leerssen (eds.), *Alterity, Identity and Image: Selves and Others in Society and Scholarship*, Amsterdam: Editions Rodopi, 1991, p. vi.
56 Czarniawska, B. "Alterity/identity interplay in image construction," in Barry, D. and H. Hansen (eds.), *The Sage Handbook of New Approaches in Management and Organization*, Thousand Oaks, CA: Sage Publications, 2008.
57 *Globe and Mail*, "The building that fought back," January 7, 2006.
58 *Globe and Mail*, "A passionate voice speaks out for porn's youngest victims," April 28, 2007.
59 *El Nacional*, "Tiempo de reflexión," April 22, 2006.
60 For example, *La Nación*, "Indignación por una seguidilla de homicidios y asaltos [A series of murders and robberies causes indignation]," August 4, 2007; "the last of 12 murders of women in the region triggered the indignation of more than 20 neighborhoods" (*El Universal*, "Padres vigilarán calles de Edomex," November 11, 2006).
61 For example, "Kidnapping is the criminal behavior that causes most anxiety and indignation" (*La Nación*, "Alarma en la ciudad," January 26, 2007); "...those who live in a situation of permanent anxiety that they absolutely do not deserve" (*La Nación*, "Editorial I: vecinos en defensa propia," October 3, 2006).
62 For example, "Across the nation, religious African-Americans were shocked that the

Notes 157

evangelical minister Juanita Bynum … said she was brutally beaten" (*New York Times*, "Jena, O.J., and the jailing of black America," September 30, 2007); "This crime would have been as shocking in an upscale area like Georgetown as it would be in less-advantaged parts of the city" (*New York Times*, "Washington officials try to ease crime fear," July 13, 2006).

63 *Globe and Mail*, "A knife registry?" January 5, 2006.
64 *El Universal*, "Vecinos trabajando," January 22, 2006.
65 *Globe and Mail*, "RCMP can't probe all organized crime cases, chief says," May 9, 2006.
66 *La Nación*, "La inseguridad es el principal problema para los porteños," 12 August, 2006.
67 *New York Times*, "Despite a decrease in city crime, troubling signs emerge," September 29, 2006.
68 *El Nacional*, "Entre el bien y el mal," May 13, 2007.
69 *El Nacional*, "Tiempo de reflexión," April 22, 2006.
70 *Globe and Mail*, "The building that fought back," January 7, 2006.
71 "[T]he group found the courage to move away from the paralysis of victimization to action" (*Globe and Mail*, "The building that fought back," January 7, 2006); "'We can't do it without you,' Deputy Chief Earl Paysinger said. 'We need your sight. We need your voice. We need your courage'" (*Los Angeles Times*, "Killings drop 11% as crime totals decline," June 10, 2006); "The alter ego of the bus drivers is not that of the superhero that drives around the metropolis. Although there is courage, that is not this type of story" (*El Nacional*, "La inseguridad acompaña a los choferes como un pasajero más," March 12, 2006).
72 *El Nacional*, "8% bajó el delito en el Municpio Chacao en 2007," December 27, 2007.
73 *El Universal*, "Reforzarán operativos en estados que colindan con Michoacán," February 18, 2006.
74 *Los Angeles Times*, "FBI joins L.A. policing effort in war on street gang crime," January 19, 2007.
75 *Globe and Mail*, "A passionate voice speaks out for porn's youngest victims," April 28, 2007.
76 "René Fiechter, a Nassau County assistant district attorney who works on community crime prevention, said that Pentecostal churches had been in the forefront of gang intervention for some time and that the Church of Hempstead's approach under Mr. Reyes had been 'methodical, low key and effective'" (*New York Times*, "Church battles to break gang cycle, with a flock for all," April 16, 2006).
77 *Globe and Mail*, "A passionate voice speaks out for porn's youngest victims," April 28, 2007.
78 *New York Times*, "Reform the reforms," January 8, 2006.
79 *Globe and Mail*, "Canada's crime rate hits lowest level in 25 years," July 19, 2007.
80 *Los Angeles Times*, "Re 'A prison of our own making,' current, Dec. 10," December 13, 2006.
81 *Globe and Mail*, "Reaching out to quell gang violence," January 7, 2006.
82 For example, "the legal combat against sex offenders" (*New York Times*, "As Albany weighs confinement of sex offenders, some fear a threat to civil liberties," February 6, 2006); "Arslanian proposed combating crime with more equality and less exclusion" (*La Nación*, "Documento de consenso contra la inseguridad," December 1, 2006).
83 For example, "the battle against heinous crimes" (*New York Times*, "Pros and cons of DNA collection," April 16, 2006); "the battle against drug trafficking and organized crime" (*El Universal*, "Fox: seguridad fronteriza es responsabilidad compartida," September 23, 2006).
84 For example, "additional resources are needed to fight those crimes" (*Los Angeles Times*, "FBI reports rise in violent crime," December 19, 2006); "he does not want

158   *Notes*

the country to lose against 'that horseman of the Apocalypse,' drugs and alcohol, which he will valiantly fight" (*El Universal*, "Pulso político," January 23, 2006).
85 For example, "officials struggle to clean up skid row" (*Los Angeles Times*, "Drug offenders to be banned from skid row," September 27, 2006); "the mission of the new authorities is to struggle 'to make the criminals the ones who feel unsafe'" (*La Nación*, "Cambios en la política de seguridad bonaerense: responderán 'enérgicamente' a la delincuencia organizada," December 14, 2007).
86 *El Universal*, "Calderón: no habrá tregua contra crimen," December 21, 2007.
87 *Los Angeles Times*, "Democrats stake out turf in war on gangs," March 16, 2007.
88 *Los Angeles Times*, "Crime victims' families rally in Riverside," April 27, 2007.
89 *Los Angeles Times*, "Bratton's 'broken windows,'" April 20, 2006.
90 *Globe and Mail*, "Reaching out to quell gang violence," January 7, 2006.
91 *Globe and Mail*, "The building that fought back," January 7, 2006.
92 *La Nación*, "Cartas de lectores—inseguridad," June 30, 2006.
93 For example, "The Governor ... declared himself in favor of a vigorous and integrated action by all branches of government to confront drug trafficking" (*El Universal*, "Pulso político," January 31, 2006); "Several thousand demonstrators ... demand[ed] ... a federal crackdown on hate crimes and a more vigorous response to incidents of noose hangings" (*Los Angeles Times*, "Sharpton leads call for federal investigation of hate crimes," November 17, 2007).
94 For example, "there could be more efficient dealing with the homeless in the area" (*Los Angeles Times*, "LAPD's skid row divide," March 10, 2006); "The multitude that gathered last Thursday ... to demand security and a higher quality and greater efficiency in the nation's institutions" (*La Nación*, "Editorial I: las propuestas de Blumberg," September 3, 2006).
95 For example, "The Minister indicated that fundamental strides could be made against drug traffickers" (*El Nacional*, "Carreño niega aumento de cifras de delitos," May 15, 2007); "Santa Ana began the year boasting that the police had made great strides against gang violence" (*Los Angeles Times*, "L.A. crime decreases for fifth year," December 27, 2006).
96 *New York Times*, "Crime rising, New Orleans asks for National Guard," June 20, 2006.
97 *La Nación*, "La sucesión kirchnerista. Jaque se comprometió a combatir el delito," December 10, 2007.
98 *Los Angeles Times*, "The new American witch hunt," March 11, 2007.
99 *New York Times*, "As Albany weighs confinement of sex offenders, some fear a threat to civil liberties," February 6, 2006.
100 *La Nación*, "El desarme, ¿apenas una ilusión?" August 23, 2006.
101 *La Nación*, "Editorial I: las causas de la inseguridad," February 12, 2007.
102 *Los Angeles Times*, "Latino leaders' silence is killing us," March 21, 2007.
103 *Globe and Mail*, "In a countering move, Dion gets tough on crime," March 14, 2007.
104 *New York Times*, "Crime rising, New Orleans asks for National Guard," June 20, 2006.
105 *Los Angeles Times*, "Violent crime rises in some big cities," June 13, 2006.
106 *La Nación*, "La creciente violencia social," June 29, 2006.
107 *La Nación*, "Vandalismo e inseguridad," October 1, 2007.
108 *El Universal*, "Incontenible violencia criminal," February 1, 2006.
109 *El Nacional*, "Copei acusa al gobierno por la inseguridad," April 7, 2007.
110 Impunity was mentioned 134 times in the Latin American texts.
111 *El Universal*, "El riesgo de la impunidad," June 28, 2007.
112 *El Nacional*, "Cuestionan criterios del CICPC para definir qué es un homicidio," May 9, 2007.
113 *La Nación*, "Editorial I: impunidad criminal," March 29, 2007.

Notes 159

114 For example, "The mayor of Alto Apure ... declared that the state police are inefficient..."(*El Nacional*, "44 muertes violentas se registraron en Alto Apure," June 22, 2006); "Encinas [the governor of the state of Mexico] acknowledged that there is a serious problem in the performance of the State's duties to provide security for women" (*El Universal*, "Cometen en Edomex 429 feminicidios cada año," May 30, 2006).

115 For example, "The murders linked to drugs are characterized by the silence that shrouds these incidents. Victims' families and witnesses refuse to talk about them, which makes it difficult to solve these crimes, admitted the state prosecutor.... Because 80% of the homicides in the state are linked to drug trafficking and organized crime, *he added that the Federal Attorney General should also work on these investigations* in order to advance in combating impunity" (*El Universal*, "Indolencia sinaloense ante narcoviolencia," November 27, 2006 (emphasis added).

116 *La Nación*, "Inseguridad: nuevos retrocesos," July 16, 2006.

117 *El Universal*, "Seguridad pública," September 16, 2006.

118 *El Nacional*, "Policía Nacional compete a la AN," May 24, 2007.

119 *El Nacional*, "Insensibilidad e ineptitud," May 13, 2007.

120 For example, "...insecurity is everyone's problem" [Venezuelan President] (*El Nacional*, "Chávez atribuye inseguridad a venta ilegal de cerveza," October 11, 2006); "...security is everyone's problem" [state governor in Argentina] (*La Nación*, "La sucesión kirchnerista. Jaque se comprometió a combatir el delito," December 10, 2007); "I propose to make Mexico a safer country through the participation of all Mexicans" [candidate for senator] (*El Universal*, "Seguridad pública," September 16, 2006).

121 For example, *La Nación*, "Editorial I: inseguridad, un problema de todos," October 23, 2007.

122 *El Universal*, "Víctimas y verdugos," March 22, 2006.

123 *El Nacional*, "Zulianos están preocupados por la inseguridad," March 26, 2006.

124 *El Nacional*, "Delincuencia uniformada," April 4, 2006.

125 *La Nación*, "Eje de la campaña bonaerense," October 6, 2007.

126 *El Universal*, "Víctimas y verdugos," March 22, 2006.

127 *Los Angeles Times*, "L.A. crime decreases for fifth year," December 27, 2006.

128 *Los Angeles Times*, "Bratton says there's more work to do," April 30, 2007.

129 *Los Angeles Times*, "Will the strategy to battle gangs work?" February 11, 2007.

130 *New York Times*, "A place for sex offenders," January 22, 2006.

131 *Los Angeles Times*, "Hate crimes need their own category," May 8, 2007.

132 *El Nacional*, "La prevención del delito," May 23, 2006.

133 *New York Times*, "100,000 gone since 2001," August 14, 2007.

134 *Globe and Mail*, "Unstable gang scene unique to B.C.," October 24, 2007.

135 *La Nación*, "No hacemos más que acostumbrarnos a vivir en una sociedad más insegura," September 24, 2007.

136 *La Nación*, "La creciente violencia social," June 29, 2006.

137 Apart from "Víctimas y Verdugos," already reviewed here, these were: "Adicción despenalizada," May 10, 2006; "Demagogia e inseguridad," June 14, 2006; "Criminalidad desbordada," September 20, 2006; "Inseguridad aniquilante," November 15, 2006; "Las policías y las víctimas," April 18, 2007; "Botellita de jerez," October 17, 2007; "Tierra de ciegos," October 31, 2007; and "Año de violencia," December 12, 2007.

138 *La Nación*, "Maldita inseguridad," November 4, 2006.

139 *La Nación*, "El escenario de la violencia joven," May 23, 2006.

140 *La Nación*, "Seguridad: la calle o la academia," July 31, 2006.

141 Best, J. *Random Violence: How We Talk about New Crimes and New Victims*, Berkeley, CA: University of California Press, 1999, p. xii. Note the use of "we" here. On page 16 of the same work, Best refers to "We—the larger society...." On the

Manichean division of the world in relation to crime and criminals, see also, Anker, E. "Villains, victims and heroes: melodrama, media and September 11," *Journal of Communication*, vol. 55, no. 1, 2005, pp. 22–37; Garland, D. "The limits of the sovereign state: strategies of crime control in contemporary society," *The British Journal of Criminology*, vol. 36, no. 4, 1996, p. 461; Hall, S., C. Crichter, T. Jefferson, J. Clarke, and B. Roberts, *Policing the Crisis: Mugging, the State, and Law and Order*, London: Palgrave Macmillan, 1978, p. 68.

142 Moscovici, S. "The conspiracy mentality," in Graumann, C.F. and S. Moscovici (eds.), *Changing Conceptions of Conspiracy*, New York: Springer-Verlag, 1987, p. 154, cited in Best, J. *Random Violence: How We Talk about New Crimes and New Victims*, Berkeley, CA: University of California Press, 1999, p. 81.

143 Vasilachis de Gialdino, I. "El lenguaje de la violencia en los medios de comunicación. Las otras formas de ser de la violencia y la prensa escrita," in PNUD (Programa de las Naciones Unidas para el Desarrollo) (ed.) *Aportes para la Convivencia y la Seguridad Ciudadana*, San Salvador, El Salvador: PNUD, 2004, p. 154.

144 Alexander, J.C. "Citizen and enemy as symbolic classification: on the polarizing discourse of civil society," in Lamont, M. and M. Fournier (eds.), *Cultivating Differences: Symbolic Boundaries and the Making of Inequality*, Chicago, IL: University of Chicago Press, 1992. The first quote is from page 291; the second from page 290.

145 Similarly, studies reveal that smokers (a new class of deviant) rarely appear in articles about the problem of smoking (Malone, E., E. Boyd, and L.A. Bero, "Science in the news: journalists' construction of passive smoking as a social problem," *Social Studies of Science*, vol. 30, no. 5, 2000, pp. 713–735).

146 Ericson, R., P.M. Baranek and J.B.L. Chan, *Representing Order: Crime, Law and Justice in the News Media*, Toronto: University of Toronto Press, 1991.

147 Thompson, C.Y., R.L. Young, and R. Burns, "Representing gangs in the news: media constructions of criminal gangs," *Sociological Spectrum*, vol. 20, 2000, pp. 409–432.

148 Frost, N.A. and N.D. Phillips, "Talking heads: crime reporting on cable news," *Justice Quarterly*, vol. 28, no. 1, 2011, pp. 87–112.

149 Sacco, V.F. "Media constructions of crime," *Annals of the American Academy of Political and Social Science*, no. 539, 1995 p. 143.

150 See, for example, Beres, L.S. and T.D. Griffith, "Demonizing youth," *Loyola of Los Angeles Law Review*, vol. 34, 2000–2001, pp. 747–766; Chesney-Lind, M. and M. Eliason, "From invisible to incorrigible: the demonization of marginalised women and girls," *Crime Media Culture*, vol. 2, no. 1, 2006, pp. 29–47; Hing, B.O. "The immigrant as criminal: punishing dreamers," *Hastings Women's Law Journal*, vol. 9, no. 1, 1998, pp. 79–96; Garland, D. *The Culture of Control: Crime and Social Order in Contemporary Society*. Chicago, IL: University of Chicago Press, 2001; Young, J. *The Exclusive Society: Social Exclusion, Crime and Difference in Late Modernity*, London: Sage, 1999.

151 Lowney, K.S. "Claimsmaking, culture, and the media in the social construction process," in Holstein, J.A. and J.F. Gubrium (eds.), *Handbook of Constructionist Research*, New York/London: The Guilford Press, 2008, pp. 342–343.

152 Compare with the following characterization of film by Doctorow, E.L.: "Film is time-driven, it never ruminates, it shows the outside of life, it shows behavior. It tends to the simplest moral reasoning. Films out of Hollywood are linear. The narrative simplification of complex morally consequential reality is always the drift of a film inspired by a book" (quoted in the *New York Times Book Review*, March 5, 2000, p. 7).

153 See, for example, Best, J. *Random Violence: How We Talk about New Crimes and New Victims*, Berkeley, CA: University of California Press, 1999; Cromer, G. "Analogies to terror: the construction of social problems in Israel during the Intifada Al Aqsa," *Terrorism and Political Violence*, vol. 18, no. 3, 2006, pp. 389–398; Young,

Notes 161

J. *The Exclusive Society: Social Exclusion, Crime and Difference in Late Modernity*, London: Sage, 1999.
154 "She likened the situation to the U.S.-led invasion of Iraq, where troops quickly routed the enemy, only to see a lack of proper planning lead to chaos. 'The LAPD knows how to surge and purge,' Rice said. But 'after the LAPD clears out a neighborhood, we don't know how to hold and build'" (*Los Angeles Times*, "Will the strategy to battle gangs work?" February 11, 2007).
155 "One year on from the start of his national crusade against drug trafficking and organized crime, President Felipe Calderón paid tribute to the soldiers and police officers who have fallen in this 'war'..." (*El Universal*, "Calderón: no habrá tregua contra el crimen," December 21, 2007).
156 "The Priest knows who to give to and who not. His empathy with the children of nothing expresses itself in his favorite prayer, which says, 'Lord Jesus Christ, son of God alive, have mercy on me'" (*El Nacional*, "La cruz de la inseguridad," September 30, 2007).
157 Lakoff, G. "The metaphor system for morality," in Goldberg, A. (ed.) *Conceptual Structure, Discourse and Language*, San Diego, CA: University of California, Center for the Study of Language and Information, 1996b, p. 259 (emphasis in the original).

4 The moral outlook

1 *Los Angeles Times*, "It's a crime how we misjudge the young," September 17, 2006.
2 This term is borrowed from Garland, D. *The Culture of Control: Crime and Social Order in Contemporary Society*, Chicago, IL: University of Chicago Press, 2001.
3 *Globe and Mail*, "Recent surge in violence unlikely to dampen Olympics, experts say," November 10, 2007.
4 *Los Angeles Times*, "Racial attacks by gangs rising," January 21, 2007.
5 *New York Times*, "Violent crime rising sharply in some cities," February 12, 2006.
6 *El Nacional*, "44 muertes violentas se registraron en Alto Apure el primer semestre del año," June 22, 2006.
7 *El Universal*, "Crimen organizado transnacional," December 13, 2006.
8 *La Nación*, "Editorial I: inseguridad: hay funcionarios que parecen de otro país," July 9, 2006.
9 *Los Angeles Times*, "It's a crime how we misjudge the young," September 17, 2006.
10 *New York Times*, "Police chiefs want U.S. aid in crime fight," August 31, 2006.
11 *New York Times*, "Police chiefs want U.S. aid in crime fight," August 31, 2006.
12 *Los Angeles Times*, "Violent crime is up for 2nd year in a row," September 25, 2007.
13 *Los Angeles Times*, "Violent crime is up for 2nd year in a row," September 25, 2007.
14 *Globe and Mail*, "Canada's crime rate hits lowest level in 25 years," July 19, 2007.
15 *Globe and Mail*, "Blair's working it like Fantino never could," August 12, 2006.
16 *Globe and Mail*, "Does Harper's message match the statistics?" April 30, 2007.
17 *New York Times*, "Violent crime rose in '05, with murders up by 4.8%," June 13, 2006.
18 *New York Times*, "100,000 gone since 2001," August 14, 2007.
19 *Globe and Mail*, "Statistics rebut claims Halifax has crime-wave, experts say," August 31, 2007.
20 *Globe and Mail*, "Statistics rebut claims Halifax has crime-wave, experts say," August 31, 2007.
21 For example, "Newark has seen hundreds of senseless killings over the years..." (*New York Times*, "Deaths in Newark," August 10, 2007); "It's an unfortunate outbreak of senseless violence..." (*Los Angeles Times*, "Killings up over long weekend," September 6, 2006).

22 *New York Times*, "Despite a decrease in city crime, troubling signs emerge," September 29, 2006.
23 *New York Times*, "Small cities in region grow more violent, data show," June 15, 2006.
24 *Los Angeles Times*, "Alarm on gangs sounded," January 13, 2007.
25 *New York Times*, "Police chiefs want U.S. aid in crime fight," August 31, 2006.
26 *New York Times*, "Washington officials try to ease fear of crime." July 13, 2006.
27 *Globe and Mail*, "New chief must deal with perception that crime is on the increase," October 1, 2007.
28 *Globe and Mail*, "Assault rate triples for Northerners, Justice study finds," October 31, 2006.
29 *New York Times*, "Small cities in region grow more violent, data show," June 15, 2006.
30 *Los Angeles Times*, "As L.A. violent crime drops, the desert becomes a hot spot," August 8, 2006.
31 See: *Globe and Mail*, "The Wild West," July 19, 2007; *New York Times*, "A precinct of contrasts, where violence still lurks," July 10, 2007; *New York Times*, "Caught on a block that conjures up 'the Wild West,'" November 15, 2007; *New York Times*, 'Killings surge in Oakland, and officials are unable to explain why," June 22, 2007.
32 *New York Times*, "Caught on a block that conjures up 'the Wild West,'" November 15, 2007.
33 *New York Times*, "Caught on a block that conjures up 'the Wild West,'" November 15, 2007.
34 *Los Angeles Times*, "A city strains to arrest a deadly trend," November 6, 2006.
35 *Los Angeles Times*, "A city strains to arrest a deadly trend," November 6, 2006.
36 *Los Angeles Times*, "Latinos and gangs: the hopeful flip side," January 28, 2007.
37 *New York Times*, "So many crimes, and reasons not to cooperate," December 30, 2007.
38 *Globe and Mail*, "The rougher end of the Danforth," August 26, 2006.
39 *Los Angeles Times*, "Anxiety builds as crime increases in Koreatown," October 31, 2006.
40 *New York Times*, "Amid the glitter, Jersey City's growing pains," March 5, 2006.
41 *Los Angeles Times*, "Alarm on gangs sounded," January 13, 2007.
42 *Los Angeles Times*, "As L.A. violent crime drops, the desert becomes a hotspot," August 8, 2006.
43 *Globe and Mail*, "Take on the biker gangs," April 12, 2006.
44 *Globe and Mail*, "Harper trumpets get-tough crime plan," January 6, 2006.
45 For example, "The teenagers were gunned down just outside the Central Business District, in an area well known locally as a haven for drug-related activity" (*New York Times*, "Crime rising, New Orleans asks for National Guard," June 20, 2006); "This maze of townhouses and apartment blocks, originally built as social housing, is poorer than Kensington Market itself and has provided a haven for dealers" (*Globe and Mail*, "The new market high," January 13, 2007).
46 For example, "…a crime surge in Compton" (*Los Angeles Times*, "Homicides up 15% in sheriff's territory," January 12, 2006); "…residents have reported a surge of petty crime" (*Globe and Mail*, "The new market high," January 13, 2007); "Nassau experienced a surge of anti-Jewish graffiti over the past month" (*New York Times*, "Officials report rise in anti-Jewish crimes," October 7, 2007).
47 For example, "Many cities are struggling with a wave of violent crime" (*New York Times*, "Baltimore mayor unveils strategy to attack increase in gun crime," May 3, 2007); "In a city already tense over a wave of gang mayhem" (*Globe and Mail*, "Vancouver gangs cruising streets in armoured vehicles, police say," December 21, 2007).

Notes 163

48 For example, "The level of crimes tracked by the F.B.I. declined 3 percent from 2004" (*New York Times*, "New York: state crime rates continued to fall in 2005," September 18, 2006); "The number of homicides reached its highest level in almost a decade" (*Globe and Mail*, "Homicide hits highest rate since 1996," July 21, 2006).
49 *Los Angeles Times*, "Police, FBI, target Valley gang crimes," November 22, 2006.
50 For example, "property crime ... has declined marginally but continues to be an epidemic" (*Globe and Mail*, "Police will step up recruitment to combat rampant property crime," August 25, 2007); "Homicide numbers continued to rise into the early 1990s, as the crack cocaine epidemic grew and gangs became active across the city" (*Los Angeles Times*, "Killings decline sharply in L.A.," December 24, 2007).
51 For example, "Serious offenses and gangs still plague two of city's toughest areas" (*Los Angeles Times*, "Crime is easing its grip on L.A.," January 3, 2006).
52 For example, "gang-infested cities" (*Los Angeles Times*, "Congress focuses on local crime fighting," June 6, 2007).
53 Commentators who were unworried about literary purity would also mix metaphors. Thus, at one point in his declaration, Stephen Harper claimed that "the current government bears significant responsibility for the *tide* of gun, drug and gang crime *plaguing* our cities" (*Globe and Mail*, "Harper trumpets get-tough crime plan," January 6, 2006; emphasis added).
54 *New York Times*, "100,000 gone since 2001," August 14, 2007.
55 *Los Angeles Times*, "Alarm on gangs sounded," January 13, 2007.
56 *Globe and Mail*, "This wasn't the start, nor will it be the end, expert says," August 10, 2007.
57 *Los Angeles Times*, "Violent crime rises in some big cities," June 13, 2006.
58 *New York Times*, "Crime drops in Newark, but murders keep on rising," April 2, 2007.
59 *Los Angeles Times*, "Crime is easing its grip on L.A.," January 3, 2006.
60 *Los Angeles Times*, "The Nation; Congress focuses on local crime fighting," June 6, 2007.
61 *Globe and Mail*, "Province's crime rate fell in 2005, study shows," July 21, 2006.
62 *Los Angeles Times*, "A prison of our own making," December 10, 2006.
63 *New York Times*, "Violent crime rose in '05, with murders up by 4.8%," June 13, 2006.
64 *Los Angeles Times*, "Bratton's 'broken windows,'" April 20, 2006.
65 *New York Times*, "Little changes, big results," April 8, 2007.
66 *Los Angeles Times*, "FBI reports rise in violent crime," December 19, 2006.
67 *New York Times*, "Open doors don't invite criminals," March 11, 2006.
68 *Globe and Mail*, "Assault rate triples for Northerners, Justice study finds," October 31, 2006.
69 *Los Angeles Times*, "Bratton says there's more work to do," April 30, 2007.
70 *New York Times*, "Counting heads along the thin blue line," March 26, 2006.
71 *New York Times*, "Violent crime rising sharply in some cities," February 12, 2006.
72 *Globe and Mail*, "Reaching out is the only way to quell gun violence, youth worker says," January 7, 2006.
73 *Globe and Mail*, "Will 2007 be a record year for murders?" December 3, 2007.
74 *Globe and Mail*, "Our streets are safe: the numbers tell the real story," April 7, 2006.
75 *Los Angeles Times*, "New Orleans' violent tempest," July 31, 2007.
76 *New York Times*, "Jena, O.J. and the jailing of black America," September 30, 2007.
77 *New York Times*, "Killings surge in Oakland and officials are unable to explain why," June 22, 2007.
78 *Globe and Mail*, "So, how are the kids?" February 22, 2007.
79 *El Nacional*, "Médicos temen ser interceptados en los pasillos de los hospitales," May 19, 2007.
80 *El Nacional*, "Videos e impunidad," October 10, 2007.

164 Notes

81 *El Universal*, "DF, capital de la inseguridad," October 27, 2006.
82 *El Nacional*, "La delincuencia se traslada en vehículos robados," December 16, 2007.
83 *La Nación*, "Inseguridad: nuevos retrocesos," July 16, 2006.
84 *El Universal*, "Ciudadanía del miedo," January 28, 2006.
85 *El Nacional*, "Zulianos están preocupados por la inseguridad," March 26, 2006.
86 *El Universal*, "Aumentan secuestros en Tijuana, alerta IP," July 8, 2006.
87 *La Nación*, "Inseguridad: hay funcionarios que parecen de otro país," July 9, 2006.
88 *La Nación*, "El mensaje de la marcha," September 2, 2006.
89 *El Nacional*, "Delincuencia y violencia a granel," March 13, 2007.
90 *El Universal*, "Tips de protección para altos ejectuvos," March 1, 2006.
91 *La Nación*, "Vecinos en defensa propia," October 3, 2006.
92 *El Nacional*, "Delincuencia y violencia a granel," March 13, 2007.
93 "How long will it take to deal with the crisis in public safety?" (*La Nación*, "Un plan para combatir las drogas y la inseguridad," October 15, 2007).
94 *El Universal*, "Año de violencia," December 12, 2007.
95 *El Nacional*, "Territorios de inseguridad," May 13, 2007.
96 *La Nación*, "La criminalidad, el mal mayor," June 13, 2006.
97 *El Nacional*, "85% rechaza labor del gobierno frente a la inseguridad," April 24, 2006.
98 *El Universal*, "Ocasionará narco más inseguridad: encuesta," June 25, 2007.
99 *La Nación*, "Inseguridad en el Área Metropolitana: encuesta de convergencia ciudadana," June 13, 2006.
100 *El Nacional*, "Cambian hábitos nocturnos para eludir la delincuencia," May 16, 2007.
101 *El Universal*, "México supera a Estados Unidos en homicidio," February 7, 2006.
102 *La Nación*, "Editorial I: inquietante sensación de inseguridad," June 15, 2006.
103 *El Nacional*, "Violencia y resilencia. Transporte público," June, 24, 2007.
104 *El Nacional*, "En Miranda hay 60.000 delincuentes," October 30, 2006.
105 *El Universal*, "En 2006, 6 ejecutados por día en promedio," November 28, 2006.
106 *El Universal*, "Hubo 2 crímenes violentos cada día en este sexenio," December 25, 2006.
107 *La Nación*, "La inseguridad bonaerense," October 14, 2007.
108 *La Nación*, "Editorial II: vandalismo e inseguridad," October 1, 2007.
109 *El Universal*, "Radiografía de la impunidad," January 15, 2006.
110 *El Universal*, "Creen que aumentará inseguridad," December 13, 2007.
111 *El Universal*, "Ejecuciones, un parte de guerra," December 1, 2006.
112 *El Nacional*, "Zulianos están preocupados por la inseguridad," March 26, 2006.
113 *La Nación*, "Editorial II: countries, blanco de la delincuencia," September 29, 2007.
114 *El Universal*, "Operativo en Sinaloa, sólo para abatir cultivos, critican," March 21, 2007.
115 *La Nación*, "La crisis de la seguridad: estudio de nueva mayoría," August 26, 2006.
116 *El Nacional*, "Comerciantes piden medidas contra el secuestro," July 28, 2007.
117 *El Nacional*, "Carreño niega aumento de cifras de delitos," May 15, 2007.
118 *El Universal*, "Delitos bajaron 23% en seis años, según balance oficial," November 30, 2006.
119 *La Nación*, "Editorial I—delito y 'sensación de inseguridad,' " April 21, 2007.
120 For example, the Venezuelan Minister of Justice criticized the media for "making it look as if insecurity has increased in the country: 'This current of opinion has the hidden intention of attacking the stability of the Venezuelan State, institutions and peace' " (*El Nacional*, "Carreño niega aumento de cifras de delitos," May 15, 2007).
121 For example, a Mexican researcher accused the government of "boasting about doctored numbers" that purported to show a decrease in crime (*El Universal*, "Delitos bajaron 23% en seis años, según balance oficial," November 30, 2006).

Notes 165

122 *El Universal*, "Perseguiremos a policías corruptos; devolveremos la confianza," December 8, 2007.
123 *El Universal*, "Entre narcos y policías," May 22, 2007.
124 *El Universal*, "Coordinación, clave anticrimen: Hank," June 4, 2007.
125 *El Universal*, "Estamos en guerra contra el narco: González Parás," April 18, 2007.
126 *El Universal*, "Alerta ante el narcotráfico," November 12, 2007.
127 *El Nacional*, "Delincuencia uniformada," April 4, 2006.
128 *La Nación*, "Editorial I: reconstruir la seguridad," September, 24, 2006.
129 *La Nación*, "Inseguridad en el Área Metropolitana: encuesta de Convergencia Ciudadana," June 13, 2006.
130 *La Nación*, "Editorial I: reconstruir la seguridad," September 24, 2006.
131 For example, "...conflict and violence are inherent to human beings, the difference is that currently they are overflowing" (*El Universal*, "Conflictos personales y de pareja motivan ejecuciones," June 8, 2006); "Criminality has overflowed because of the lack of continuity in public policies for citizen safety...." (*El Nacional*, "Liquidar la inseguridad," December 23, 2007).
132 *La Nación*, "La creciente violencia social," June 29, 2006.
133 *El Nacional*, "La prevención del delito," May 23, 2006.
134 *El Nacional*, "Entre el bien y el mal," May 23, 2007. Other examples: "'Nobody is safe from the crime wave...'" (*La Nación*, "Ni mano dura ni garantismo ingenuo," October 6, 2007); "...[I]t is likely that the wave of narcoviolence and insecurity that lashes the country ... will increase in this decade" (*El Universal*, "Guerra al crimen organizado," December 21, 2006).
135 *La Nación*, "Una epidemia de inseguridad," November 7, 2006; *El Universal*, "Encrucijada de la inseguridad," November 17, 2006.
136 For example, *La Nación*, "Cifras de delincuencia," June 3, 2007; *El Universal*, "Actuarán contra quien se coluda con la delincuencia," April 22, 2007.
137 *La Nación*, "Vandalismo e inseguridad," October 1, 2007.
138 "...the phenomenon of drug trafficking is a cancer that advances and contaminates all that it touches..." (*El Universal*, "Seguridad pública y la paz, un buen recuerdo," December 15, 2006).
139 For example, "...the monster of insecurity" (*La Nación*, "El combate contra la inseguridad," August 27, 2007); "One cannot begin to think about doing away with that monster of a thousand heads, without a prior commitment from the three levels of government..." (*El Universal*, "Redefinir la estrategia," May 26, 2007).
140 For example, "...the wave of assassinations and violence that have unleashed themselves..." (*El Universal*, "Anuncian en Aguas Calientes acciones contra la inseguridad," October 16, 2007); "I agree with the [transport] strike because crime is off the leash..." (*El Nacional*, "Más de 2.000 choferes paralizaron a Ciudad Guayana," May 23, 2006).
141 *El Universal*, "Demagogia e inseguridad," June 14, 2006.
142 For example, *La Nación*, "El Crimen de Aragone, en San Isidro," December 27, 2006.
143 *El Nacional*, "La delincuencia continúa reinando en San Bernardino," October 28, 2007; *El Universal*, "Imperan en Pantitlán desorden y delitos," October 4, 2007.
144 For example, "...a woman ... protects her bag so as not to fall prey to crime" (*El Universal*, "Imperan en Pantitlán desorden y delitos," October 4, 2007); "Alcoholism advances uncontrollably and makes prey of our young men and our adolescent women" (*El Universal*, "Alcoholismo juvenil," July 14, 2006).
145 *La Nación*, "Delincuencia en moto," May 4, 2007.
146 *El Nacional*, "La violencia también asiste a clases," May 13, 2007.
147 *El Universal*, "El narco busca consolidar mercado interno," May 1, 2006.
148 *El Universal*, "Alarma inseguridad en frontera norte," September 23, 2006.
149 *El Universal*, "AMLO: ¿más militares?" February 4, 2006.

150 *El Universal*, "'Picaderos,' plaga mortal en Mexicali," April 1, 2006.
151 *La Nación*, "Seguridad: hechos y no promesas," November 28, 2006.
152 *La Nación*, "Un plan para combatir las drogas y la inseguridad," October 15, 2007.
153 For example, *El Nacional*, "Incrementa la violencia infantil," September 24, 2006; *El Nacional*, "La prevención del delito," May 23, 2006.
154 For example, *El Universal*, "Hasta dónde tolerar el crimen," October 22, 2007; *La Nación*, "Editorial I: la inseguridad y el código penal," June 25, 2006.
155 *El Nacional*, "44 muertes violentas se registraron en Alto Apure en el primer semestre del año," June 22, 2006.
156 *La Nación*, "Primer reportaje radial, Al Filo de la Veda," October 24, 2007.
157 *El Universal*, "Atizapán arranca plan para detectar vehículos robados," July 18, 2007.
158 *El Nacional*, "En Sucre, homicidios aumentaron 11%," December 31, 2007.
159 For example, *El Universal*, "Delincuencia más joven y violenta," October 6, 2007; *La Nación*, "Delitos en la capital: decisión del jefe de gobierno," June 25, 2006.
160 *El Nacional*, "Liquidar la inseguridad," December 23, 2007.
161 *El Nacional*, "La prevención del delito," May 23, 2006.
162 *El Nacional*, "Nos hemos llenado de policías," October 21, 2006.
163 *El Universal*, "Guerra al crimen organizado," December 21, 2006.
164 *El Universal*, "Tepito, zona insegura pese a operativos, acusan vecinos," July 26, 2007.
165 For example, *La Nación*, "Un reclamo popular sin respuesta," September 4, 2006.
166 *La Nación*, "La inseguridad bonaerense," October 14, 2007.
167 *El Nacional*, "Inseguridad (II)," May 12, 2006.
168 *El Universal*, "Llama IP a combatir la pobreza y criminalidad," November 6, 2006.
169 *El Universal*, "La inseguridad pública," December 25, 2006.
170 *La Nación*, "Una epidemia de inseguridad," November 7, 2006.
171 *El Universal*, "Abusos y drogadicción agravan la situación de las niñas infractoras," March 5, 2006.
172 *La Nación*, "El combate contra la inseguridad," August 27, 2007.
173 *El Universal*, "Delincuencia más joven y violenta," October 6, 2007.
174 *El Nacional*, "Incrementa la violencia juvenil," September 24, 2006.
175 *El Universal*, "Roban 70 vehículos al día en la Ciudad de México," March 12, 2007.
176 *La Nación*, "Editorial II: vandalismo e inseguridad," October 1, 2007.
177 *El Universal*, "Vecinos trabajando," January 22, 2006.
178 *La Nación*, "En la ciudad de Buenos Aires los hábitos cambiaron por la inseguridad," July 30, 2006.
179 *Globe and Mail*, "Canada's crime rate hits lowest level in 25 years," July 19, 2007.
180 *Globe and Mail*, "Province's crime rate fell in 2005, study shows," July 21, 2006.
181 *El Nacional*, "En Miranda hay 60.000 delincuentes," October 30, 2006.
182 *El Universal*, "La inseguridad pública," December 25, 2006.
183 *Los Angeles Times*, "In defense of guns," April 20, 2007.
184 *New York Times*, "After prison, more debt," February 26, 2006.
185 *La Nación*, "Una epidemia de inseguridad," November 7, 2006.
186 *El Universal*, "El narco busca consolidar mercado interno," May 1, 2006.
187 *The Globe and Mail*, "Province's crime rate fell in 2005, study shows," July 21, 2006.
188 Marvell, T. and C. Moody, "Specification problems, police levels and crime rates," *Criminology*, vol. 34, no. 4, 1996, p. 609.
189 Kleck, G. and J.C. Barnes, "Do more police lead to more crime deterrence?" *Crime and Delinquency*, October 18, 2010 (doi: 10.1177/0011128710382263).
190 See also, Lim, H., H. Lee, and S.J. Cuvelier, "The impact of police levels on crime rates: a systematic analysis of methods and statistics in existing studies," *Asian Pacific Journal of Police and Criminal Justice*, vol. 8, no. 1, 2010, pp. 49–82.
191 *New York Times*, "After prison, more debt," February 26, 2006.

192 *La Nación*, "Una epidemia de inseguridad," November 7, 2006.
193 Patterson, E.B. "Poverty, income inequality and community crime rates," *Criminology*, vol. 29, no. 4, 1991, p. 755.
194 Brush, J. "Does income inequality lead to more crime? A comparison of cross-sectional and time-series analyses of United States counties," *Economics Letters*, vol. 96, 2007, p. 264.
195 See also, Pridemore, W. "Poverty matters: a reassessment of the inequality-homicide relationship in cross-national studies," *British Journal of Criminology*, vol. 51, no. 5, 2011, pp. 739–772.
196 *El Nacional*, "En Miranda hay 60.000 delincuentes," October 30, 2006.
197 For a discussion of different types of uncertainty in scientific knowledge, see MacGill, S.M. and Y.L. Siu, "The nature of risk," *Journal of Risk Research*, vol. 7, no. 3, 2004, pp. 315–352.
198 Quarantelli, E.L. "The different worlds of science and mass communication: implications for information flow from the former to the latter," in Nemec, J., J. Nigg and F. Siccardi (eds.), *Prediction and Perception of Natural Hazards*, Dordrecht, NL: Kluwer Academic Publishers, 1993.
199 Titus, J.J. "Boy trouble: rhetorical framing of boys' underachievement," *Discourse: Studies in the Cultural Politics of Education*, vol. 25, no. 2, 2004, p. 156.
200 Similarly, Loseke reported considerable differences between articles on wife abuse in professional and popular outlets ("'Violence' is 'violence'… or is it? The social construction of 'wife abuse' and public policy," in Best, J. (ed.), *Images of Issues*, New York: Aldine de Gruyter, 1989).
201 Lindblom, C.E. *Inquiry and Change*, New Haven, CT: Yale University Press, 1990, p. 11.
202 Researchers authored only 7 percent of the texts in the set of items compiled for this study, the largest group of authors obviously being journalists (83 percent). Likewise, researchers represented only 12 percent of the people cited (textually or through paraphrase) in items, the largest group being police spokespeople (22 percent).
203 As Desrosières expressed it: "It is logical for actors in daily life to reason *as if* things existed because first, in the historical, envisaged space of action, the process of prior construction causes them to exist and second, a different way of thinking would prohibit any form of action on the world" (*The Politics of Large Numbers: A History of Statistical Reasoning*, Cambridge, MA: Harvard University Press, 1998, p. 11; emphasis in the original).
204 *New York Times*, "Violent crime rose in '05, with murders up by 4.8%," June 13, 2006 (emphasis added).
205 *Los Angeles Times*, "FBI reports rise in violent crime," December 19, 2006 (emphasis added).
206 While disagreements between researchers attract much attention, many knowledge claims put forth within the scientific domain also go unchallenged. But they are rarely unsubstantiated.
207 In the North American papers, it was a convention that letters to the editor make explicit reference to an item that had been previously published. The same did not hold for Latin America, where letters usually conveyed complaints or concerns (see, for example, Liliana Cánaves' letter with which Chapter 2 opens). In total, there were 43 letters to the editor in the sample of texts compiled for this study, 26 of them in Anglo-America. The latter did not necessarily contain rebuttals, and rebuttals were not necessarily about matters of fact.
208 *Los Angeles Times*, "It's a crime how we misjudge the young," September 17, 2006.
209 "The moral side [of a problem] is that which enables the situation to be viewed as painful, ignoble, immoral. It … suggests a condemnable state of affairs…" (Gusfield, J. *The Culture of Public Problems*, Chicago, IL: University of Chicago Press, 1981, p. 9).

168 Notes

210 Burke, K. *On Symbols and Society*, Chicago, IL: University of Chicago Press, 1989, pp. 86–106.
211 Burke, K. *On Symbols and Society*, Chicago, IL: University of Chicago Press, 1989, p. 91.
212 The latter might have been a difficult task since metaphors, in some form or other, are recognized to be a regular feature of "scientific" discourse (Ortony, A. (ed.), *Metaphor and Thought*, Cambridge, UK: Cambridge University Press, 1993).
213 *Los Angeles Times*, "It's a crime how we misjudge the young," September 17, 2006.
214 *Globe and Mail*, "The rougher end of the Danforth," August 26, 2006.
215 *New York Times*, "Church battles to break gang cycle, with a flock for all," April 16, 2006.
216 Ritter, J. "Recovering hyperbole: re-imagining the limits of rhetoric for an age of excess," *Communication Dissertations*, paper 22, 2010, pp. 3–4.
217 *El Universal*, "Ciudadanía del miedo," 28 January 28, 2006.
218 *El Nacional*, "Delincuencia y violencia a granel," March 13, 2007.
219 *El Nacional*, "Delincuencia uniformada," April 4, 2006.
220 *El Universal*, "Víctimas y verdugos," March 22, 2006.
221 *La Nación*, "Maldita inseguridad," November 4, 2006.
222 *La Nación*, "El escenario de la violencia joven," May 23, 2006.
223 This approach is particularly evident in the work on moral panics (for example, Goode, E. and N. Ben-Yehuda, *Moral Panics: The Social Construction of Deviance*, New York: Wiley-Blackwell, 2009). For specific examples, see Boyd, S. "Media constructions of illegal drugs, users, and sellers: a closer look at *Traffic*," *International Journal of Drug Policy*, vol. 13, no. 5, 2002, pp. 397–407; Chesney-Lind, M. and M. Eliason, "From invisible to incorrigible: the demonization of marginalised women and girls," *Crime Media Culture*, vol. 2, no. 1, 2006, pp. 29–47.
224 Barak, G. "Newsmaking criminology: reflections on the media, intellectuals and crime," *Justice Quarterly*, vol. 5, no. 4, 1988, pp. 565–587; Barak, G. "Doing newsmaking criminology from within the academy," *Theoretical Criminology*, vol. 11, no. 2, 2007, pp. 191–207; Tewkesbury, R., A. Miller and M.T. DeMichele, "From the field: crime, media, and public opinion: criminologists' role as source of public information," *Journal of Crime and Justice*, vol. 29, no. 1, 2006, pp. 123–142.
225 The failure of researchers to see themselves as agents of social construction was pointed out by Woolgar, S. and D. Pawluch ("Ontological gerrymandering: the anatomy of social problems explanations," *Social Problems*, vol. 32, no. 3, 1985, pp. 214–227).
226 Admittedly, the field of social problems rhetoric is still at an incipient stage of development. See, for example, Best, J. "Rhetoric in claims-making: constructing the missing children problem," *Social Problems*, vol. 34, no. 2, 1987, pp. 101–121; Coltrane, S. and N. Hickman, "The rhetoric of rights and needs: moral discourse in the reform of child custody and child support laws," *Social Problems*, vol. 39, no. 4, 1992, pp. 400–420; DeYoung, M. "Speak of the devil: rhetoric in claims-making about the satanic ritual abuse problem," *Journal of Sociology and Social Welfare*, vol. 23, no. 2, 1996, pp. 55–74; Hopkins, N. and S. Reicher, "Social movement rhetoric and the social psychology of collective action: a case study of anti-abortion mobilization," *Human Relations*, vol. 50, no. 3, 1997, pp. 261–286; Ibarra, P.R. and J.I. Kitsuse, "Vernacular constituents of moral discourse: an interactionist proposal for the study of social problems," in Miller, G. and J. Holstein (eds.), *Constructionist Controversies: Issues in Social Problems Theory*, New York: Aldine de Gruyter, 1993.

5 Moral agency

1 This, and the next five quotes, all come from the following article: *New York Times*, "Baltimore mayor unveils strategy to attack increase in gun crime," May 3, 2007.
2 *La Nación*, "Medidas para vivir más seguros," November 30, 2006.
3 *El Universal*, "Concluye marcha contra la inseguridad," November 6, 2006.
4 *La Nación*, "Editorial I: seguridad: hechos y no promesas," November 28, 2006.
5 *Globe and Mail*, "Crime victims get advocate," March 17, 2007.
6 *La Nación*, "Delitos en la capital: decisión del jefe de gobierno, Jorge Telerman," June 25, 2006.
7 *Los Angeles Times*, "Democrats stake out turf in war on gangs," March 16, 2007.
8 *El Nacional*, "77% de los motorizados han sido asaltados," September 3, 2007.
9 *New York Times*, "Senate votes for expanded federal authority to prosecute hate crimes," September 28, 2007.
10 *La Nación*, "Editorial I: grave retroceso frente al delito," June 16, 006.
11 *New York Times*, "Getting away with murder," October 23, 2007.
12 El Universal, "Crimen organizado reta a las autoridades: de la Barreda," 28 November 2006.
13 *La Nación*, "La inseguridad es el principal problema para los porteños," August 12, 2006.
14 *Los Angeles Times*, "Newest police beat: patrolling the internet," November 18, 2007.
15 *El Universal*, "Mexicali, víctima de la inseguridad: alcalde Rosa María Méndez Fierros," April 14, 2006.
16 These sorts of statement have something in common with the "hypothetical imperatives" discussed by Kant (see Foot, P. "Morality as a system of hypothetical imperatives," *The Philosophical Review*, vol. 81, no. 3, 1972, pp. 305–316).
17 For example, "The integration of data from the police and that from public registries would be a huge step in the modernization of judicial systems ... and would prevent offenders moving to another city in order to avoid being sentenced as recidivists" (*La Nación*, "Tecnología para empresas. Herramientas tecnológicas que ayudan a reducir los crímenes," October 9, 2006); "[T]here is no way to extinguish this supply of guns" (*Los Angeles Times*, "In defense of guns," April 20, 2007).
18 See, for example, *New York Times*, "In ID theft, some victims see opportunity," November 16, 2007 (giving a brief overview of a new automated service to prevent credit fraud); *Globe and Mail*, "Looking to Europe for answers on crime," September 27, 2006 (indicating how safe zones would operate for the sex trade in Vancouver); *El Nacional*, "La inseguridad incrementa el blindaje de vehículos," September 3, 2007 (describing the levels of protection available for armored cars).
19 See, for example, *El Nacional*, "Al robarme el apartamento perdí la sensación de seguridad," May 17, 2007 (describing a "Safe Condominiums" program run by a municipality); *New York Times*, "Study lauds police effort," June 28, 2007 (reporting that the New York Police Department was "flooding" high-crime areas with new officers); *La Nación*, "Editorial II: la entrega voluntaria de armas," July 26, 2007 (governmental and non-governmental agencies in Argentina were encouraging citizens to hand in firearms).
20 See, for example, *El Universal*, "Acuerdan dar más recursos contra el narcomenudeo," January 31, 2006 (state governors in Mexico agreed to channel 20 percent of their security budgets to a national program to deal with small-scale drug sales); *Globe and Mail*, "Crackdown takes aim at guns, sentencing," May 5, 2006 (Canada's Minister of Public Security announced the investment of about $235 million over five years to build new federal prisons); *Los Angeles Times*, "Crime data will be shared," December 19, 2006 (a database for sharing information between police departments in Los Angeles County was to be expanded to neighboring counties).

170   *Notes*

21 The multifaceted and densely heterogeneous nature of these newspaper texts made coding a tool for focused retrieval rather than precise analysis (see Appendix). Thus, a single utterance could be simultaneously classified on more than one dimension of interest to the study. Nevertheless, the fact that twice as many segments of text were coded to a category referring to crime-oriented action (3,051) than segments coded to a category referring to crime (1,496) indicates something of the quantitative predominance of the former over the latter.
22 Similarly, Thompson, C.Y., R.L. Young, and R. Burns made the following comment on news items about gangs in a Dallas newspaper: "Talk about and responses to gang crime are clearly an important part of the gang story, perhaps a bigger part than actual gang activity" ("Representing gangs in the news: media constructions of criminal gangs," *Sociological Spectrum*, vol. 20, 2000, p. 425).
23 *El Universal*, "Víctimas y verdugos," March 22, 2006. See Chapter 3 for a full version of this text.
24 *El Universal*, "Inseguridad aniquilante," November 15, 2006.
25 "People, groups, and nations understand their progress through time in terms of stories, plots which have beginnings, middles, and ends, heroes and antiheroes, epiphanies and denouements, dramatic, comic, and tragic forms" (Alexander, J.C. and P. Smith, "The discourse of American civil society: a new proposal for cultural studies," *Theory and Society*, vol. 22, 1993, p. 156).
26 *Los Angeles Times*, "Keeping killers in check," December 29, 2007.
27 *El Universal*, "'Crear empleos inhibe la delincuencia': investigador," December 1, 2006 (emphasis added).
28 *Los Angeles Times*, "Crime victims' families rally in Riverside," April 27, 2007 (emphasis added).
29 *Globe and Mail*, "Our streets are safe: the numbers tell the real story," April 7, 2006.
30 *La Nación*, "Editorial I: inseguridad, un problema de todos," October 23, 2007.
31 *Globe and Mail*, "Police to focus on domestic violence," December 26, 2006.
32 *El Universal*, "Conjuntan ataque a delitos y adicciones," February 28, 2006.
33 *La Nación*, "Indignación por una seguidilla de homicidios y asaltos," August 4, 2007.
34 "There is an old saw in political science that difficult conditions become problems only when people come to see them as amenable to human action" (Stone, D.A. "Causal stories and the formation of policy agendas," *Political Science Quarterly*, vol. 104, no. 2, 1989, p. 281).
35 *El Nacional*, "Inseguridad (III)," May 26, 2006.
36 *La Nación*, "Editorial I: inseguridad: hay funcionarios que parecen de otro país," July 9, 2006.
37 *El Universal*, "Alto, ya, a la violencia," July 25, 2006.
38 *El Universal*, "Alcoholismo juvenil," July 14, 2006.
39 *La Nación*, "La creciente violencia social," June 29, 2006.
40 *La Nación*, "Cartas de lectores—inseguridad," June 30, 2006.
41 There were, however, a few instances of stirring phrases in the North. For example: "Girl violence needs to be taken seriously," wrote the *Globe and Mail* in an editorial (see, "Girls gone violent," October 15, 2007). "Whatever the number, we should work to solve this tragic problem [of wrongful convictions], not ignore it," wrote a professor of law to *New York Times* (see, "False-conviction study," January 27, 2006). Carnell Cooper's comment, cited at the beginning of this chapter, that "We can't just throw our hands up in the air and say we can't do anything about this problem," would be another example.
42 *El Universal*, "Caravanas de la muerte," June 23, 2006.
43 *El Nacional*, "Asamblea creó sala situacional para combatir la inseguridad," June 16, 2006.

44 *El Universal*, "Piden a Fox que asuma gravedad de inseguridad," February 2, 2006.
45 *El Universal*, "Pulso político," January 31, 2006.
46 *El Nacional*, "Zulianos están preocupados por la inseguridad," March 26, 2006.
47 *La Nación*, "Polémica en Mar de la Plata por 'zonas liberadas,'" August 11, 2007.
48 *New York Times*, "Reform the reforms," January 8, 2006.
49 *Los Angeles Times*, "D.C. cracks down during crime lull," July 22, 2006 (emphasis added).
50 *Globe and Mail*, "Cracking down on drugs sparks 'turf wars,'" November 22, 2007 (emphasis added).
51 *New York Times*, "Does it work? Campus security," January 8, 2006 (emphasis added).
52 *El Nacional*, "En una semana han robado 11 locales de Petare," January 26, 2006 (emphasis added).
53 *El Universal*, "Entre narcos y policías," May 22, 2007.
54 *La Nación*, "Datos que no sólo sirven a los políticos," June 14, 2006 (emphasis added).
55 *New York Times*, "Report urges requiring all convicted convicts to give DNA," March 21, 2006.
56 *Los Angeles Times*, "Sharpton leads call for federal investigation of hate crimes," November 17, 2011.
57 *Globe and Mail*, "Politicians urged to get tough on gun crime," January 17, 2006.
58 *El Nacional*, "Altos índice delictivos preocupan a los industriales," June 16, 2006.
59 *El Universal*, "Mejor combate a cyberdelitos, exigen," April 15, 2006.
60 *La Nación*, "Editorial I: inseguridad: nuevos retrocesos," July 16, 2006.
61 See, for example, "I want the district attorney to put more people in prison" (*Los Angeles Times*, "Homicides an issue in race for Atty. Gen.," March 8, 2006); "The Conservatives want criminals doing real time, rather than lounging around under house arrest" (*Globe and Mail*, "Tories are playing politics of justice," October 26, 2006); "It remains for the commitment [to internationally approved conventions] to turn into concrete actions, such as the passage of a law creating the crime of person trafficking, with corresponding sanctions of up to 20 years in prison" (*La Nación*, "Prostitución y esclavitud," June 19, 2006).
62 *El Nacional*, "Incrementa la violencia juvenil," September 24, 2006.
63 *El Universal*, "Evitan criminalidad más programas sociales," September 11, 2006.
64 *New York Times*, "The crime rate and birth control," April 15, 2007.
65 *Globe and Mail*, "Criminal errors," April 5, 2006.
66 *New York Times*, "A fallen judge rethinks crime and punishment," January 13, 2006.
67 *El Universal*, "Delincuencia más joven y violenta," October 6, 2007.
68 See, for example, Beckett, K. *Making Crime Pay: Law and Order in Contemporary American Politics*, New York: Oxford University Press, 1999; Garland, D. *The Culture of Control: Crime and Social Order in Contemporary Society*. Chicago, IL: University of Chicago Press, 2001.
69 *El Universal*, "¿Cerrar filas?" December 23, 2006.
70 *La Nación*, "Un reclamo popular sin respuesta," September 4, 2006.
71 *Globe and Mail*, "Day thinking locally on youth crime," June 9, 2007.
72 *Los Angeles Times*, "Will the strategy to battle gangs work?" February 11, 2007.
73 See *La Nación*, "Editorial I: la inseguridad y el Código Penal," June 25, 2006; "Seguridad: la calle o la academia," July 31, 2006; "'Ni mano dura ni garantismo ingenuo,'" October 6, 2007; "La seguridad, eje de la pelea bonaerense," October 14, 2007.
74 See, for example, *Globe and Mail*: "Dion losing law-and-order votes, leading liberal says," March 6, 2007; "In a countering move, Dion gets tough on crime," March 14, 2007; "With the crime rate falling, liberals decide to break out the cuffs," March 15, 2007.

75 *Los Angeles Times*, "Angelides backs GOP initiative to boost sex crime penalties," July 18, 2006.
76 *Globe and Mail*, "Looking to Europe for answers on crime," September 27, 2006.
77 For example, *Los Angeles Times*, "A city strains to arrest a deadly trend," November 6, 2006.
78 *New York Times*, "New York State draws nearer to collecting DNA in all crimes, big and small," May 4, 2006.
79 *El Universal*, "Critican construcción de más cárceles en la ciudad," November 27, 2006.
80 *La Nación*, "Datos que no sólo sirven a los políticos," June 14, 2006.
81 *Globe and Mail*, "Crime and punishment," January 7, 2006.
82 See, from the *New York Times,* "A place for sex offenders," January 22, 2006; "As Albany weighs confinement of sex offenders, some fear a threat to civil liberties," February 6, 2006; "Doing more than their time," May 21, 2006;" "Wrong turn on sex offenders," March 13, 2007; and from the *Los Angeles Times*, "The new American witch hunt," March 11, 2007.
83 *Los Angeles Times*, "Tracking bad policy," February 7, 2006. On this type of initiative, see also, The *New York Times*, "Iowa's residency rules drive sex offenders underground," March 15, 2006.
84 *Los Angeles Times*, "The new American witch hunt," March 11, 2007.
85 *New York Times*, "Doing more than their time," May 21, 2006.
86 *Los Angeles Times*, "Tracking bad policy," February 7, 2006.
87 *New York Times*, "A place for sex offenders," January 22, 2006.
88 *New York Times*, "As Albany weighs confinement of sex offenders, some fear a threat to civil liberties," February 6, 2006.
89 *New York Times*, "Doing more than their time," May 21, 2006.
90 *New York Times*, "Iowa's residency rules drive sex offenders underground," March 15, 2006.
91 *New York Times*, "As Albany weighs confinement of sex offenders, some fear a threat to civil liberties," February 6, 2006.
92 *New York Times*, "Iowa's residency rules drive sex offenders underground," March 15, 2006.
93 *New York Times*, "As Albany weighs confinement of sex offenders, some fear a threat to civil liberties," February 6, 2006.
94 *Los Angeles Times*, "The new American witch hunt," March 11, 2007.
95 *New York Times*, "Doing more than their time," May 21, 2006.
96 For example, "[Civil commitments] cost, on average, four times more per inmate than prison, but almost never make an offender fit to rejoin society" (*New York Times*, "Wrong turn on sex offenders," March 13, 2007); "A new state law barring those convicted of sex crimes involving children from living within 2,000 feet of a school or day care center has brought unintended and disturbing consequences. It has rendered some offenders homeless and left others sleeping in cars or in the cabs of their trucks" (*New York Times*, "As Albany weighs confinement of sex offenders, some fear a threat to civil liberties," February 6, 2006).
97 *New York Times*, "Doing more than their time," May 21, 2006 (emphasis added).
98 *Los Angeles Times*, "The new American witch hunt," March 11, 2007.
99 *New York Times*, "As Albany weighs confinement of sex offenders, some fear a threat to civil liberties," February 6, 2006.
100 *New York Times*, "Iowa's residency rules drive sex offenders underground," March 15, 2006.
101 *New York Times*, "Doing more than their time," May 21, 2006.
102 *Los Angeles Times*, "The new American witch hunt," March 11, 2007.
103 Discussion of the ethics of sex offender treatment was being conducted in specialist academic journals rather than in the mass media. See, for example, Glaser, B.

Notes 173

"Therapeutic jurisprudence: an ethical paradigm for therapists in sex offender treatment programs," *Western Criminology Review*, vol. 4, no. 2, 2003, pp. 143–154; Levenson, J. and D. D'Amora, "An ethical paradigm for sex offender treatment: response to Glaser," *Western Criminology Review*, vol. 6, no. 1, 2005, pp. 145–153; Ward, T. and A. Birgden, "Human rights and correctional clinical practice," *Aggression and Violent Behavior*, vol. 12, 2007, pp. 628–643.

104 The same conclusion applies to another important Anglo-American policy debate, on guns, that appears in the set of texts compiled for this study. See, for example: *Globe and Mail*, "Targeting gun offences presents legal quagmire," January 2, 2006; *Los Angeles Times*, "In defense of guns," April 20, 2007; *New York Times*, "Getting away with murder," October 23, 2007 (but see the *New York Times*, "Shoot first—no questions asked," August 14, 2006, for a short editorial column that pays more attention, albeit largely implicit, to principles).

105 *El Universal*, "¿Ejército vs. el narco?" May 17, 2007.
106 *El Universal*, "Redefinir la estrategia," May 26, 2007.
107 *El Universal*, "Enfrentar el narcotráfico," May 16, 2007.
108 *El Universal*, "La sensación efímera de seguridad," December 21, 2007.
109 *El Universal*, "¿Ejército vs. el narco?" May 17, 2007.
110 *El Universal*, "Ven con reservas anuncio de operativo en NL," January 9, 2007.
111 *El Universal*, "¿Ejército vs. el narco?" May 17, 2007.
112 *El Universal*, "Más inteligencia, menos fuerza militar," December 7, 2007.
113 *El Universal*, "Enfrentar el narcotráfico," May 16, 2007.
114 *El Universal*, "¿Ejército vs. el narco?" May 17, 2007.
115 *El Universal*, "Más inteligencia, menos fuerza militar," December 7, 2007.
116 *El Universal*, "Enfrentar el narcotráfico," May 16, 2007; *El Universal*, "¿Ejército vs. el narco?" May 17, 2007.
117 *El Universal*, "¿Ejército vs. el narco?" May 17, 2007.
118 *El Universal*, "Más inteligencia, menos fuerza militar," December 7, 2007.
119 *El Universal*, "Enfrentar el narcotráfico," May 16, 2007.
120 But see *El Universal*, "Medir en el DF peligrosidad," June 30, 2007, for a notable exception: "Measurements are necessary, important and valuable. We already know that what cannot be measured cannot be improved."
121 *El Universal*, "¿Ejército vs. el narco?" May 17, 2007.
122 *El Universal*, "Redefinir la estrategia," May 26, 2007.
123 *El Universal*, "Redefinir la estrategia," May 26, 2007.
124 *El Universal*, "Más inteligencia, menos fuerza militar," December 7, 2007.
125 *El Universal*, "Más inteligencia, menos fuerza militar," December 7, 2007. See also, *El Universal*, "Redefinir la estrategia," May 26, 2007; *El Universal*, "¿Ejército vs. el narco?" May 17, 2007.
126 *El Universal*, "Enfrentar el Narcotráfico," May 16, 2007.
127 Broadly similar characteristics could also be seen in a debate on civilian disarmament that took place in Argentina in 2006 and 2007. See, for example, *La Nación*, "El desarme, ¿apenas una ilusión?" August 23, 2006; *La Nación*, "Diputados aprobó el programa de desarme nacional," November 9, 2006; *La Nación*, "Darán hasta $450 a los que cedan sus armas," January 30, 2007; *La Nación*, "Editorial II: la entrega voluntaria de armas," July 26, 2007. (But see *La Nación*, "Un millón de armas para defenderse," June 5, 2007, for an article giving data from a survey of firearms possession.)
128 *New York Times*, "As Albany weighs confinement of sex offenders, some fear a threat to civil liberties," February 6, 2006.
129 *El Nacional*, "Incrementa la violencia infantil," September 24, 2006.
130 *Los Angeles Times*, "New Orleans gets anti-crime update," January 27, 2007.
131 *New York Times*, "Reform the reforms," January 8, 2006.
132 *La Nación*, "Editorial. La crisis del principio de autoridad," April 22, 2007.

174 Notes

133 See, again, *La Nación*, "Medidas para vivir más seguros," November 30, 2006.
134 *New York Times*, "Baltimore mayor unveils strategy to attack increase in gun crime," May 3, 2007.
135 Lindblom, C.E. *Inquiry and Change*, New Haven, CT: Yale University Press, 1990, p. 11.
136 *El Universal*, "Violencia e inversión," February 1, 2006.
137 *New York Times*, "Blacks mull call for 10,000 to curb violence," September 30, 2007.
138 *Los Angeles Times*, "Cutting dropout rates also fights crime, study says," December 26, 2007.
139 *Los Angeles Times*, "A city strains to arrest a deadly trend," November 6, 2006.
140 *El Universal*, "Cifras, ¿quién miente?" January 6, 2006.
141 *Globe and Mail*, "Crime and punishment," January 7, 2006.
142 *Globe and Mail*, "Sentencing by politics," January 13, 2006.
143 *New York Times*, "Texas weighs death penalty for rapes of children," May 20, 2007.
144 *Los Angeles Times*, "FBI joins policing effort in war on street gang crime," January 19, 2007.
145 *El Universal*, "Más inteligencia, menos fuerza militar," December 7, 2007.
146 *La Nación*, "Seguridad: la calle o la academia," July 31, 2006.
147 See, for example, in philosophy: Crisp, R. and M. Slote (eds.), *Virtue Ethics*, Oxford: Oxford University Press, 1997; business: Williams, O.F. and P.E. Murphy, "The ethics of virtue: a moral theory for marketing," *Journal of Macromarketing*, vol. 10, 1990, pp. 19–29; criminal justice: Banks, C. *Criminal Justice Ethics: Theory and Practice*, Thousand Oaks, CA: Sage, 2004; education: Carr, D. and J. Steutel (eds.), *Virtue Ethics and Moral Education*, London: Routledge, 1999; and medicine: Lawson, A.D. "What is medical ethics?" *Trends in Anaesthesia and Critical Care*, vol. 1, 2011, pp. 3–6; Saunders, B. "How to teach moral theories in applied ethics," *Journal of Medical Ethics*, vol. 36, 2010, pp. 635–638. Additional approaches are mentioned by some of these authors (Banks, Lawson), but they are either classical curiosities or eclectic combinations of the deontological, teleological, and aretaic perspectives. They serve, however, to underline the historically contingent character of moral theories.
148 See, for example, Reidenbach, R.E. and D.P. Robin, "Some initial steps toward improving the measurement of ethical evaluations of marketing activities," *Journal of Business Ethics*, vol. 7, no. 11, 1988, pp. 871–879; Sparks, J.R. and Y. Oan, "Ethical judgments in business ethics research: definition, and research agenda," *Journal of Business Ethics*, vol. 91, 2010, pp. 405–418.
149 For example, Nielsen, R.P. "Introduction to the special issue. In search of organizational virtue: moral agency in organizations," *Organization Studies*, vol. 27, no. 3, 2006, pp. 317–321; Williams, O.F. and P.E. Murphy, "The ethics of virtue: a moral theory for marketing," *Journal of Macromarketing*, vol. 10, 1990, pp. 19–29.
150 Gusfield, J. *The Culture of Public Problems*, Chicago, IL: University of Chicago Press, 1981; Gusfield, J. "Constructing the ownership of social problems: fun and profit in the welfare state," *Social Problems*, vol. 36, no. 5, 1989, pp. 431–441.
151 "There is a crucial distinction ... between the practice of science and the practice of engineering.... Engineering is not pure science. Engineers do not produce abstract knowledge; they produce artifacts" (Perelman, L.C. "The two rhetorics: design and interpretation in engineering and humanistic discourse," *Language and Learning across the Disciplines*, vol. 3, no. 2, 1999, p. 65).
152 Cobb, R.W. and J.F. Coughlin, "Are elderly drivers a road hazard?: problem definition and political impact," *Journal of Aging Studies*, vol. 12, no. 4, 1998, pp. 411–427.
153 Lounsbury, M., M. Ventresca and P.M. Hirsch, "Social movements, field frames and industry emergence: a cultural-political perspective on US recycling," *Socio-Economic Review*, vol. 1, 2003, pp. 71–104.

154 Rohlinger, D.A. "Framing the abortion debate: organizational resources, media strategies, and movement-countermovement dynamics," *The Sociological Quarterly*, vol. 43, no. 4, 2002, pp. 479–507.
155 Coltrane, S. and M. Adams, "The social construction of the divorce 'problem': morality, child victims and the politics of gender," *Family Relations*, vol. 52, no. 4, 2003, pp. 363–372.
156 On the challenges of establishing ideas as determinants of policy decisions, see Campbell, J.L. "Ideas, politics, and public policy," *Annual Review of Sociology*, vol. 28, 2002, pp. 21–38; Yee, A.S. "The causal effects of ideas on policies," *International Organization*, vol. 50, no. 1, 1996, pp. 69–108.
157 See Noy, D. "When framing fails: ideas, influence and resources in San Francisco's homeless policy field," *Social Problems*, vol. 56, no. 2, 2009, pp. 223–242.
158 See, for example, Best, J. *Random Violence: How We Talk about New Crimes and New Victims*, Berkeley, CA: University of California Press, 1999, p. 142; Loseke, D. "'Violence' is 'violence' ... or is it? The social construction of 'wife abuse' and public policy," in Best, J. (ed.), *Images of Issues*, New York: Aldine de Gruyter, 1989, p. 202); Noy, D. "When framing fails: ideas, influence and resources in San Francisco's homeless policy field," *Social Problems*, vol. 56, no. 2, 2009, p. 223.
159 See, for example, Cobb, R.W. and J.F. Coughlin, "Are elderly drivers a road hazard?: problem definition and political impact," *Journal of Aging Studies*, vol. 12, no. 4, 1998, pp. 411–427; McCright, A.M. and R.E. Dunlap, "Challenging global warming as a social problem: an analysis of the Conservative movement's counter-claims," *Social Problems*, vol. 47, no. 4, 2000, pp. 499–522.
160 See, for example, Harbison, J. "The changing career of 'elder abuse and neglect' as a social problem in Canada," *Journal of Elder Abuse and Neglect*, vol. 11, no. 4, 1999, pp. 59–80; Loseke, D. *Thinking about Social Problems*, New York: Transaction Books, second edition, 2003; Tuggle, J.L. and M.D. Holmes, "Blowing smoke: status politics and the Shasta County ban," *Deviant Behavior*, vol. 18, 1997, pp. 77–93.
161 For work on rhetorical and argumentative strategies in social problems discourse, see Chapter 4, note 226.

6 American melodramas

1 Thus, Singer, B. "For most of the two centuries in which melodrama has been identified as a dramatic category, it has been a target of critical ridicule and derision" (*Melodrama and Modernity*, New York: Columbia University Press, 2001, p. 2).
2 See, for example, Brooks, P. *The Melodramatic Imagination: Balzac, Henry James, Melodrama and the Mode of Excess*, New Haven, CT: Yale University Press, 1976; Smith, J.L. *Melodrama*, London: Methuen, 1973. On the widespread recourse to melodrama in Latin America, see, for example, Monsiváis, C. "Ciudadanía y violencia urbana: pesadillas al aire libre," in Rotker, S. (ed.), *Ciudadanías del Miedo*, Caracas: Editorial Nueva Sociedad, 2000; Segura, C. "Violencia y melodrama en la novela colombiana contemporánea," *América Latina Hoy*, vol. 47, 2007, pp. 55–76.
3 E. Hadley, identifies a "melodramatic mode," which is a much broader category than the theatrical productions that are typically associated with the notion of melodrama. Thus, in nineteenth century England: "Melodrama's ... narratives ... were represented in a wide variety of social settings, not just on the stage. Indeed, a version of the 'melodramatic' seems to have served as a behavioral and and expressive model for several generations of English people" (*Melodramatic Tactics: Theatricalized Dissent in the English Marketplace, 1800–1885*, Stanford, CA: Stanford University Press, 1995, p. 3). Similarly, J.L. Smith suggests that "we see most of the serious conflicts and crises of our everyday lives in melodramatic ... terms" (*Melodrama*, London: Methuen, 1973, p. 10). (See, also, Heilman, R.B. *Tragedy and Melodrama: Versions*

of Experience, Seattle, WA: University of Washington Press, 1968, p. 89.) On the presence of melodrama in recent televised news reporting, see Anker, E. "Villains, victims and heroes: melodrama, media and September 11," *Journal of Communication*, vol. 55, no. 1, 2005, pp. 22–37.
4 Heilman, R.B. *Tragedy and Melodrama: Versions of Experience*, Seattle, WA: University of Washington Press, 1968.
5 Smith, J.L. *Melodrama*, London: Methuen, 1973, p. 7.
6 Smith, J.L. *Melodrama*, London: Methuen, 1973, p. 8.
7 Smith, J.L. *Melodrama*, London: Methuen, 1973, p. 8.
8 "…melodrama is the realm of social action, public action, action within the world…" (Heilman, R.B. *Tragedy and Melodrama: Versions of Experience*, Seattle, WA: University of Washington Press, 1968, p. 97).
9 This view of melodrama is much broader than that of Best, who has written a critical examination of the "melodramatic vision" of crime in the United States (see Best, J. *Random Violence: How We Talk about New Crimes and New Victims*, Berkeley, CA: University of California Press, 1999, p. xii). Best's objects of attack are the exceptional examples of evil and the "distorted" images of crime that so frequently annoy researchers and which seem to get in the way of rational and informed policymaking. They are better considered as a particularly dramatic form of melodrama, perhaps akin to the more superficial melodramas on stage and screen, than as the totality of the melodramatic form (which often includes academic writing).
10 See *La Nación*, "Alarma en la ciudad," January 26, 2007: "…barbarism invades like dirty water."
11 See, for example: "…the core issue—isolated pockets of crime in our cities" (*Globe and Mail*, "Criminal errors," April 5, 2006); "…LAPD still has some work to do to improve some pockets such as downtown's skid row" (*Los Angeles Times*, "Bratton vows to reduce crime by 8%," January 6, 2006); "…people speak of a neighborhood of sharp contrasts, of welcome reductions in crime and stubborn pockets of violence, of affluence settling in amid despair" (*New York Times*, "A precinct of contrasts, where violence still lurks," July 10, 2007).
12 See, for example, Gómez-Cespedes, A. "The federal law enforcement agencies: an obstacle in the fight against organized crime in Mexico," *Journal of Contemporary Criminal Justice*, vol. 15, no. 4, 1999, p. 354; Davis, D.E. "The state of the state in Latin American sociology," in Wood, C.H. and B.R. Roberts (eds.), *Rethinking Development in Latin America*, University Park, PA: The Pennsylvania State University Press, 2005, p. 180; López Maya, M. "The Venezuelan *Caracazo* of 1989: popular protest and institutional weakness," *Journal of Latin American Studies*, vol. 35, 2003, pp. 117–137.
13 For example, Schulte-Bockholt, A. "Latin American critical criminology," in DeKeseredy, W.S. and M. Dragiewicz (eds.), *Routledge Handbook of Critical Criminology*, New York: Routledge, 2011, p. 72.
14 For example, Carballo, M. "Cultural Trends in Argentina: 1983–2000," in Pettersson, T. and Y. Esmer (eds.), *Changing Values, Persisting Cultures: Case Studies in Value Change*, Leiden, NL: Koninklijke Brill, 2008, p. 109.
15 For example, Davis, D.E. "The state of the state in Latin American sociology," in Wood, C.H. and B.R. Roberts (eds.), *Rethinking Development in Latin America*, University Park, PA: The Pennsylvania State University Press, 2005, p. 180; Morris, S.D. *Political Corruption in Mexico: The Impact of Democratization*, Boulder, CO: Lynne Rienner, 2009.
16 Manning, N. and D.L. Wetzel, "Tales of the unexpected: rebuilding trust in government," in Canuto, O. and M. Giugale (eds.), *The Day After Tomorrow: A Handbook on the Future of Economic Policy in the Developing World*, Washington, DC: The World Bank, 2010, p. 67.
17 For the definition of this term, see Abramson, P.R. and R. Inglehart, *Value Change in Global Perspective*, Ann Arbor, MI: University of Michigan Press, 1995.

18 Segovia Arancibia, C. *Political Trust in Latin America*, University of Michigan: Unpublished Ph.D. dissertation, 2008.
19 Hinton, M.S. *The State on the Streets: Police and Politics in Argentina and Brazil*, Boulder, CO: Lynne Rienner, 2006, p. 10.
20 For example, Birkbeck, C. and L.G. Gabaldón, "Venezuela: policing as an exercise in authority," in Hinton, M.S. and T. Newburn (eds.), *Policing Developing Democracies*, London: Routledge, 2009; Dammert, L. and M.F.T. Malone, "Inseguridad y temor en Argentina: el impacto de la confianza en la policía y la corrupción sobre la percepción ciudadana del crimen," *Desarrollo Económico*, vol. 42, no. 166, 2002, pp. 285–301; Goldstein, D.M., G. Achá, E. Hinojosa, and T. Roncken, "*La Mano Dura* and the violence of civil society in Bolivia," in Fischer, E.F. (ed.), *Indigenous Peoples, Civil Society and the Neo-Liberal State in Latin America*, Oxford: Berghahn Books, 2009; Moser, C. and C. McIlwaine, *Encounters with Violence in Latin America: Urban Poor Perceptions from Colombia and Guatemala*, New York: Routledge, 2004.
21 Cruz, J.M. "Violencia, democracia y cultura política," *Nueva Sociedad*, no. 167, 2000, p. 133.
22 Gaines, L.K. and V.E. Kappeler, *Policing in America*, Waltham, MA: Anderson Publishing, seventh edition, 2011, pp. 2–3.
23 Brown, B. and W.R. Benedict, "Perceptions of the police: past findings, methodological issues, conceptual issues and policy implications," *Policing: An International Journal of Police Strategies and Management*, vol. 25, no. 3, 2002, p. 546. One early study found that the "local" police ranked third highest in public approval ratings out of 15 "well-known" organizations in the US, outscoring, for example, the American Medical Association, Congress, the Supreme Court, the press and the ACLU (Peek, C.W., J.P. Alston, and G.D. Lowe, "Comparative evaluation of the local police," *Public Opinion Quarterly*, vol. 37, 1978, pp. 370–379).
24 The police appear as featured sources (quoted directly or indirectly) in 33.8 percent of the Anglo-American articles but in only 12.8 percent of the Latin American articles.
25 The Latin American police were also occasionally quoted on their own weaknesses (e.g., their inability to stop the community taking justice into its own hands [*El Universal*, "Enfrentan a ladrones con piedras y palos," October 8, 2007], or the fears of becoming targets for the violence from organized crime [*El Universal*, "Muchos no salen de noche por temor a morir," November 30, 2006]). No North American police spokesperson made any similar admission of weakness.
26 See, for example, Dalton, R.J. "The social transformation of trust in government," *International Review of Sociology*, vol. 15, no. 1, 2005, pp. 133–154.
27 *Los Angeles Times*, "It's a crime how we misjudge the young," September 17, 2006. In a subsequent article, he returned to the theme of unfounded empirical claims about the young: "News features, political commentaries and institutional reports incessantly berate the sexual excesses of modern teenagers ... [but] [e]vidence supporting the claims of rising teenage sexual violence is seldom offered," (*Los Angeles Times*, "The decline of rape," February 16, 2007).
28 *New York Times*, "Iowa's residency rules drive sex offenders underground," March 15, 2006.
29 *New York Times*, "Open doors don't invite criminals," March 11, 2006.
30 *Los Angeles Times*, "Bratton's broken windows," April 20, 2006.
31 *Globe and Mail*, "Read my lips: there is no crime epidemic in Canada," January 4, 2006.
32 *La Nación*, "Inseguridad: hay funcionarios que parecen de otro país," July 9, 2006.
33 *El Universal*, "Percepciones y realidades," April 23, 2007.
34 Marston, G, and R. Watts, "Tampering with the evidence: a critical appraisal of evidence-based policy-making," *The Drawing Board: An Australian Review of Public Affairs*, vol. 3, no. 3, 2003, p. 152.

35 Goetzmann, W.H. "Exploration and the culture of science: the long good-bye of the Twentieth Century," in Luedtke L.S. (ed.), *Making America: The Society and Culture of the United States*, Chapel Hill, NC: The University of North Carolina Press, 1992, p. 414.
36 See UNESCO (United Nations Educational, Scientific and Cultural Organization), *Science and Technology Statistics*, Paris, France: UNESCO, 2011. The specific figures are as follows. Researchers per million inhabitants (2007): Argentina, 983; Mexico, 347; Venezuela, 163; Canada, 4,335, United States, 4,637. Gross domestic expenditure on R&D as a percentage of gross domestic product (2005): Argentina, 0.46 percent; Mexico, 0.46 percent; Venezuela, 0.23 percent; Canada, 1.98 percent; United States, 2.62 percent.
37 Calhoun, C. "Social Sciences in North America," in *World Social Science Report 2010*, Paris, France: UNESCO/International Social Science Council, 2010, p. 55.
38 See, for example, Casas Guerrero, R. "Conocimiento, tecnología y desarrollo en América Latina," *Revista Mexicana de Sociología*, vol. 66, octubre, 2004, pp. 255–277; Cereijido, M. "En América Latina ya podemos investigar, el próximo paso es tratar de hacer ciencia," *Interciencia*, vol. 21, no. 2, 1996, pp. 64–70; Vessuri, H. "The social study of science in Latin America," *Social Studies of Science*, vol. 17, no. 3, 1987, pp. 519–554.
39 See, for example, Basáñez, M. and A. Moreno, "Value change in Mexico, 1998–2000: evidence from the World Values surveys," in Pettersson, T. and Y. Esmer (eds), *Changing Values, Persisting Cultures: Case Studies in Value Change*, Leiden, NL: Koninklijke Brill, 2008; Faria, V. "Social science and academic sociology in Brazil," in Wood, C.H. and B.R. Roberts (eds.), *Rethinking Development in Latin America*, University Park, PA: The Pennsylvania State University Press, 2005.
40 Haen-Marshall, I. "The criminological enterprise in Europe and the United States: A contextual exploration," *European Journal on Criminal Policy and Research*, vol. 9, no. 3, 2001, pp. 239–240.
41 Simon, J. "Positively punitive: how the inventor of scientific criminology who died at the beginning of the Twentieth Century continues to haunt American crime control at the beginning of the Twenty-First," *Texas Law Review*, vol. 84, 2005–2006, p. 2167.
42 See the contributions by Davis Rodrigues on Brazil, Heskia on Chile, Escobar on Colombia, and Arroyo Juárez and Martínez Solares on Mexico in Smith, C.J., S.X. Zhang and R. Barberet, (eds.), *Routledge Handbook of International Criminology*, London: Routledge, 2011.
43 See, again, Smith, C.J., S.X. Zhang and R. Barberet, (eds.), *Routledge Handbook of International Criminology*, London: Routledge. Similarly, while Morris found little scholarly research on corruption in the Mexico of the 1980s, "Today, by contrast, a host of Mexican government agencies and scores of Mexican scholars, journalists and political activists—in a manner similar to the international trends—focus intense attention and analysis on the matter, producing massive reports and detailed studies" (Morris, S.D. *Political Corruption in Mexico: The Impact of Democratization*, Boulder, CO: Lynne Rienner, p. 5).
44 Elbert, C. "Rebuilding utopia? Critical criminology and the difficult road of reconstruction," *Crime, Law and Social Change*, vol. 41, no. 4, p. 392.
45 There were no significant differences between Anglo-America and Latin America in the proportion of articles that offered any type of description (33 percent) (including numbers [33 percent]) or explanation for crime (25 percent). Descriptions of measures taken to deal with crime were somewhat more likely to appear in Anglo-America (55 percent of articles) than in Latin America (45 percent). While the status of some sources was hard to determine (e.g., whether they were researchers, professionals, politicians or members of NGOs) a tentative classification revealed that researchers were more frequently used as sources in the Anglo-American press, but not greatly so (featuring in 16.7 percent of items, compared to 10.5 percent in Latin America). And

self-identified "academic" contributors were equally represented (23 percent) as authors of opinion items in each region.

46 Pak, C.S. and R. Acevedo, "Spanish-language newspaper editorials from Mexico, Spain and the U.S.," in Connor, U., E. Nagelhout and W.V. Roziycki (eds.), *Contrastive Rhetoric: Reaching to Intercultural Rhetoric*, Philadelphia, PA: John Benjamins Publishing Company, 2008. Pak and Acevedo also noted that editorials in the *New York Times* were almost always argumentative, while many in the Spanish language newspapers were explanatory and informative. This difference in function reinforces the recourse to evidence in the former and the use of facts and information in the latter.
47 *Globe and Mail*, "So, how are the kids?" February 22, 2007. The report itself can be accessed at www.vanierinstitute.ca/publications.
48 Ambert, A.M. *The Rise in the Number of Children and Adolescents Who Exhibit Problematic Behaviors: Multiple Causes*, Ottawa: The Vanier Institute of the Family, 2007, p. 24.
49 Lovett, B. "A defence of prudential moralism," *Journal of Applied Philosophy*, vol. 22, no. 2, 2005, p. 162.
50 Coady, C.A.J. "Preface," *Journal of Applied Philosophy*, vol. 22, no. 2, 2005, p. 101 (emphasis added).
51 Wolfe, A. "Civil religion revisited: quiet faith in middle class America," in Rosenblum, N.L. (ed.), *Obligations of Citizenship: Religious Accommodation in Pluralist Democracies*, Princeton, NJ: Princeton University Press, 2000, pp. 32–72.
52 Lovett, B. "A defence of prudential moralism," *Journal of Applied Philosophy*, vol. 22, no. 2, 2005, p. 161.
53 Driver, J. "Hyperactive ethics," *The Philosophical Quarterly*, vol. 44, no. 174, 1994, p. 23. Consistent with this critique, Driver places heavy and positive emphasis on the notion of "moral restraint."
54 Janoff-Bulman, R. and S. Sheikh, "From national trauma to moralizing nation," *Basic and Applied Social Psychology*, vol. 28, no. 4, 2006, p. 327.
55 Baier, K. *The Moral Point of View*, New York, NY: Random House, 1965, p. 3.
56 Himmelfarb, G. "A de-moralized society: the British/American experience," *The Public Interest*, Fall 94, no. 117, 1994, p. 68.
57 Collini, S. *Public Moralists: Political Thought and Intellectual Life in Britain, 1850–1930*, Oxford: Clarendon Press, 1993, pp. 132–133.
58 The term "Mugwump" is a corruption of the Native American (Algonquian) word *mugquomp*, meaning "great man," or "boss." It was used, most notably, to describe a group of Republican activists who left the party during the 1880s in moral protest over corruption (see Tucker, D.M. *Mugwumps: Public Moralists of the Gilded Age*, Columbia, MO: University of Missouri Press, 1998). The inelegant sound of the anglicized term seems clearly designed to signal implicit ridicule of the moral status that these party activists sought to claim.
59 Ridge, M. "The populist as a social critic," *Minnesota History*, vol. 43, no. 8, 1973, pp. 297–302.
60 Barry, B. "Social criticism and political philosophy," *Philosophy and Public Affairs*, vol. 19, no. 4, 1990, p. 361.
61 Martín Alcoff, L. "Does the public intellectual have intellectual integrity?" *Metaphilosophy*, vol. 33, no. 5, 2002, p. 525.
62 P.G. Earle described the decline of the essay as a "displacement," in which "its function as intellectual discourse and intuitive revelation has been absorbed, and weakened more often than strengthened, by fiction, criticism, and journalism" ("On the contemporary displacement of the Hispanic American essay," *Hispanic Review*, vol. 46, no. 3, 1978, p. 331).
63 Earle, P.G. "On the contemporary displacement of the Hispanic American essay," *Hispanic Review*, vol. 46, no. 3, 1978, p. 332.

64 See, for example, Kirklighter, C. *Traversing the Democratic Borders of the Essay*, Albany, NY: State University of New York Press, 2002; Stabb, M.S. "The new essay of Mexico," *Hispania*, vol. 70, no. 1, 1987, pp. 47–61.
65 Skirius, J. *El Ensayo Hispanoamericano del Siglo XX*, México, DF: Fondo de Cultura Económica, 2004, p. 30. See also Juan Loveluck's inventory of typical essay topics in Latin America: "ideological combat, moral denunciation, testimony in adversity, nordofilia and nordofobia, self-circumstantial definitions of culture, etc." (Earle, P.G. "On the contemporary displacement of the Hispanic American essay," *Hispanic Review*, vol. 46, no. 3, 1978, p. 333).
66 But it is not the public moralist of Victorian England, who was impregnated with altruism (Collini, S. *Public Moralists: Political Thought and Intellectual Life in Britain, 1850–1930*, Oxford: Clarendon Press, 1993). As Chapter 2 shows, although moral commentary on crime in Latin America was not an expression of naked self-interest, it more strongly reflected a concern for "ourselves" than it did a concern for others.
67 Skirius, J. *El Ensayo Hispanoamericano del Siglo XX*, México, DF: Fondo de Cultura Económica, 2004, p. 12.
68 Earle, P.G. "On the contemporary displacement of the Hispanic American essay," *Hispanic Review*, vol. 46, no. 3, 1978, pp. 329–341; Skirius, J. *El Ensayo Hispanoamericano del Siglo XX*, México, DF: Fondo de Cultura Económica, 2004; Stabb, M.S. "The new essay of Mexico," *Hispania*, vol. 70, no. 1, 1987, pp. 47–61.
69 Montaño-Harmon, M.R. "Discourse features of written Mexican Spanish: current research in contrastive rhetoric and its implications," *Hispania*, vol. 74, no. 2, 1991, p. 419.
70 Montaño-Harmon, M.R. "Discourse features of written Mexican Spanish: current research in contrastive rhetoric and its implications," *Hispania*, vol. 74, no. 2, 1991, p. 418; also, Dealy, G.C. *The Latin Americans: Spirit and Ethos*, Boulder, CO: Westview Press, 1992, p. 123.
71 Leonard, I.A. "Science, technology and Hispanic America," in Wiarda, H.J. and M.M. Mott (eds.), *Politics and Social Change in Latin America: Still a Distinct Tradition?*, Westport, CT: Praeger, 2003, p. 84.
72 Ortega y Gasset, J. *Meditaciones del Quijote*, Madrid: Publicaciones de la Residencia de Estudiantes, Serie II, Volumen I, 1914, p. 32.
73 Earle, P.G. "On the contemporary displacement of the Hispanic American essay," *Hispanic Review*, vol. 46, no. 3, 1978, pp. 329–341; Skirius, J. *El Ensayo Hispanoamericano del Siglo XX*, México, DF: Fondo de Cultura Económica, 2004; Stabb, M.S. "The new essay of Mexico," *Hispania*, vol. 70, no. 1, 1987, pp. 47–61.
74 Ortega y Gasset, J. *Meditaciones del Quijote*, Madrid: Publicaciones de la Residencia de Estudiantes, Serie II, Volumen I, 1914, p. 32.
75 T.L. Glasser and J.S. Ettema, borrowing a phrase from Hallin (1985), spoke of the "scientization of journalism." They argued that there was a tension in US journalism between moral custodianship and moral disengagement: "the journalism of righteous indignation has been made credible (indeed, it has been made intellectually possible in an age of science) by its 'appearance of disinterest and rigor'" (See "Investigative journalism and the moral order," *Critical Studies in Mass Communication*, vol. 6, 1989, p. 5).
76 See, for example, Collins, H. and R. Evans, *Rethinking Expertise*, Chicago, IL: University of Chicago Press, 2007; Ericsson, K.A., N. Charness, R.R. Hoffman, and P.J. Feltovich, (eds.), *The Cambridge Handbook of Expertise and Expert Performance*, New York: Cambridge University Press, 2006; Williams, R., W. Faulkner and J. Fleck (eds.), *Exploring Expertise: Issues and Perspectives*, London: Macmillan, 1998.
77 See Welch, M., M. Fenwick and M. Roberts, "State managers, intellectuals, and the media: a content analysis of ideology in experts' quotes in feature newspaper articles on crime," *Justice Quarterly*, vol. 15, no. 2, 1998, pp. 219–241.

78 Obviously, experts were not the only sources used in either region. As shown by examples used in previous chapters, lay commentators (neighborhood residents, victims or potential victims, members of the public, etc.) were also used as sources for some texts. And in both regions, politicians mainly played the role of ideological leaders rather than experts. (For an early discussion of the difference between leaders and experts, see Znaniecki, F. *The Social Role of the Man of Knowledge*, New York: Harper Torchbooks, 1968.)

79 In an extensive review of historical trends in media systems in Europe and North America, D.C. Hallin and P. Mancini noted that "by the beginning of the twenty-first century, the differences [in media systems] have eroded to the point that it is reasonable to ask whether a single, global media model is displacing the national variation of the past, at least among the advanced capitalist democracies..." (*Comparing Media Systems: Three Models of Media and Politics*, Cambridge: Cambridge University Press, 2004, p. 251). Perhaps the same process of homogenization is also present in the Americas. For a comparison of trends in journalistic production and consumption in Latin America and Western Europe, see Boczkowski, P.J., E. Mitchelstein, and M. Walgter, "Convergence across divergence: understanding the gap in the online choices of journalists and consumers in Western Europe and Latin America," *Communication Research*, vol. 38, no. 3, 2011, pp. 376–396.

80 For a recent overview of this literature, see Blind, P.K. *Building Trust in Government in the Twenty First Century: Review of Literature and Emerging Issues*. Paper presented at the Seventh Global Forum on Reinventing Government: Building Trust in Government, Vienna, June 26–29, 2007.

81 For studies on crime rates in Latin America, see, for example, Buvinic, M., A. Morrison and M. Shifter, *Violence in Latin America and the Caribbean: A Framework for Action*, Washington: Inter-American Development Bank, 1999; Heinemann, A. and D. Verner, *Crime and Violence in Development: A Literature Review of Latin America and the Caribbean*, Washington: World Bank, 2006.

82 The use of scientific research as a rhetorical resource in North America has, of course, been examined by several scholars interested in the social construction of social problems (see references cited in Chapters 2 and 3). But in the few studies that adopt a comparative, cross-cultural, perspective on social problems, rhetoric (and, in particular, the role of scientific research in rhetorical strategies) has not been a focus of attention (see, for example, Ben-Yehuda, N. *The Politics of Morality and Deviance: Moral Panics, Drug Abuse, Deviant Science, and Reversed Stigmatization*, Albany, NY: State University of New York Press, 1990; Best, J. (ed.), *How Claims Spread: Cross-National Diffusion of Social Problems*, New York: Aldine de Gruyter, 2001).

7 The artifacts of talk

1 See, for example, Esser, F. "'Tabloidization' of news: a comparative analysis of Anglo-American and German press journalism," *European Journal of Communication*, vol. 14, no. 3, 1999, pp. 291–234; Greer, C. *Sex Crime and the Media: Sex Offending and the Press in a Divided Society*, Collumpton, UK: Willan, 2003; Uribe, R. and B. Gunter, "Are 'sensational' news stories more likely to trigger readers' emotions than non-sensational news stories? A content analysis of British TV news," *European Journal of Communication*, vol. 22, no. 2, 2007, pp. 207–228. In relation to the two leading dailies in Argentina (*Clarín* and *La Nación*), S. Martini comments that "Police news in the so-called serious press ... has progressively occupied a significant and notable place, a place that it historically held in the popular press" ("Argentina: prensa gráfica, delito y seguridad," in Rey, G. (ed.), *Los Relatos Periodísticos del Crimen*, Bogotá: Centro de Competencia en Comunicación Para América Latina, 2007, p. 35). For Venezuela, C.L. Briggs comments that "The discursive gap that generally separates *El Nacional* and *El Universal* (which used to be the national

reference papers), the daily tabloids and the *Crónica Policial*, a sensationalist weekly specializing in crime stories, is vastly reduced here through similarities in narrative techniques" ("Mediating infanticide: theorizing relations between narrative and violence," *Cultural Anthropology*, vol. 22, no. 3, 2007, p. 325).

2 See, for example, Ericson, R., P.M. Baranek and J.B.L. Chan, *Representing Order: Crime, Law and Justice in the News Media*, Toronto: University of Toronto Press, 1991; Hall, S., C. Crichter, T. Jefferson, J. Clarke, and B. Roberts, *Policing the Crisis: Mugging, the State, and Law and Order*, London: Palgrave Macmillan, 1978; Peelo, M., B. Francis, K. Soothill, J. Pearson, and E. Ackerley, "Newspaper reporting and the public construction of homicide," *British Journal of Criminology*, vol. 44, 2004, pp. 256–275; Soothill, K. and S. Walby, *Sex Crime in the News*, London: Routledge, 1991; Wykes, M. *News, Crime and Culture*, London: Pluto Press, 2001.

3 See, for example, Chermak, S.M. "Body count news: how crime is presented in the media," *Justice Quarterly*, vol. 11, no. 4, 1994, pp. 561–582; Levi, M. "The media construction of financial white-collar crimes," *British Journal of Criminology*, vol. 46, no. 6, 2006, p. 1037–1057; Pollak, J.M. and C.E. Kubrin, "Crime in the news: how crimes, offenders and victims are portrayed by the media," *Journal of Criminal Justice and Popular Culture*, vol. 14, no. 1, 2007, pp. 59–83.

4 Meyrowitz, J. "Shifting worlds of strangers: medium theory and changes in 'them' versus 'us,'" *Social Inquiry*, vol. 67, no. 1, 1997, pp. 59–71.

5 "Discursive space is never completely independent of social place and the formation of new kinds of speech can be traced through the emergence of new public sites of discourse and the transformation of old ones" (Stallybrass, P. and A. White, *The Politics and Poetics of Transgression*, London: Methuen, 1986, p. 80).

6 Lamont, M. and L. Thévenot (eds.), *Rethinking Comparative Cultural Sociology: Repertoires of Evaluation in France and the United States*, Cambridge, UK: Cambridge University Press, 2000.

7 Ferree, M.M., W.A. Gamson, J. Gerhards, and D. Rucht, *Shaping Abortion Discourse: Democracy and the Public Sphere in Germany and the United States*, New York: Cambridge University Press, 2002.

8 Benson, R. and A.C. Saguy, "Constructing social problems in an age of globalization: a French-American comparison," *American Sociological Review*, vol. 70, no. 2, 2005, pp. 233–259; Saguy, A.C., K. Gruys and S. Gong, "Social problem construction and national context: news reporting on 'overweight' and 'obesity' in the United States and France," *Social Problems*, vol. 57, no. 4, 2010, pp. 586–610.

9 See, for example, Heintz, M. (ed.), *The Anthropology of Moralities*, Oxford: Berghahn, 2009; Howell, S. (ed.), *The Ethnography of Moralities*, London: Routledge, 1997; Inglehart, R. and M. Carballo, "Does Latin America exist? (And is there a Confucian culture?): A global analysis of cross-cultural differences," *PS: Political Science and Politics*, vol. 30, no. 1, 1997, pp. 34–47; Smith, D.M. *Moral Geographies: Ethics in a World of Difference*, Edinburgh, UK: Edinburgh University Press, 2000; Wong, D.B. *Moral Relativity*, Berkeley, CA: University of California Press, 1984. This diversity, often known as "moral relativism," has recently exercised human rights scholars, who are constrained to adopt a normative approach to moral matters (see, for example, Corradetti, C. *Relativism and Human Rights: A Theory of Pluralistic Universalism*, New York: Springer, 2009; Ernst, G. "Universal human rights and moral diversity," in Ernst, G. and J.C. Helinger (eds.), *The Philosophy of Human Rights: Contemporary Controversies*, Berlin/Boston: Walter de Gruyter, 2012).

10 Brooks, P. *The Melodramatic Imagination: Balzac, Henry James, Melodrama and the Mode of Excess*, New Haven, CT: Yale University Press, 1976, pp. 14–15.

11 Himmelfarb, G. "A de-moralized society: the British/American experience," *The Public Interest*, Fall 94, no. 117, 1994, p. 68.

12 Huhn, S. *The Culture of Fear and Control in Costa Rica (II): The Talk of Crime and*

Social Changes, Hamburg: German Institute of Global and Area Studies, Working Paper 108, 2009, abstract.
13 Huhn, S. *The Culture of Fear and Control in Costa Rica (II): The Talk of Crime and Social Changes*, Hamburg: German Institute of Global and Area Studies, Working Paper 108, 2009, p. 17.
14 Something of the range of topics that attract moral talk can be appreciated by looking at textbooks and readers on social problems; for example, Eitzen, D.S., M.B. Zinn and K.E. Smith, *Social Problems*, Upper Saddle River, NJ: Prentice Hall, twelfth edition, 2011; Kornblum, W. and J. Julian, *Social Problems*, Upper Saddle River, NJ: Pearson, fourteenth edition, 2012; Ritzer, G. (ed.), *Handbook of Social Problems: A Comparative International Perspective*, Newbury Park, CA: Sage, 2004.
15 See, for example, Alexander, J.C. and P. Smith, "The discourse of American civil society: a new proposal for cultural studies," *Theory and Society*, vol. 22, 1993, pp. 151–207; Archer, M.S. *Culture and Agency: The Place of Culture in Social Theory*, Cambridge, UK: Cambridge University Press, 1988; Lamont, M. and M. Fournier (eds.), *Cultivating Differences: Symbolic Boundaries and the Making of Inequality*, Chicago, IL: University of Chicago Press, 1992.
16 Nelson, B. *Making an Issue of Child Abuse*, Chicago, IL: University of Chicago Press, 1984, p. 27.
17 For example, K. Beckett comments that there is no pro-child abuse lobby, although there have been heated debates about the nature, extent, and responses to child abuse ("Culture and the politics of signification: the case of child sexual abuse," *Social Problems*, vol. 43, no. 1, 1996, p. 57).
18 Rock, P. "The sociology of deviance and conceptions of moral order," *British Journal of Criminology*, vol. 14, no. 2, 1974, p. 147.
19 See, for example, Lamont, M. *Money, Morals and Manners: The Culture of the French and the American Upper-Middle Class*, Chicago, IL: University of Chicago Press, 1992; Lamont, M. *The Dignity of Working Men: Morality and the Boundaries of Race, Class and Imagination*, New York: Russell Sage Foundation and Harvard University Press, 2000; Levine, D.N. "Adumbrations of a sociology of morality in the work of Parsons, Simmel, and Merton," in Hitlin, S. and S. Vaisey (eds), *Handbook of the Sociology of Morality*, New York: Springer, 2010; Ossowska, M. *Social Determinants of Moral Ideas*, London: Routledge and Kegan Paul, 1971.
20 Nevertheless, the discussion of the societal context for collective morality, provided in Chapter 6, naturally arouses curiosity about explanations for the differences observed between Anglo and Latin America, although no explanation is developed there.
21 Waisbord, S. "The narrative of exposés in South American journalism: telling the story of Collorgate in Brazil," *Gazette*, vol. 59, no. 3, 1997, p. 201.
22 Waisbord, S. "The narrative of exposés in South American journalism: telling the story of Collorgate in Brazil," *Gazette*, vol. 59, no. 3, 1997, p. 201.
23 See, particularly, Habermas, J. *The Theory of Communicative Action*, Cambridge,UK: Polity Press, 1989; Habermas, J. *Moral Consciousness and Communicative Action*, Cambridge, MA: MIT Press, 1990.
24 See, for example, Ferree, M.M., W.A. Gamson, J. Gerhards, and D. Rucht, *Shaping Abortion Discourse: Democracy and the Public Sphere in Germany and the United States*, New York: Cambridge University Press, 2002; Livingstone, S. "Television discussion and the public sphere: conflicting discourses of the Former Yugoslavia," *Political Communication*, vol. 13, 1996, pp. 259–280; McGuigan, J. "The cultural public sphere," *European Journal of Cultural Studies*, vol. 8, no. 4, 2005, pp. 427–445.
25 See, for example, Steenbergen, M.R., A. Bächtiger, M. Spörndli, and J. Steiner, "Measuring political deliberation: a discourse quality index," *Comparative European Politics*, vol. 1, 2003, pp. 21–48.

184 *Notes*

26 Gutmann, A. and D. Thompson, "Deliberative democracy beyond process," *The Journal of Political Philosophy*, vol. 10, no. 2, 2002, pp. 153–174.
27 Gans, H.J. *Deciding What's News: A Study of CBS Evening News, NBC Nightly News, Newsweek* and *Time*, New York: Vintage Books, 1980, p. 293. For a similar argument, see Glasser, T.L. and J.S. Ettema, "Investigative journalism and the moral order," *Critical Studies in Mass Communication*, vol. 6, 1989, pp. 1–20.
28 Brooks, P. *The Melodramatic Imagination: Balzac, Henry James, Melodrama and the Mode of Excess*, New Haven, CT: Yale University Press, 1976.
29 Heilman, R.B. *Tragedy and Melodrama: Versions of Experience*, Seattle, WA: University of Washington Press, 1968, p. 7.
30 Heilman, R.B. *Tragedy and Melodrama: Versions of Experience*, Seattle, WA: University of Washington Press, 1968, p. 86.
31 Heilman, R.B. *Tragedy and Melodrama: Versions of Experience*, Seattle, WA: University of Washington Press, 1968, p. 141.
32 *Globe and Mail*, "The building that fought back," January 7, 2006.
33 In this regard, I. Vasilachis de Gialdino's study of newspaper reports on *maras* (gangs) in El Salvador mentioned some seemingly exceptional articles in which gang members themselves were quoted. However, not only were these articles apparently few in number, but the brief and clichéd content of the quotes ("if they were to show up now, I'd come out shooting," "I'm not going to last long, sooner or later they're going to kill me," etc.) revealed a heroic pose for the press, but revealed nothing more. (See, "El lenguaje de la violencia en los medios de comunicación. Las otras formas de ser de la violencia y la prensa escrita," in PNUD (Programa de las Naciones Unidas para el Desarrollo) (ed.), *Aportes para la Convivencia y la Seguridad Ciudadana*, San Salvador, El Salvador: PNUD, 2004.)
34 The phrase is from Schmid, D. "True crime," in Rzepka, C. and L. Horsley (eds.), *A Companion to Crime Fiction*, New York: Wiley-Blackwell, 2010, p. 205. Schmid goes on to comment that "inasmuch as sympathy for the criminal implies a recognition of the criminal's humanity, a humanity shared by both the criminal and the reader, contemporary true crime writers eschew sympathy altogether, preferring instead to present their readers with the comforting thought that the monsters they write about have nothing to do with them" (p. 5).
35 Katz, J. *Seductions of Crime: Moral and Sensual Attractions in Doing Evil*, New York: Basic Books, 1988, p. vii.
36 Cited by Heilman, R.B. *Tragedy and Melodrama: Versions of Experience*, Seattle, WA: University of Washington Press, 1968, p. 246.
37 See, for example, Martel, J. and B. Hogeveen, "The state of critical scholarship in criminology and socio-legal studies in Canada," *Canadian Journal of Criminology and Criminal Justice*, vol. 48, no. 5, 2006, pp. 633–646; Tunnell, K.D. "Silence of the Left: reflections on critical criminology and criminologists," *Social Justice*, vol. 22, no. 1, 1995, pp. 89–101. Critical criminology's younger offshoot, cultural criminology, celebrates its own interests in life at the margins of the public sphere, but has yet to make much noise outside academia. (See, for example, Ferrell, J., K.J. Hayward, and J. Young, *Cultural Criminology: An Introduction*, Los Angeles, CA: Sage, 2008.)
38 Heilman, R.B. *Tragedy and Melodrama: Versions of Experience*, Seattle, WA: University of Washington Press, 1968, p. 294.
39 Roche, M.W. "Introduction to Hegel's theory of tragedy," *PhaenEx*, vol. 1, no. 2, 2006, pp. 11–20.
40 Jones, J. *On Aristotle and Greek Tragedy*, Stanford, CA: Stanford University Press, 1980, p. 21.
41 See, particularly, the journal *Criminal Justice Ethics*. For specific recent examples of different ethical approaches applied to crime and criminal justice, see Christie, T., L. Groarke and W. Sweet, "Virtue ethics as an alternative to deontological and consequential reasoning in the harm reduction debate," *International Journal of Drug*

Policy, vol. 19, 2008, pp. 52–58; Ward, T. and K. Salmon, "The ethics of punishment: correctional practice implications," *Aggression and Violent Behavior*, vol. 14, 2009, pp. 239–247.
42 See, for example, Banks, C. *Criminal Justice Ethics: Theory and Practice*, Thousand Oaks, CA: Sage, 2004; Robertson, C. and S. Mire, *Ethics for Criminal Justice Professionals*, Baton Rouge, FL: CRC, 2009.
43 Much of the field of "applied ethics" could be considered to be founded on this difficulty (and in some cases distaste). For critical views, of disparate orientation and object, on the role of ethics in the personal and public domains, see, for example, Bauman, Z. "Morality without ethics," *Theory, Culture and Society*, vol. 11, 1994, pp. 1–34; Hedgecoe, A.M. "Critical bioethics: beyond the social science critique of applied ethics," *Bioethics*, vol. 18, no. 2, 2004, pp. 120–143; Hoffmaster, B. "The forms and limits of medical ethics," *Social Science and Medicine*, vol. 39, no. 9, 1994, pp. 1155–1164; Hunt, M.R. and F.A. Carnevale, "Moral experience: a framework for bioethics research," *Journal of Medical Ethics,* vol. 37, 2011, pp. 658–662; Nielsen, R.P. "Limitations of ethical reasoning as an action (praxis) strategy," *Journal of Business Ethics*, vol. 7, 1988, pp. 725–733.
44 This phrase was coined by G. Barak ("Newsmaking criminology: reflections on the media, intellectuals and crime," *Justice Quarterly*, vol. 5, no. 4, 1988, pp. 565–587). In 1988, he noted the conspicuous absence of criminologists from the US mass media's reporting and commentary on crime and justice. In 2007, he observed that "This situation has not substantively changed in 20 years" (Barak, G. "Doing newsmaking criminology from within the academy," *Theoretical Criminology*, vol. 11, no. 2, 2007, p. 192). See also, Frost, N.A. and N.D. Phillips, "Talking heads: crime reporting on cable news," *Justice Quarterly*, vol. 28, no. 1, 2011, pp. 87–112.
45 Dupuy, J.P. and A. Grinbaum, "Living with uncertainty: from the precautionary principle to the method of ongoing normative assessment," *C.R. Geoscience*, vol. 337, 2005, p. 459.
46 This process could be seen as an embryonic application of the "precautionary rule" that is much discussed in environmental matters (Gardiner, S.M. "A core precautionary principle," *The Journal of Political Philosophy*, vol. 14, no. 1, 2006, pp. 33–60).
47 See, for example, Funtowicz, S.O. and J.R. Ravetz, *Uncertainty and Quality in Science and Policy*, Dordrecht, NL: Kluwer Academic Publishing Company, 1990.
48 See, for example, Aven, T. and O. Renn, "On risk defined as an event where the outcome is uncertain," *Journal of Risk Research*, vol. 12, no. 1, 2009, pp. 1–11; MacGill, S.M. and Y.L. Siu, "The nature of risk," *Journal of Risk Research*, vol. 7, no. 3, 2004, pp. 315–352.
49 See, for example, Campbell, B.L. "Uncertainty as symbolic action in disputes among experts," *Social Studies of Science*, vol. 15, no. 3, 1985, pp. 429–453; Sarewitz, D. "How science makes environmental controversies worse," *Environmental Science and Policy*, vol. 7, 2004, pp. 385–403.
50 Aporia designates both the puzzlement or perplexity that arise when people realize that they do not know, and—to paraphrase Plato—"the puzzles that puzzle people" (Politis, V. "*Aporia* and searching in the early Plato," in Judson, L. and V. Karasmanis (eds.), *Remembering Socrates. Philosophical Essays*, Oxford: Clarendon Press, 2006, p. 100).
51 So, for example, "A morality appropriate to modernity advises tolerance in the face of the ambiguity and uncertainty given by the pluralism and complexity of modernity.... Prudence ... counsels not surrender to indeterminacy but a recognition that indeterminacy will be reduced ... only through responsible and cooperative social intercourse" (Hearn, F. *Moral Order and Disorder: The American Search for Civil Society*, Hawthorne, NY: Aldine de Gruyter, 1997, pp. 89–90).

52 Note that the quality of a puzzle does do not inhere in a particular event, but in the way in which the event is perceived and assimilated. For example, much commentary on the terrorist incidents of "9/11" in the United States did not betray signs of puzzlement (see, for example, Anker, E. "Villains, victims and heroes: melodrama, media and September 11," *Journal of Communication*, vol. 55, no. 1, 2005, pp. 22–37). Indeed, S.J. Hartnett and L.A. Stengrim have developed an extended demonstration and trenchant critique of the way in which George W. Bush "manufactured" certainty regarding weapons of mass destruction in Iraq, in part by building on the events of September 11, 2001 ("'The whole operation of deception': reconstructing President Bush's rhetoric of weapons of mass destruction," *Cultural Studies ↔ Critical Methodologies*, vol. 4, no. 2, 2004, pp. 152–197). By contrast, E. Moodie hints that a moment of aporia may have existed in "post-conflict" El Salvador of the mid-1990s: "What I found there was not peace. It wasn't war, either. It was something else, something somehow more sinister, less knowable. This mystery, this unpredictable new mode of danger, only amplified anxiety" (*El Salvador in the Aftermath of Peace: Crime, Uncertainty and the Transition to Democracy*, Philadelphia, PA: University of Pennsylvania Press, 2010, p. 2).

53 Thus, M. Alvesson and D. Kärreman: "Many discourse studies proceed from the assumption of the inseparability of language-meaning-cognition-action-practice. Sometimes this is a taken-for-granted assumption to be uncritically reproduced rather than a potentially productive idea to reflect upon and selectively use..." ("Decolonializing discourse: critical reflections on organizational discourse analysis," *Human Relations*, vol. 64, no. 9, 2011, p. 1142). On the difficulties of establishing the effects of media representations of crime see, for example, Doyle, A. "How not to think about crime in the media," *Canadian Journal of Criminology and Criminal Justice*, vol. 48, no. 6, 2006, pp. 867–885.

54 This is often the way in which ethnography looks at talk.

55 Boltanski, L. *Distant Suffering: Morality, Media and Politics*, Cambridge, UK: Cambridge University Press, 1999, p. xv.

56 Boltanski, L. *Distant Suffering: Morality, Media and Politics*, Cambridge, UK: Cambridge University Press, 1999, p. 115.

57 Boltanski, L. *Distant Suffering: Morality, Media and Politics*, Cambridge, UK: Cambridge University Press, 1999, p. xvi (emphasis in the original).

58 Boltanski, L. *Distant Suffering: Morality, Media and Politics*, Cambridge, UK: Cambridge University Press, 1999, p. xv.

59 Boltanski, L. *Distant Suffering: Morality, Media and Politics*, Cambridge, UK : Cambridge University Press, 1999, p. 116.

60 Boltanski, L. *Distant Suffering: Morality, Media and Politics*, Cambridge, UK: Cambridge University Press, 1999, p. 132.

Appendix: notes on method and sources

1 Lee, J.A. and S. Ungar, "A coding method for the analysis of moral discourse," *Human Relations*, vol. 42, no. 8, 1989, pp. 691–715.

2 Ibarra, P.R. and J.I. Kitsuse, "Vernacular constituents of moral discourse: an interactionist proposal for the study of social problems," in Miller, G. and J. Holstein (eds.), *Constructionist Controversies: Issues in Social Problems Theory*, New York: Aldine de Gruyter, 1993.

3 More recently, B.M. Lowe has presented a proposal for the analysis of "moral vocabularies," but his approach is best considered an example of frame analysis (as defined and discussed in Chapter 1 of this book) rather than discourse analysis ("*Hearts and Minds* and morality: analyzing moral vocabularies in qualitative studies," *Qualitative Sociology*, vol. 25, no. 1, 2002, pp. 105–123).

4 For example, their category of "preference" included censorious and prescriptive

statements (moral discourse) as well as predictions (empirical discourse), which seems unhelpful.
5 See Holstein, J. and G. Miller (eds.), *Challenges and Choices: Constructionist Perspectives on Social Problems*, New York: Aldine de Gruyter, 2003; Miller, G. and J. Holstein (eds.), *Constructionist Controversies: Issues in Social Problems Theory*, New York: Aldine de Gruyter, 1993.
6 Ibarra, P.R. and J.I. Kitsuse, "Vernacular constituents of moral discourse: an interactionist proposal for the study of social problems," in Miller, G. and J. Holstein (eds.), *Constructionist Controversies: Issues in Social Problems Theory*, New York: Aldine de Gruyter, 1993, p. 52.
7 See, for example, Best, J. "Rhetoric in claims-making: constructing the missing children problem," *Social Problems*, vol. 34, no. 2, 1987, pp. 101–121; Sasson, T. *Crime Talk: How Citizens Construct a Social Problem*, New York: Aldine de Gruyter, 1995.
8 Benford, R.D. and D.A. Snow, "Framing processes and social movements: an overview and assessment," *Annual Review of Sociology*, vol. 26, 2000, 611–639; Gamson, W.A. and A. Modigliani, "Media discourse and public opinion on nuclear power. A constructionist approach," *The American Journal of Sociology*, vol. 95, no. 1, 1989, 1–37; Gusfield, J. *The Culture of Public Problems*, Chicago, IL: University of Chicago Press, 1981.
9 However, items which used references to specific incidents, such as a high-profile murder or kidnapping, as an ingredient for more general commentary on crime were included in the study.
10 Stein, M.L. and S.F. Paterno, *The Newswriters' Handbook, An Introduction to Journalism*, Ames, IA: Iowa State University Press, 1998, p. 6.
11 See Barlow, M.H., D.E. Barlow and T.G. Chiricos, "Economic conditions and ideologies of crime in the media: a content analysis of crime news," *Crime and Delinquency*, vol. 41, no. 1, 1995, pp. 3–19; Rodgers, S. and E. Thorson, "The reporting of crime and violence in the Los Angeles Times: is there a public health perspective?" *Journal of Health Communication*, vol. 6, no. 2, 2001, pp. 160–182.
12 See, for example, Barak, G. (ed.), *Media, Process and the Social Construction of Crime: Studies in Newsmaking Criminology*, New York, Garland, 1995; Huhn, S., A. Oettler, and P. Peetz, "Contemporary discourses on violence in Central American newspapers," *The International Communication Gazette*, vol. 71, no. 4, 2009, pp. 243–261; Reiner, R. "Media-made criminality: the representation of crime in the mass media," in Maguire, M., R. Morgan, and R. Reiner (eds.), *The Oxford Handbook of Criminology*, Oxford, UK: Oxford University Press, 2007, pp. 304–311.
13 Audit Bureau of Circulations, *eCirc*, 2009; Canadian Newspaper Association, *Circulation Data Report*, 2008; LexisNexis, *Searchable Directory of Online Sources*, 2009; *New York Times*, "Newspaper circulation continues to decline rapidly," October 27, 2008.
14 For example, for use of the *Globe and Mail*, see Sprott, J.B. "Understanding public views of youth crime and the youth justice system," *Canadian Journal of Criminology*, vol. 38, no. 3, 1996, pp. 271–290. For use of the *Los Angeles Times*, see Eyres, J. and D. Altheide, "News themes and ethnic identity: *Los Angeles Times* news reports of Vietnamese, Black and Hispanic Gangs," *Perspectives on Social Problems*, vol. 11, 1999, pp. 85–103; Rodgers, S. and E. Thorson, "The reporting of crime and violence in the Los Angeles Times: is there a public health perspective?" *Journal of Health Communication*, vol. 6, no. 2, 2001, pp. 160–182; Sorenson, S.B., J.G. Peterson Manz and R. Berk, "News media coverage and the epidemiology of homicide," *American Journal of Public Health*, vol. 88, 1998, p. 1510–1514. For use of the *New York Times*, see Wasserman, I.M. and S. Stack, "Communal violence and the media: lynchings and their news coverage by the *New York Times* between 1882 and 1930," in Barak, G. (ed.), *Media, Process and the Social Construction of Crime. Studies in Newsmaking Criminology*, New York: Garland, 1995; Welch, M., M. Fenwick, and

M. Roberts, "State managers, intellectuals, and the media: a content analysis of ideology in experts' quotes in feature newspaper articles on crime," *Justice Quarterly*, vol. 15, no. 2, 1998, pp. 219–241.
15 For studies of crime as reported in other Latin American newspapers, see, for example, Huhn, S., A. Oettler, and P. Peetz, *Exploding Crime? Topic Management in Central American Newspapers*, Hamburg: German Institute of Global and Area Studies, Giga Working Paper No. 33, 2006; Rey, G. *El Cuerpo del Delito. Representación y Narrativas Mediáticas de la Seguridad Ciudadana*, Bogotá: Centro de Competencia en Comunicación para América Latina, 2005; Rey, G. (ed.), *Los Relatos Periodísticos del Crimen*, Bogotá: Centro de Competencia en Comunicación para América Latina, 2007.
16 Wikipedia, *The Globe and Mail*, 2009.
17 Puglisi, R. *Being the New York Times: The Political Behavior of a Newspaper*, London: London School of Economics, Political Economy and Public Policy Series, No. 20, 2006.
18 In fact, M.M. Ferree *et al.* see both the *New York Times* and the *Los Angeles Times* as seeking "what they see as the ideological center" (Ferree, M.M., W.A. Gamson, J. Gerhards, and D. Rucht, *Shaping Abortion Discourse: Democracy and the Public Sphere in Germany and the United States*, New York: Cambridge University Press, 2002, p. 82).
19 Bogart, L. and J.A. Giner, *Éxitos y Desafíos. La Situación de la Industria Periodística Latinoamericana: 32 Perfiles de Diarios*, Pamplona, ES: Innovation International Media Consulting Group, S.L., 1997, pp. 181–187.
20 Bogart, L. and J.A. Giner, *Éxitos y Desafíos. La Situación de la Industria Periodística Latinoamericana: 32 Perfiles de Diarios*, Pamplona, ES: Innovation International Media Consulting Group, S.L., 1997, pp. 181–187.
21 For more information on *La Nación*, see Martini, S. "Argentina: prensa gráfica, delito y seguridad," in Rey, G. (ed.), *Los Relatos Periodísticos del Crimen*, Bogotá: Centro de Competencia en Comunicación Para América Latina, 2007.
22 The total for each newspaper was as follows: *Globe and Mail* (122); *New York Times* (110); *Los Angeles Times* (116); *El Universal* (272); *El Nacional* (99); *La Nación* (134).
23 *El Nacional*, "Incrementa la violencia juvenil," September 25, 2006.
24 *Globe and Mail*, "Sentenced by politics," January 13, 2006.
25 *Los Angeles Times*, "Rates of slayings and gun violence are up," September 11, 2006.
26 *La Nación*, "Lanzan un plan para prevenir el delito," August 14, 2006.
27 *New York Times*, "New Haven rethinking tactics on crime," December 8, 2006.
28 *El Universal*, "Despolicializar la seguridad," February 10, 2007.
29 *Globe and Mail*, "Ontario to spend millions fighting gun crime," January 6, 2006.
30 *La Nación*, "El desarme ¿apenas una desilusión?" August 23, 2006.
31 *Globe and Mail*, "Treat gangs as terrorists," December 7, 2007.
32 *La Nación*, "Editorial II: la entrega voluntaria de armas," July 26, 2007.
33 For example, T.A. van Dijk argued that news items have a "semantic macrostructure" that "makes explicit the overall topics or themes of a text" (*News as Discourse*, Hillsdale, NJ: Lawrence Erlbaum Associates, 1988, p. 13). In relation to editorials, he posited that "many ... feature a category of *Prediction* or *Recommendation*, which we may subsume under the broader category of a *Conclusion* or *Moral*, and which focuses on the future: what will happen?, or what should or should not be done?" (*Racism and the Press*, London: Routledge, p. 133, emphasis in the original). Items, or sections of items, can therefore be considered to have a theme, which may have moral significance and, if so, can help to categorize ambiguous segments of the constitutive text.
34 *Los Angeles Times*, "Crime victims' families rally in Riverside," April 27, 2007.
35 *El Universal*, "Estado de excepción," May 9, 2007.

36 The significance of these intellective dimensions is also reflected in the different models of social issues that have been proposed by social problems and social movements scholars, and which include moral, empirical, and practical components. See, for example, Benford, R.D. and D.A. Snow, "Framing processes and social movements: an overview and assessment," *Annual Review of Sociology*, vol. 26, 2000, 611–639; Gamson, W.A. and A. Modigliani, "Media discourse and public opinion on nuclear power. A constructionist approach," *The American Journal of Sociology*, vol. 95, no. 1, 1989, 1–37; Gusfield, J. *The Culture of Public Problems*, Chicago, IL: University of Chicago Press, 1981.
37 *La Nación*, "Sola admitió que no logró su objetivo en seguridad," October 9, 2007.
38 *New York Times*, "Violent crime rising sharply in some cities," February 12, 2006.
39 *Los Angeles Times*, "Bratton's 'broken windows,'" April 20, 2006.
40 *El Nacional*, "Al robarme el apartamento perdí la sensación de seguridad," May 17, 2007.
41 *Globe and Mail*, "Organized crime groups on the rise," August 18, 2007.
42 *El Universal*, "Año de violencia," December 12, 2007.
43 *Los Angeles Times*, "Mayor backs chief's second term," January 3, 2007.
44 *La Nación*, "Eje de la campaña bonaerense," October 6, 2007.
45 *Globe and Mail*, "Natives try 'banishment' to fight crime," February 8, 2006.
46 *Globe and Mail*, "A few unnerving words about Canada's security," May 11, 2006.
47 *La Nación*, "El desarme ¿apenas una desilusión?" August 23, 2006.
48 *El Nacional*, "La labor sigue en las zonas populares," August 9, 2007.
49 *El Universal*, "Detectan 20 zonas donde hay más robos," September 26, 2007.
50 *New York Times*, "Church battles to break gang cycle, with a flock for all," April 16, 2006.
51 Compare N. Fairclough: "Discourses correspond roughly to dimensions of texts which have traditionally been discussed in terms of 'content', 'ideational meaning', 'topic', 'subject matter', and so forth.... [A] discourse ... is standardly associated with a range of genres (scientific articles, lectures, consultations, and so forth) and can show up in all sorts of other genres (conversations, television chat shows, or indeed poems)" (*Discourse and Social Change*, Cambridge, UK: Polity Press, 1993, pp. 127–128). By extension, a discourse also "shows up" in a set of items or texts within a given genre.
52 For example, "It is impossible to countenance a 'convoy of death' such as that seen this week in the north of the country" (*El Universal*, "Caravanas de la muerte," June 23, 2006).
53 For example, "...Blasi said the city has paid little more than lip service to efforts beyond law enforcement" (*Los Angeles Times*, "Crime off, but plan is faulted," September 26, 2007).
54 For example, "'It's long past time for Congress to do more to prevent hate crimes and insist that they be fully prosecuted when they occur,' Mr. Kennedy said" (*New York Times*, "House votes to expand hate-crime protection," May 4, 2007).
55 For example, "We have gone backward in our ability to deal with the illegal gun market..." (*Los Angeles Times*, "FBI reports rise in violent crime," December 19, 2006).

Bibliography

Abdullah, N., "Exploring constructions of the 'drug problem' in historical and contemporary Singapore," *New Zealand Journal of Asian Studies*, vol. 7, no. 2, 2005, pp. 40–70.

Abend, G., "Two main problems in the sociology of morality," *Theory and Society*, vol. 37, no. 2, 2008, pp. 87–125.

Abramson, P.R. and Inglehart, R., *Value Change in Global Perspective*, Ann Arbor, MI: University of Michigan Press, 1995.

Albert, E., "AIDS and the press: the creation and transformation of a social problem," in Best, J. (ed.), *Images of Issues: Typifying Contemporary Social Problems*, New York: Aldine de Gruyter, 1989.

Alexander, J.C., "Citizen and enemy as symbolic classification: on the polarizing discourse of civil society," in Lamont, M. and Fournier, M. (eds.), *Cultivating Differences: Symbolic Boundaries and the Making of Inequality*, Chicago, IL: University of Chicago Press, 1992.

Alexander, J.C., *The Meanings of Social Life: A Cultural Sociology*, New York: Oxford University Press, 2003.

Alexander, J.C. and Smith, P., "The discourse of American civil society: a new proposal for cultural studies," *Theory and Society*, vol. 22, 1993, pp. 151–207.

Altamirano Molina, X., "Discursos y encuadres de la prensa escrita chilena sobre la inseguridad urbana: atribución de responsabilidades y agenda política," in Rey, G. (ed.), *Los Relatos Periodísticos del Crimen*, Bogotá: Centro de Competencia en Comunicación para América Latina, 2007.

Alvesson, M. and Kärreman, D., "Decolonializing discourse: critical reflections on organizational discourse analysis," *Human Relations*, vol. 64, no. 9, 2011, pp. 1121–1146.

Ambert, A.M., *The Rise in the Number of Children and Adolescents Who Exhibit Problematic Behaviors: Multiple Causes*, Ottawa: The Vanier Institute of the Family, 2007. Online. Available, www.vanierinstitute.ca/publications (accessed April 21, 2012).

Anderson, B., *Imagined Communities. Reflections on the Origin and Spread of Nationalism*, London: Verso, 2006.

Anderson, E., *Code of the Street: Decency, Violence and the Moral Life of the Inner City*, New York: W.W. Norton and Company, 1999.

Anker, E., "Villains, victims and heroes: melodrama, media and September 11," *Journal of Communication*, vol. 55, no. 1, 2005, pp. 22–37.

Archer, M.S., *Culture and Agency: The Place of Culture in Social Theory*, Cambridge, UK: Cambridge University Press, 1988.

Armstrong, E.M. and Abel, E.L., "Fetal alcohol syndrome: the origins of a moral panic," *Alcohol and Alcoholism*, vol. 35, no. 3, 2000, pp. 276–282.

Audit Bureau of Circulations, *eCirc*, 2009. Online. Available at: http://abcas3.accessabc.com/ecirc/index.html (accessed September 21, 2009).

Aven, T. and Renn, O., "On risk defined as an event where the outcome is uncertain," *Journal of Risk Research*, vol. 12, no. 1, 2009, pp. 1–11.

Baier, K., *The Moral Point of View*, New York, NY: Random House, 1965.

Banks, C., *Criminal Justice Ethics: Theory and Practice*, Thousand Oaks, CA: Sage, 2004.

Barak, G., "Newsmaking criminology: reflections on the media, intellectuals and crime," *Justice Quarterly*, vol. 5, no. 4, 1988, pp. 565–587.

Barak, G. (ed.), *Media, Process and the Social Construction of Crime: Studies in Newsmaking Criminology*, New York, Garland, 1995.

Barak, G., "Doing newsmaking criminology from within the academy," *Theoretical Criminology*, vol. 11, no. 2, 2007, pp. 191–207.

Barlow, M.H., Barlow, D.E., and Chiricos, T.G., "Economic conditions and ideologies of crime in the media: a content analysis of crime news," *Crime and Delinquency*, vol. 41, no. 1, 1995, pp. 3–19.

Barry, B., "Social criticism and political philosophy," *Philosophy and Public Affairs*, vol. 19, no. 4, 1990, pp. 360–373.

Basáñez, M. and Moreno, A., "Value change in Mexico, 1998–2000: evidence from the World Values surveys," in Pettersson, T. and Esmer, Y. (eds), *Changing Values, Persisting Cultures: Case Studies in Value Change*, Leiden, NL: Koninklijke Brill, 2008.

Bauman, Z., "Morality without ethics," *Theory, Culture and Society*, vol. 11, 1994, pp. 1–34.

Baumann, E.A., "Research rhetoric and the social construction of elder abuse," in Best, J. (ed.), *Images of Issues: Typifying Contemporary Social Problems*, New York: Aldine de Gruyter, 1989.

Beckett, K., "Culture and the politics of signification: the case of child sexual abuse," *Social Problems*, vol. 43, no. 1, 1996, pp. 57–76.

Beckett, K., *Making Crime Pay: Law and Order in Contemporary American Politics*, New York: Oxford University Press, 1999.

Becker, H., *Outsiders: Studies in the Sociology of Deviance*, New York: The Free Press, 1963.

Benford, R.D., "'You could be the hundredth monkey': collective action frames and vocabularies of motive within the nuclear disarmament movement," *The Sociological Quarterly*, vol. 34, no. 2, 1993, 195–216.

Benford, R.D. and Snow, D.A., "Framing processes and social movements: an overview and assessment," *Annual Review of Sociology*, vol. 26, 2000, 611–639.

Benson, R. and Saguy, A.C., "Constructing social problems in an age of globalization: a French–American comparison," *American Sociological Review*, vol. 70, no. 2, 2005, pp. 233–259.

Ben-Yehuda, N., *The Politics of Morality and Deviance: Moral Panics, Drug Abuse, Deviant Science, and Reversed Stigmatization*, Albany, NY: State University of New York Press, 1990.

Beres, L.S. and Griffith, T.D., "Demonizing youth," *Loyola of Los Angeles Law Review*, vol. 34, 2000–2001, pp. 747–766.

Berns, N., "My problem and how I solved it," *The Sociological Quarterly*, vol. 40, 1999, pp. 85–108.

Bibliography

Best, J., "Rhetoric in claims-making: constructing the missing children problem," *Social Problems*, vol. 34, no. 2, 1987, pp. 101–121.

Best, J., *Threatened Children: Rhetoric and Concern about Child Victims*, Chicago, IL: University of Chicago Press, 1990.

Best, J., *Random Violence: How We Talk about New Crimes and New Victims*, Berkeley, CA: University of California Press, 1999.

Best, J. (ed.), *How Claims Spread: Cross-National Diffusion of Social Problems*, New York: Aldine de Gruyter, 2001.

Best, J., *Images of Issues: Typifying Contemporary Social Problems*, New Brunswick, NJ: Transaction Publishers, 2009.

Birkbeck, C. and Gabaldón, L.G., "Venezuela: policing as an exercise in authority," in Hinton, M.S. and Newburn, T. (eds.), *Policing Developing Democracies*, London: Routledge, 2009.

Blind, P.K., *Building Trust in Government in the Twenty First Century: Review of Literature and Emerging Issues*. Paper presented at the Seventh Global Forum on Reinventing Government: Building Trust in Government, Vienna, June 26–29, 2007. Online. Available at: www.unpan.org/DPADM/Events/GlobalForum/7thGlobalForum/tabid/601/language/en-US/Default.aspx#Link8 (accessed April 1, 2012).

Boczkowski, P.J., Mitchelstein, E. and Walgter, M., "Convergence across divergence: understanding the gap in the online choices of journalists and consumers in Western Europe and Latin America," *Communication Research*, vol. 38, no. 3, 2011, pp. 376–396.

Bogart, L. and Giner, J.A., *Éxitos y Desafíos. La Situación de la Industria Periodística Latinoamericana: 32 Perfiles de Diarios*, Pamplona, ES: Innovation International Media Consulting Group, S.L., 1997.

Boltanski, L., *Distant Suffering: Morality, Media and Politics*, Cambridge, UK: Cambridge University Press, 1999.

Boyd, S., "Media constructions of illegal drugs, users, and sellers: a closer look at Traffic," *International Journal of Drug Policy*, vol. 13, no. 5, 2002, pp. 397–407.

Briggs, C.L., "Mediating infanticide: theorizing relations between narrative and violence," *Cultural Anthropology*, vol. 22, no. 3, 2007, pp. 315–356.

Brooks, P., *The Melodramatic Imagination: Balzac, Henry James, Melodrama and the Mode of Excess*, New Haven, CT: Yale University Press, 1976.

Brown, B. and Benedict, W.R., "Perceptions of the police: past findings, methodological issues, conceptual issues and policy implications," *Policing: An International Journal of Police Strategies and Management*, vol. 25, no. 3, 2002, pp. 543–580.

Brush, J., "Does income inequality lead to more crime? A comparison of cross-sectional and time-series analyses of United States counties," *Economics Letters*, vol. 96, 2007, pp. 264–268.

Burke, K., *On Symbols and Society*, Chicago, IL: University of Chicago Press, 1989.

Buvinic, M., Morrison, A., and Shifter, M., *Violence in Latin America and the Caribbean: A Framework for Action*, Washington: Inter-American Development Bank, 1999.

Calhoun, C., "Social Sciences in North America," in *World Social Science Report 2010*, Paris: UNESCO/International Social Science Council, 2010.

Campbell, B.L., "Uncertainty as symbolic action in disputes among experts," *Social Studies of Science*, vol. 15, no. 3, 1985, pp. 429–453.

Campbell, J.L., "Ideas, politics, and public policy," *Annual Review of Sociology*, vol. 28, 2002, pp. 21–38.

Canadian Newspaper Association, *Circulation Data Report*, 2008. Online. Available at: www.cna-acj.ca/en/system/files/CircDataReport08.pdf (accessed September 24, 2009).

Carballo, M., "Cultural trends in Argentina: 1983–2000," in Pettersson, T. and Esmer, Y. (eds.), *Changing Values, Persisting Cultures: Case Studies in Value Change*, Leiden, NL: Koninklijke Brill, 2008.

Carr, D. and Steutel, J. (eds.), *Virtue Ethics and Moral Education*, London: Routledge, 1999.

Casas Guerrero, R., "Conocimiento, tecnología y desarrollo en América Latina," *Revista Mexicana de Sociología*, vol. 66, octubre, 2004, pp. 255–277.

Cereijido, M., "En América Latina ya podemos investigar, el próximo paso es tratar de hacer ciencia," *Interciencia*, vol. 21, no. 2, 1996, pp. 64–70.

Chermak, S.M., "Body count news: how crime is presented in the media," *Justice Quarterly*, vol. 11, no. 4, 1994, pp. 561–582.

Chesney-Lind, M. and Eliason, M., "From invisible to incorrigible: the demonization of marginalized women and girls," *Crime Media Culture*, vol. 2, no. 1, 2006, pp. 29–47.

Christie, T., Groarke, L., and Sweet, W., "Virtue ethics as an alternative to deontological and consequential reasoning in the harm reduction debate," *International Journal of Drug Policy*, vol. 19, 2008, pp. 52–58.

Clark, C., *Misery and Company. Sympathy in Everyday Life*, Chicago, IL: University of Chicago Press, 1997.

Coady, C.A.J., "Preface," *Journal of Applied Philosophy*, vol. 22, no. 2, 2005, pp. 101–104.

Cobb, R.W. and Coughlin, J.F., "Are elderly drivers a road hazard?: problem definition and political impact," *Journal of Aging Studies*, vol. 12, no. 4, 1998, pp. 411–427.

Cohen, S., *Folk Devils and Moral Panics*, London: Routledge, third edition, 2002.

Collini, S, *Public Moralists: Political Thought and Intellectual Life in Britain, 1850–1930*, Oxford: Clarendon Press, 1993.

Collins, H. and Evans, R., *Rethinking Expertise*, Chicago, IL: University of Chicago Press, 2007.

Coltrane, S. and Adams, M., "The social construction of the divorce 'problem': morality, child victims and the politics of gender," *Family Relations*, vol. 52, no. 4, 2003, pp. 363–372.

Coltrane, S. and Hickman, N., "The rhetoric of rights and needs: moral discourse in the reform of child custody and child support laws," *Social Problems*, vol. 39, no. 4, 1992, pp. 400–420.

Corbey, R. and Leerssen, J., "Studying alterity: backgrounds and perspectives," in Corbey, R. and Leerssen, J. (eds.), *Alterity, Identity and Image: Selves and Others in Society and Scholarship*, Amsterdam: Rodopi, 1991.

Corradetti, C., *Relativism and Human Rights: A Theory of Pluralistic Universalism*, New York: Springer, 2009.

Crisp, R. and Slote, M. (eds.), *Virtue Ethics*, Oxford: Oxford University Press, 1997.

Critcher, C., *Moral Panics and the Media*, Buckingham, UK: Open University Press, 2003.

Cromer, G., "Analogies to terror: the construction of social problems in Israel during the Intifada Al Aqsa," *Terrorism and Political Violence*, vol. 18, no. 3, 2006, pp. 389–398.

Cruz, J. M., "Violencia, democracia y cultura política," *Nueva Sociedad*, no. 167, 2000, pp. 132–146.

Czarniawska, B., "Alterity/identity interplay in image construction," in Barry, D. and Hansen, H. (eds.), *The Sage Handbook of New Approaches in Management and Organization*, Thousand Oaks, CA: Sage Publications, 2008.

Bibliography

Dalton, R.J., "The social transformation of trust in government," *International Review of Sociology*, vol. 15, no. 1, 2005, pp. 133–154.

Dammert, L. and Malone, M.F.T., "Inseguridad y temor en Argentina: el impacto de la confianza en la policía y la corrupción sobre la percepción ciudadana del crimen," *Desarrollo Económico*, vol. 42, no. 166, 2002, pp. 285–301.

Davis, D.E., "The state of the state in Latin American sociology," in Wood, C.H. and Roberts, B.R. (eds.), *Rethinking Development in Latin America*, University Park, PA: The Pennsylvania State University Press, 2005.

Dealy, G.C., *The Latin Americans: Spirit and Ethos*, Boulder, CO: Westview Press, 1992.

Desrosières, A., *The Politics of Large Numbers: A History of Statistical Reasoning*, Cambridge, MA: Harvard University Press, 1998.

de Sousa Santos, B., "*Nuestra America*: reinventing a subaltern paradigm of recognition and redistribution," *Theory, Culture and Society*, vol. 18, 2001, pp. 185–217.

DeYoung, M., "Speak of the devil: rhetoric in claims-making about the satanic ritual abuse problem," *Journal of Sociology and Social Welfare*, vol. XXIII, no. 2, 1996, pp. 55–74.

Doyle, A., "How not to think about crime in the media," *Canadian Journal of Criminology and Criminal Justice*, vol. 48, no. 6, 2006, pp. 867–885.

Driver, J., "Hyperactive ethics," *The Philosophical Quarterly*, vol. 44, no. 174, 1994, pp. 9–25.

Dunn, J.L., "Accounting for victimization: social constructionist perspectives," *Sociology Compass*, vol. 2, no. 5, 2008, p. 1601–1620.

Dupuy, J.P. and Grinbaum, A., "Living with uncertainty: from the precautionary principle to the method of ongoing normative assessment," *C.R. Geoscience*, vol. 337, 2005, pp. 457–474.

Earle, P.G., "On the contemporary displacement of the Hispanic American essay," *Hispanic Review*, vol. 46, no. 3, 1978, pp. 329–341.

Eitzen, D.S., Zinn, M.B., and Smith, K.E., *Social Problems*, Upper Saddle River, NJ: Prentice Hall, twelfth edition, 2011.

Elbert, C., "Rebuilding utopia? Critical criminology and the difficult road of reconstruction," *Crime, Law and Social Change*, vol. 41, no. 4, pp. 385–395.

Entman, R.M., "Framing: toward clarification of a fractured paradigm," *Journal of Communication*, vol. 43, no. 4, 1993, pp. 51–58.

Ericson, R., Baranek, P.M., and Chan, J.B.L., *Representing Order: Crime, Law and Justice in the News Media*, Toronto: University of Toronto Press, 1991.

Ericsson, K.A., Charness, N., Hoffman, R.R., and Feltovich, P.J. (eds.), *The Cambridge Handbook of Expertise and Expert Performance*, New York: Cambridge University Press, 2006.

Ernst, G., "Universal human rights and moral diversity," in Ernst, G. and Helinger, J.C. (eds.), *The Philosophy of Human Rights: Contemporary Controversies*, Berlin/Boston: Walter de Gruyter, 2012.

Esser, F., "'Tabloidization' of news: a comparative analysis of Anglo-American and German press journalism," *European Journal of Communication*, vol. 14, no. 3, 1999, pp. 291–234.

Eyres, J. and Altheide, D., "News themes and ethnic identity: *Los Angeles Times* news reports of Vietnamese, Black and Hispanic Gangs," *Perspectives on Social Problems*, vol. 11, 1999, pp. 85–103.

Fairclough, N., *Discourse and Social Change*, Cambridge, UK: Polity Press, 1993.

Faria, V., "Social science and academic sociology in Brazil," in Wood, C.H. and

Roberts, B.R. (eds.), *Rethinking Development in Latin America*, University Park, PA: The Pennsylvania State University Press, 2005.

Ferree, M.M., Gamson, W.A., Gerhards, J., and Rucht, D., *Shaping Abortion Discourse: Democracy and the Public Sphere in Germany and the United States*, New York: Cambridge University Press, 2002.

Ferrell, J., Hayward, K.J., and Young, J., *Cultural Criminology: An Introduction*, Los Angeles, CA: Sage, 2008.

Foot, P., "Morality as a system of hypothetical imperatives," *The Philosophical Review*, vol. 81, no. 3, 1972, pp. 305–316.

Foucault, M., *Madness and Civilization: A History of Insanity in the Age of Reason*, London: Routledge, 1989.

Fowler, R., *Language in the News: Discourse and Ideology in the Press*, London: Routledge, 1991.

Frost, N.A. and Phillips, N.D., "Talking heads: crime reporting on cable news," *Justice Quarterly*, vol. 28, no. 1, 2011, pp. 87–112.

Funtowicz, S.O. and Ravetz, J.R., *Uncertainty and Quality in Science and Policy*, Dordrecht, NL: Kluwer Academic Publishing Company, 1990.

Furedi, F., *Culture of Fear*, New York: Cassell, 1997.

Furedi, F., "Coping with adversity: the turn to the rhetoric of vulnerability," *Security Journal*, vol. 20, 2007, pp. 171–184.

Gaines, L.K. and Kappeler, V.E., *Policing in America*, Waltham, MA: Anderson Publishing, seventh edition, 2011.

Gamson, W.A. and Modigliani, A. "Media discourse and public opinion on nuclear power. A constructionist approach," *The American Journal of Sociology*, vol. 95, no. 1, 1989, pp. 1–37.

Gans, H.J., *Deciding What's News: A Study of CBS Evening News, NBC Nightly News, Newsweek and Time*, New York: Vintage Books, 1980.

Gardiner, S.M., "A core precautionary principle," *The Journal of Political Philosophy*, vol. 14, no. 1, 2006, pp. 33–60.

Garland, D., "The limits of the sovereign state: strategies of crime control in contemporary society," *The British Journal of Criminology*, vol. 36, no. 4, 1996, pp. 445–471.

Garland, D., *The Culture of Control: Crime and Social Order in Contemporary Society*, Chicago, IL: University of Chicago Press, 2001.

Gingrich, A., "Conceptualising identities: anthropological alternatives to essentialising difference and moralising about the other," in Baumann, G. and Gingrich, A. (eds.), *Grammars of Identity/Alterity: A Structural Approach*, Oxford: Berghahn Books, 2004.

Girling, E., Loader, I., and Sparks, R., *Crime and Social Change in Middle England: Questions of Order in an English Town*, London: Routledge, 2000.

Glaser, B., "Therapeutic jurisprudence: an ethical paradigm for therapists in sex offender treatment programs," *Western Criminology Review*, vol. 4, no. 2, 2003, pp. 143–154.

Glasser, T.L. and Ettema, J.S., "Investigative journalism and the moral order," *Critical Studies in Mass Communication*, vol. 6, 1989, pp. 1–20.

Goetzmann, W.H., "Exploration and the culture of science: the long good-bye of the Twentieth Century," in Luedtke, L.S. (ed.), *Making America: The Society and Culture of the United States*, Chapel Hill, NC: The University of North Carolina Press, 1992.

Goldstein, D.M., Achá, G., Hinojosa, E., and Roncken, T., "*La Mano Dura* and the violence of civil society in Bolivia," in Fischer, E.F. (ed.), *Indigenous Peoples, Civil Society and the Neo-Liberal State in Latin America*, Oxford: Berghahn Books, 2009.

Gómez-Cespedes, A., "The federal law enforcement agencies: an obstacle in the fight

against organized crime in Mexico," *Journal of Contemporary Criminal Justice*, vol. 15, no. 4, 1999, pp. 352–369.
Goode, E. and Ben-Yehuda, N., *Moral Panics: The Social Construction of Deviance*, New York: Wiley-Blackwell, 2009.
Greer, C., *Sex Crime and the Media: Sex Offending and the Press in a Divided Society*, Collumpton, UK: Willan, 2003.
Grimshaw, A.D., "Referential ambiguity in pronominal inclusion: social and linguistic boundary marking," in Grimshaw, A.D. (ed.), *What's Going on Here? Complementary Studies of Professional Talk*, Norwood, NJ: Ablex, 1994.
Gruder, V.R., "'No taxation without representation': the Assembly of Notables of 1787 and political ideology in France," *Legislative Studies Quarterly*, vol. 7, no. 2, 1982, pp. 263–279.
Gusfield, J., *The Culture of Public Problems*, Chicago, IL: University of Chicago Press, 1981.
Gusfield, J., "Constructing the ownership of social problems: fun and profit in the welfare state," *Social Problems*, vol. 36, no. 5, 1989, pp. 431–441.
Gutman, Y., *Encyclopedia of the Holocaust, Volume 3*, New York: Macmillan, 1990.
Gutmann, A. and Thompson, D., "Deliberative democracy beyond process," *The Journal of Political Philosophy*, vol. 10, no. 2, 2002, pp. 153–174.
Habermas, J., *The Theory of Communicative Action*, Cambridge, UK: Polity Press, 1989.
Habermas, J., *Moral Consciousness and Communicative Action*, Cambridge, MA: MIT Press, 1990.
Hadley, E., *Melodramatic Tactics: Theatricalized Dissent in the English Marketplace, 1800–1885*, Stanford, CA: Stanford University Press, 1995.
Haen-Marshall, I., "The criminological enterprise in Europe and the United States: a contextual exploration," *European Journal on Criminal Policy and Research*, vol. 9, no. 3, 2001, pp. 235–257.
Hall, S., Crichter, C., Jefferson, T., Clarke, J., and Roberts, B., *Policing the Crisis: Mugging, the State, and Law and Order*, London: Palgrave Macmillan, 1978.
Halliday, M.A.K., *Language as Social Semiotic*, London: Edward Arnold, 1978.
Hallin, D.C. and Mancini, P., *Comparing Media Systems: Three Models of Media and Politics*, Cambridge, UK: Cambridge University Press, 2004.
Harbison, J., "The changing career of 'elder abuse and neglect' as a social problem in Canada," *Journal of Elder Abuse and Neglect*, vol. 11, no. 4, 1999, pp. 59–80.
Hartnett, S.J. and Stengrim, L.A., "'The whole operation of deception': reconstructing President Bush's rhetoric of weapons of mass destruction," *Cultural Studies ↔ Critical Methodologies*, vol. 4, no. 2, 2004, pp. 152–197.
Hearn, F., *Moral Order and Disorder: The American Search for Civil Society*, Hawthorne, NY: Aldine de Gruyter, 1997.
Hedgecoe, A.M., "Critical bioethics: beyond the social science critique of applied ethics," *Bioethics*, vol. 18, no. 2, 2004, pp. 120–143.
Heilman, R.B., *Tragedy and Melodrama: Versions of Experience*, Seattle, WA: University of Washington Press, 1968.
Heinemann, A. and Verner, D., *Crime and Violence in Development: A Literature Review of Latin America and the Caribbean*, Washington, DC: World Bank, 2006.
Heintz, M. (ed.), *The Anthropology of Moralities*, Oxford: Berghahn, 2009.
Heritage, J., *Garfinkel and Ethnomethodology*, Cambridge, UK: Polity Press, 1984.
Himmelfarb, G., "A de-moralized society: the British/American experience," *The Public Interest*, Fall 94, no. 117, 1994, pp. 57–80.

Hing, B.O., "The immigrant as criminal: punishing dreamers," *Hastings Women's Law Journal*, vol. 9, no. 1, 1998, pp. 79–96.
Hinton, M.S., *The State on the Streets: Police and Politics in Argentina and Brazil*, Boulder, CO: Lynne Rienner, 2006.
Hitlin, S. and Piliavin, J.A., "Values: reviving a dormant concept," *Annual Review of Sociology*, vol. 30, 2004, pp. 359–393.
Hitlin, S. and Vaisey, S. (eds.), *Handbook of the Sociology of Morality*, New York: Springer, 2010.
Hoffmaster, B., "The forms and limits of medical ethics," *Social Science and Medicine*, vol. 39, no. 9, 1994, p. 1155–1164.
Holstein, J. and Miller, G. (eds.), *Challenges and Choices: Constructionist Perspectives on Social Problems*, New York: Aldine de Gruyter, 2003.
Hopkins, N. and Reicher, S., "Social movement rhetoric and the social psychology of collective action: a case study of anti-abortion mobilization," *Human Relations*, vol. 50, no. 3, 1997, pp. 261–286.
Howell, S. (ed.), *The Ethnography of Moralities*, London: Routledge, 1997.
Huhn, S., *The Culture of Fear and Control in Costa Rica (II): The Talk of Crime and Social Changes*, Hamburg: German Institute of Global and Area Studies, Working Paper 108, 2009.
Huhn, S., Oettler, A., and Peetz, P., *Exploding Crime? Topic Management in Central American Newspapers*, Hamburg: German Institute of Global and Area Studies, Giga Working Paper No. 33, 2006.
Huhn, S., Oettler, A., and Peetz, P., "Contemporary discourses on violence in Central American newspapers," *The International Communication Gazette*, vol. 71, no. 4, 2009, pp. 243–261.
Hunt, A., *Governing Morals. A Social History of Moral Regulation*, Cambridge, UK: Cambridge University Press, 1999.
Hunt, A., "Risk and moralization in everyday life," in Ericson, R.V. and Doyle, A. (eds.), *Risk and Morality*, Toronto: University of Toronto Press, 2003.
Hunt, M.R. and Carnevale, F.A., "Moral experience: a framework for bioethics research," *Journal of Medical Ethics*, vol. 37, 2011, pp. 658–662.
Ibarra, P.R. and Kitsuse, J.I., "Vernacular constituents of moral discourse: an interactionist proposal for the study of social problems," in Miller, G. and Holstein, J. (eds.), *Constructionist Controversies: Issues in Social Problems Theory*, New York: Aldine de Gruyter, 1993.
Inglehart, R. and Carballo, M., "Does Latin America exist? (And is there a Confucian culture?): a global analysis of cross-cultural differences," *PS: Political Science and Politics*, vol. 30, no. 1, 1997, pp. 34–47.
Janoff-Bulman, R. and Sheikh, S., "From national trauma to moralizing nation," *Basic and Applied Social Psychology*, vol. 28, no. 4, 2006, pp. 325–332.
Jenness, V., "Social movement growth, domain expansion, and framing processes: the gay/lesbian movement and violence against gays and lesbians as a social problem," *Social Problems*, vol. 42, no. 1, 1995, pp. 145–170.
Johnson, J.M., "Horror stories and the construction of child abuse," in Best, J. (ed.), *Images of Issues: Typifying Contemporary Social Problems*, Hawthorne, NY: Aldine de Gruyter, 1989.
Johnson, T.C., "Child perpetrators—children who molest other children: preliminary findings," *Child Abuse and Neglect*, vol. 12, 1988, pp. 219–229.
Jones, J., *On Aristotle and Greek Tragedy*, Stanford, CA: Stanford University Press, 1980.

Katz, J., *Seductions of Crime: Moral and Sensual Attractions in Doing Evil*, New York: Basic Books, 1988.

Kirklighter, C., *Traversing the Democratic Borders of the Essay*, Albany, NY: State University of New York Press, 2002.

Kleck, G. and Barnes, J.C., "Do more police lead to more crime deterrence?" *Crime and Delinquency*, October 18, 2010 (doi: 10.1177/0011128710382263).

Kornblum, W. and Julian, J., *Social Problems*, Upper Saddle River, NJ: Pearson, fourteenth edition, 2012.

Lakoff, G., *Moral Politics: What Conservatives Know That Liberals Don't*, Chicago, IL: University of Chicago Press, 1996a.

Lakoff, G., "The metaphor system for morality," in Goldberg, A. (ed.), *Conceptual Structure, Discourse and Language*, San Diego, CA: University of California, Center for the Study of Language and Information, 1996b.

Lakoff, G., *Moral Politics: How Liberals and Conservatives Think*, Chicago, IL: University of Chicago Press, 2002.

Lamont, M., *Money, Morals and Manners: The Culture of the French and the American Upper-Middle Class*, Chicago, IL: University of Chicago Press, 1992.

Lamont, M., *The Dignity of Working Men: Morality and the Boundaries of Race, Class and Imagination*, New York: Russell Sage Foundation and Harvard University Press, 2000.

Lamont, M. and Fournier, M. (eds.), *Cultivating Differences: Symbolic Boundaries and the Making of Inequality*, Chicago, IL: University of Chicago Press, 1992.

Lamont, M. and Thévenot, L. (eds.), *Rethinking Comparative Cultural Sociology: Repertoires of Evaluation in France and the United States*, Cambridge, UK: Cambridge University Press, 2000.

Lawson, A.D., "What is medical ethics?" *Trends in Anaesthesia and Critical Care*, vol. 1, 2011, pp. 3–6.

Lee, J.A. and Ungar, S., "A coding method for the analysis of moral discourse," *Human Relations*, vol. 42, no. 8, 1989, pp. 691–715.

Leonard, I.A., "Science, technology and Hispanic America," in Wiarda, H.J. and Mott M.M. (eds.), *Politics and Social Change in Latin America: Still a Distinct Tradition?*, Westport, CT: Praeger, 2003.

Levenson, J. and D'Amora, D., "An ethical paradigm for sex offender treatment: response to Glaser," *Western Criminology Review*, vol. 6, no. 1, 2005, pp. 145–153.

Levi, M., "The media construction of financial white-collar crimes," *British Journal of Criminology*, vol. 46, no. 6, 2006, p. 1037–1057.

Levine, D.N., "Adumbrations of a sociology of morality in the work of Parsons, Simmel, and Merton," in Hitlin, S. and Vaisey, S. (eds), *Handbook of the Sociology of Morality*, New York: Springer, 2010.

LexisNexis, *Searchable Directory of Online Sources*, 2009. Online. Available at: http://w3.nexis.com/sources/ (accessed September 25, 2009).

Lim, H., Lee, H., and Cuvelier, S.J., "The impact of police levels on crime rates: a systematic analysis of methods and statistics in existing studies," *Asian Pacific Journal of Police and Criminal Justice*, vol. 8, no. 1, 2010, pp. 49–82.

Lindblom, C.E., *Inquiry and Change*, New Haven, CT: Yale University Press, 1990.

Linger, D.T., *Dangerous Encounters: Meanings of Violence in a Brazilian City*, Stanford, CA: Stanford University Press, 1992.

Livingstone, S., "Television discussion and the public sphere: conflicting discourses of the Former Yugoslavia," *Political Communication*, vol. 13, 1996, pp. 259–280.

López Maya, M., "The Venezuelan *Caracazo* of 1989: popular protest and institutional weakness," *Journal of Latin American Studies*, vol. 35, 2003, pp. 117–137.
Loseke, D., "'Violence' is 'violence' ... or is it? The social construction of 'wife abuse' and public policy," in Best, J. (ed.), *Images of Issues*, New York: Aldine de Gruyter, 1989.
Loseke, D., *Thinking about Social Problems*, New York: Transaction Books, second edition, 2003.
Lounsbury, M., Ventresca, M., and Hirsch, P.M., "Social movements, field frames and industry emergence: a cultural-political perspective on US recycling," *Socio-Economic Review*, vol. 1, 2003, pp. 71–104.
Lovett, B., "A defence of prudential moralism," *Journal of Applied Philosophy*, vol. 22, no. 2, 2005, pp. 161–170.
Lowe, B.M., "*Hearts and Minds* and morality: analyzing moral vocabularies in qualitative studies," *Qualitative Sociology*, vol. 25, no. 1, 2002, pp. 105–123.
Lowney, K.S., "Claimsmaking, culture, and the media in the social construction process," in Holstein, J.A. and Gubrium, J.F. (eds.), *Handbook of Constructionist Research*, New York/London: The Guilford Press, 2008.
Luhmann, N., *The Reality of the Mass Media*, Stanford, CA: Stanford University Press, 2000.
MacGill, S.M. and Siu, Y.L., "The nature of risk," *Journal of Risk Research*, vol. 7, no. 3, 2004, pp. 315–352.
Malone, E., Boyd, E., and Bero, L.A., "Science in the news: journalists' construction of passive smoking as a social problem," *Social Studies of Science*, vol. 30, no. 5, 2000, pp. 713–735.
Manning, N. and Wetzel, D.L., "Tales of the unexpected: rebuilding trust in government," in Canuto, O. and Giugale, M. (eds.), *The Day After Tomorrow: A Handbook on the Future of Economic Policy in the Developing World*, Washington, DC: The World Bank, 2010.
Marston, G. and Watts, R., "Tampering with the evidence: a critical appraisal of evidence-based policy-making," *The Drawing Board: An Australian Review of Public Affairs*, vol. 3, no. 3, 2003, pp. 143–163.
Martel, J. and Hogeveen, B., "The state of critical scholarship in criminology and socio-legal studies in Canada," *Canadian Journal of Criminology and Criminal Justice*, vol. 48, no. 5, 2006, pp. 633–646.
Martín Alcoff, L., "Does the public intellectual have intellectual integrity?" *Metaphilosophy*, vol. 33, no. 5, 2002, pp. 521–534.
Martini, S., "Argentina: prensa gráfica, delito y seguridad," in Rey, G. (ed.), *Los Relatos Periodísticos del Crimen*, Bogotá: Centro de Competencia en Comunicación Para América Latina, 2007.
Marvell, T. and Moody, C., "Specification problems, police levels and crime rates," *Criminology*, vol. 34, no. 4, 1996, pp. 609–645.
Maurer, D., "Meat as a social problem: rhetorical strategies in the contemporary vegetarian literature," in Maurer, D. and Sobal, J. (eds.), *Eating Agendas: Food and Nutrition as Social Problems*, Hawthorne, NY: Aldine de Gruyter, 1995.
McCright, A.M. and Dunlap, R.E., "Challenging global warming as a social problem: an analysis of the Conservative movement's counter-claims," *Social Problems*, vol. 47, no. 4, 2000, pp. 499–522.
McGuigan, J., "The cultural public sphere," *European Journal of Cultural Studies*, vol. 8, no. 4, 2005, pp. 427–445.

Meyrowitz, J., "Shifting worlds of strangers: medium theory and changes in 'them' versus 'us,'" *Social Inquiry*, vol. 67, no. 1, 1997, pp. 59–71.

Miceli, M.S., "Morality politics vs. identity politics: framing processes and competition among Christian right and gay social movement organizations," *Sociological Forum*, vol. 20, no. 4, 2005, pp. 589–612.

Miller, G. and Holstein, J. (eds.), *Constructionist Controversies: Issues in Social Problems Theory*, New York: Aldine de Gruyter, 1993.

Monsiváis, C., "Ciudadanía y violencia urbana: pesadillas al aire libre," in Rotker, S. (ed.), *Ciudadanías del Miedo*, Caracas: Editorial Nueva Sociedad, 2000.

Montaño-Harmon, M.R., "Discourse features of written Mexican Spanish: current research in contrastive rhetoric and its implications," *Hispania*, vol. 74, no. 2, 1991, pp. 417–425.

Moodie, E., *El Salvador in the Aftermath of Peace: Crime, Uncertainty and the Transition to Democracy*, Philadelphia, PA: University of Pennsylvania Press, 2010.

Morris, S.D., *Political Corruption in Mexico: The Impact of Democratization*, Boulder, CO: Lynne Rienner, 2009.

Moscovici, S., "The conspiracy mentality," in Graumann, C.F. and Moscovici, S. (eds.), *Changing Conceptions of Conspiracy*, New York: Springer-Verlag, 1987.

Moser, C. and McIlwaine, C., *Encounters with Violence in Latin America: Urban Poor Perceptions from Colombia and Guatemala*, New York: Routledge, 2004.

Nelson, B., *Making an Issue of Child Abuse*, Chicago, IL: University of Chicago Press, 1984.

Nielsen, R.P., "Limitations of ethical reasoning as an action (praxis) strategy," *Journal of Business Ethics*, vol. 7, 1988, pp. 725–733.

Nielsen, R.P., "Introduction to the special issue. In search of organizational virtue: moral agency in organizations," *Organization Studies*, vol. 27, no. 3, 2006, pp. 317–321.

Noy, D., "When framing fails: ideas, influence and resources in San Francisco's homeless policy field," *Social Problems*, vol. 56, no. 2, 2009, pp. 223–242.

Ortega y Gasset, J., *Meditaciones del Quijote*, Madrid: Publicaciones de la Residencia de Estudiantes, Serie II, Volumen I, 1914.

Ortony, A. (ed.), *Metaphor and Thought*, Cambridge, UK: Cambridge University Press, 1993.

Ossowska, M., *Social Determinants of Moral Ideas*, London: Routledge and Kegan Paul, 1971.

Pak, C.S. and Acevedo, R., "Spanish-language newspaper editorials from Mexico, Spain and the U.S.," in Connor, U., Nagelhout, E., and Roziycki, W.V. (eds.), *Contrastive Rhetoric: Reaching to Intercultural Rhetoric*, Philadelphia, PA: John Benjamins Publishing Company, 2008.

Parker, I., *Discourse Dynamics: Critical Analysis for Individual and Social Psychology*, London: Routledge, 1992.

Patterson, E.B., "Poverty, income inequality and community crime rates," *Criminology*, vol. 29, no. 4, 1991, pp. 755–776.

Peek, C.W., Alston, J.P., and Lowe, G.D., "Comparative evaluation of the local police," *Public Opinion Quarterly*, vol. 37, 1978, pp. 370–379.

Peelo, M., Francis, B., Soothill, K., Pearson, J., and Ackerley, E., "Newspaper reporting and the public construction of homicide," *British Journal of Criminology*, vol. 44, 2004, pp. 256–275.

Perelman, L.C., "The two rhetorics: design and interpretation in engineering and humanistic discourse," *Language and Learning across the Disciplines*, vol. 3, no. 2, 1999, pp. 64–82.

Phillips, N., Lawrence, T.B., and Hardy, C., "Discourse and institutions," *Academy of Management Review*, vol. 29, no. 4, 2004, 635–652.
Politis, V., "*Aporia* and searching in the early Plato," in Judson, L. and Karasmanis, V. (eds.), *Remembering Socrates. Philosophical Essays*, Oxford: Clarendon Press, 2006.
Pollak, J.M. and Kubrin, C.E., "Crime in the news: how crimes, offenders and victims are portrayed by the media," *Journal of Criminal Justice and Popular Culture*, vol. 14, no. 1, 2007, pp. 59–83.
Pridemore, W., "Poverty matters: a reassessment of the inequality-homicide relationship in cross-national studies," *British Journal of Criminology*, vol. 51, no. 5, 2011, pp. 739–772.
Puglisi, R., *Being the New York Times: The Political Behavior of a Newspaper*, London: London School of Economics, Political Economy and Public Policy Series, No. 20, 2006. Online. Available at: http://sticerd.lse.ac.uk/dps/pepp/PEPP20.pdf (accessed September 23, 2009).
Quarantelli, E.L., "The different worlds of science and mass communication: implications for information flow from the former to the latter," in Nemec, J., Nigg, J., and Siccardi F. (eds.), *Prediction and Perception of Natural Hazards*, Dordrecht, NL: Kluwer Academic Publishers, 1993.
Rainham, D., "Risk communication and public response to industrial chemical contamination in Sydney, Nova Scotia: a case study," *Journal of Environmental Health*, vol. 65, no. 5, 2002, pp. 26–32.
Reidenbach, R.E. and Robin, D.P., "Some initial steps toward improving the measurement of ethical evaluations of marketing activities," *Journal of Business Ethics*, vol. 7, no. 11, 1988, pp. 871–879.
Reiner, R., "Media-made criminality: the representation of crime in the mass media," in Maguire, M., Morgan, R., and Reiner R. (eds.), *The Oxford Handbook of Criminology*, Oxford, UK: Oxford University Press, 2007.
Rey, G., *El Cuerpo del Delito. Representación y Narrativas Mediáticas de la Seguridad Ciudadana*, Bogotá: Centro de Competencia en Comunicación para América Latina, 2005.
Rey, G. (ed.), *Los Relatos Periodísticos del Crimen*, Bogotá: Centro de Competencia en Comunicación para América Latina, 2007.
Ridge, M., "The populist as a social critic," *Minnesota History*, vol. 43, no. 8, 1973, pp. 297–302.
Ritter, J., "Recovering hyperbole: re-imagining the limits of rhetoric for an age of excess," *Communication Dissertations*, Paper 22, 2010. Online. Available at: http://digitalarchive.gsu.edu/communication_diss/22 (accessed June 4, 2011).
Ritzer, G. (ed.), *Handbook of Social Problems: A Comparative International Perspective*, Newbury Park, CA: Sage, 2004.
Robertson, C. and Mire, S., *Ethics for Criminal Justice Professionals*, Baton Rouge, FL: CRC, 2009.
Roche, M.W., "Introduction to Hegel's theory of tragedy," *PhaenEx*, vol. 1, no. 2, 2006, pp. 11–20.
Rock, P., "The sociology of deviance and conceptions of moral order," *British Journal of Criminology*, vol. 14, no. 2, 1974, pp. 139–149.
Rodgers, S. and Thorson, E., "The reporting of crime and violence in the *Los Angeles Times*: is there a public health perspective?" *Journal of Health Communication*, vol. 6, no. 2, 2001, pp. 160–182.
Rohlinger, D.A., "Framing the abortion debate: organizational resources, media strategies, and movement-countermovement dynamics," *The Sociological Quarterly*, vol. 43, no. 4, 2002, pp. 479–507.

Rokeach, M., *Understanding Human Values*, New York: Simon and Schuster, 1979.

Sacco, V.F., "Media constructions of crime," *Annals of the American Academy of Political and Social Science*, no. 539, 1995, pp. 141–154.

Saguy, A.C., Gruys, K., and Gong, S., "Social problem construction and national context: news reporting on 'overweight' and 'obesity' in the United States and France," *Social Problems*, vol. 57, no. 4, 2010, pp. 586–610.

Sarewitz, D., "How science makes environmental controversies worse," *Environmental Science and Policy*, vol. 7, 2004, pp. 385–403.

Sarmiento, D.F., *Facundo. Civilización y Barbarie*, Madrid: Alianza, [1845]1988.

Sasson, T., *Crime Talk: How Citizens Construct a Social Problem*, New York: Aldine de Gruyter, 1995.

Saunders, B., "How to teach moral theories in applied ethics," *Journal of Medical Ethics*, vol. 36, 2010, pp. 635–638.

Scheppele, K.L., "Telling stories," *Michigan Law Review*, vol. 87, no. 8, 1989, p. 2073–2098.

Schmid, D., "True crime," in Rzepka, C. and Horsley, L. (eds.), *A Companion to Crime Fiction*, New York: Wiley-Blackwell, 2010.

Schulte-Bockholt, A., "Latin American critical criminology," in DeKeseredy, W.S. and Dragiewicz, M. (eds.), *Routledge Handbook of Critical Criminology*, New York: Routledge, 2011.

Segovia Arancibia, C., *Political Trust in Latin America*, University of Michigan: Unpublished Ph.D. dissertation, 2008. Online. Available at: http://deepblue.lib.umich.edu/bitstream/2027.42/61668/1/csegovia_1.pdf (accessed March 1, 2012).

Segura, C., "Violencia y melodrama en la novela colombiana contemporánea," *América Latina Hoy*, vol. 47, 2007, pp. 55–76.

Simon, J., "Positively punitive: how the inventor of scientific criminology who died at the beginning of the Twentieth Century continues to haunt American crime control at the beginning of the Twenty-First," *Texas Law Review*, vol. 84, 2005–2006, pp. 2135–2172.

Singer, B., *Melodrama and Modernity*, New York: Columbia University Press, 2001.

Skirius, J., *El Ensayo Hispanoamericano del Siglo XX*, México, DF: Fondo de Cultura Económica, 2004.

Smith, C.J., Zhang, S.X., and Barberet, R. (eds.), *Routledge Handbook of International Criminology*, London: Routledge, 2011.

Smith, D.M., *Moral Geographies: Ethics in a World of Difference*, Edinburgh, UK: Edinburgh University Press, 2000.

Smith, D. E., "'Literacy' and business: 'social problems' as social organization," in Holstein, J.A. and Miller, G. (eds.), *Reconsidering Social Constructionism: Debates in Social Problems Theory*, New York: Aldine de Gruyter, 1993.

Smith, J.L., *Melodrama*, London: Methuen, 1973.

Soothill, K. and Walby, S., *Sex Crime in the News*, London: Routledge, 1991.

Sorenson, S.B., Peterson Manz, J.G., and Berk, R., "News media coverage and the epidemiology of homicide," *American Journal of Public Health*, vol. 88, 1998, pp. 1510–1514.

Sparks, J.R. and Oan, Y., "Ethical judgments in business ethics research: definition, and research agenda," *Journal of Business Ethics*, vol. 91, 2010, pp. 405–418.

Spiegelberg, H., "On the right to say 'we': a linguistic and phenomenological analysis," in Psathas, G. (ed.), *Phenomenological Sociology: Issues and Applications*, New York: John Wiley, 1973.

Sprott, J.B., "Understanding public views of youth crime and the youth justice system," *Canadian Journal of Criminology*, vol. 38, no. 3, 1996, pp. 271–290.
Stabb, M.S., "The new essay of Mexico," *Hispania*, vol. 70, no. 1, 1987, pp. 47–61.
Stallybrass, P. and White, A., *The Politics and Poetics of Transgression*, London: Methuen, 1986.
Steenbergen, M.R., Bächtiger, A., Spörndli, M., and Steiner, J., "Measuring political deliberation: a discourse quality index," *Comparative European Politics*, vol. 1, 2003, pp. 21–48.
Stein, M.L. and Paterno, S.F., *The Newswriters' Handbook, An Introduction to Journalism*, Ames, IA: Iowa State University Press, 1998.
Stivers, R., "Towards a sociology of morality," *International Journal of Sociology and Social Policy*, vol. 16, nos.1–2, 1996, pp. 1–14.
Stone, D.A., "Causal stories and the formation of policy agendas," *Political Science Quarterly*, vol. 104, no. 2, 1989, pp. 281–300.
Tewkesbury, R., Miller, A., and DeMichele, M.T., "From the field: crime, media, and public opinion: criminologists' role as source of public information," *Journal of Crime and Justice*, vol. 29, no. 1, 2006, pp. 123–142.
Thompson, C.Y., Young, R.L., and Burns, R., "Representing gangs in the news: media constructions of criminal gangs," *Sociological Spectrum*, vol. 20, 2000, pp. 409–432.
Titus, J.J., "Boy trouble: rhetorical framing of boys' underachievement," *Discourse: Studies in the Cultural Politics of Education*, vol. 25, no. 2, 2004, pp. 145–169.
Tucker, D.M., *Mugwumps: Public Moralists of the Gilded Age*, Columbia, MO: University of Missouri Press, 1998.
Tuggle, J.L. and Holmes, M.D., "Blowing smoke: status politics and the Shasta County ban," *Deviant Behavior*, vol. 18, 1997, pp. 77–93.
Tunnell, K.D., "Silence of the Left: reflections on critical criminology and criminologists," *Social Justice*, vol. 22, no. 1, 1995, pp. 89–101.
Ulrich, C.L., "Hate crime legislation: a policy analysis," *Houston Law Review*, vol. 36, no. 4, 1999, pp. 1467–1529.
UNESCO (United Nations Educational, Scientific and Cultural Organization), *Science and Technology Statistics*, Paris: UNESCO, 2011. Online. Available at: http://stats.uis.unesco.org/unesco/ReportFolders/ReportFolders.aspx (accessed March 3, 2012).
Uribe, R. and Gunter, B., "Are 'sensational' news stories more likely to trigger readers' emotions than non-sensational news stories? A content analysis of British TV news," *European Journal of Communication*, vol. 22, no. 2, 2007, pp. 207–228.
van Dijk, T.A., *News as Discourse*, Hillsdale, NJ: Lawrence Erlbaum Associates, 1988.
van Dijk, T.A., *Racism and the Press*, London: Routledge, 1991.
Vasilachis de Gialdino, I., "El lenguaje de la violencia en los medios de comunicación. Las otras formas de ser de la violencia y la prensa escrita," in PNUD (Programa de las Naciones Unidas para el Desarrollo) (ed.), *Aportes para la Convivencia y la Seguridad Ciudadana*, San Salvador, El Salvador: PNUD, 2004.
Vessuri, H., "The social study of science in Latin America," *Social Studies of Science*, vol. 17, no. 3, 1987, pp. 519–554.
Voestermans, P., "Alterity/identity: a deficient image of culture," in Corbey, R. and Leerssen, J. (eds.), *Alterity, Identity, Image: Selves and Others in Society and Scholarship*, Amsterdam: Editions Rodopi, 1991.
Wagner, D., "The universalization of social problems: some radical explanations," *Critical Sociology*, vol. 23, no. 1, 1997, pp. 3–23.
Waisbord, S., "The narrative of exposés in South American journalism: telling the story of Collorgate in Brazil," *Gazette*, vol. 59, no. 3, 1997, pp. 189–203.

Ward, T. and Birgden, A., "Human rights and correctional clinical practice," *Aggression and Violent Behavior*, vol. 12, 2007, pp. 628–643.

Ward, T. and Salmon, K., "The ethics of punishment: correctional practice implications," *Aggression and Violent Behavior*, vol. 14, 2009, pp. 239–247.

Wasserman, I.M. and Stack, S., "Communal violence and the media: lynchings and their news coverage by the *New York Times* between 1882 and 1930," in Barak, G. (ed.), *Media, Process and the Social Construction of Crime. Studies in Newsmaking Criminology*, New York: Garland, 1995.

Watney, S., *Policing Desire: Pornography, Aids and the Media*, London: Methuen, 1987.

Weber, M., *The Protestant Ethic and the Spirit of Capitalism*, Roxbury, CA: Blackwell, 2002.

Welch, M., Fenwick, M., and Roberts, M., "State managers, intellectuals, and the media: a content analysis of ideology in experts' quotes in feature newspaper articles on crime," *Justice Quarterly*, vol. 15, no. 2, 1998, pp. 219–241.

Wikipedia, *The Globe and Mail*, 2009. Online. Available at: http://en.wikipedia.org/wiki/The_Globe_and_Mail (accessed September 24, 2009).

Williams, O.F. and Murphy, P.E., "The ethics of virtue: a moral theory for marketing," *Journal of Macromarketing*, vol. 10, 1990, pp. 19–29.

Williams, R., "Constructing the public good: social movements and cultural resources," *Social Problems*, vol. 42, no. 1, 1995, pp. 124–144.

Williams, R., Faulkner, W., and Fleck, J. (eds.), *Exploring Expertise: Issues and Perspectives*, London: Macmillan, 1998.

Wolfe, A., "Civil religion revisited: quiet faith in middle class America," in Rosenblum, N.L. (ed.), *Obligations of Citizenship: Religious Accommodation in Pluralist Democracies*, Princeton, NJ: Princeton University Press, 2000.

Wong, D.B., *Moral Relativity*, Berkeley, CA: University of California Press, 1984.

Woolgar, S. and Pawluch, D., "Ontological gerrymandering: the anatomy of social problems explanations," *Social Problems*, vol. 32, no. 3, 1985, pp. 214–227.

Wykes, M., *News, Crime and Culture*, London: Pluto Press, 2001.

Yee, A.S., "The causal effects of ideas on policies," *International Organization*, vol. 50, no. 1, 1996, pp. 69–108.

Young, J., *The Exclusive Society: Social Exclusion, Crime and Difference in Late Modernity*, London: Sage, 1999.

Young, J., "Moral panic: its origins in resistance, ressentiment and the translation of fantasy into reality," *British Journal of Criminology*, vol. 49, no. 1, 2009, p. 4–16.

Znaniecki, F., *The Social Role of the Man of Knowledge*, New York: Harper Torchbooks, 1968.

Index

abortion 59
academia, as specialized 70
action: calls to 77, 80; effectiveness of 89–91, 92–3; and knowledge 48; as message 91; specific 81–3; virtue of 77
aesthetic perspective 117–18
agency *see* moral agency
Aguinis, Marcos 34
alarm 39
Alexander, J.C. 47
alterity 33–7, 38, 47, 48, 97
Ambert, Anne-Marie 60, 102–3
amorality, in crime reporting 2
anecdotes 15
Anglo-America: moral outlook 51–61; as secure moral community 51–61
anxiety 21, 39, 56–8
aporia 115
approval, expressions of 16, 27
aretaic approach 91–2
argument 101
Aristotle 114

Babún, Alfredo 24
barbarity 34
beliefs, basis of 69–70
Benford, R.D. 5
Best, J. 47
blamelessness, and sympathy 27
Boltanski, L. 117–18
Bratton, William J. 22, 50, 58, 59, 72
Brooks, Peter 110
bureaucratic data reporting 15
Burke, Kenneth 73
Burzaco, Eugenio 46
business, and insecurity 24
business sector, crime 19–20

Calderón, Felipe 87

calls to action 77, 80
Cánaves, Liliana: calls to action 80; determination 41; letter to *La Nación* 11–13, 16; solidarity 19
Cantero, Santiago, letter to *La Nación* 96
Caracas, crime prevention plan 19, 26
caricatural silhouettes 35
causes of crime, multiple 68
Cázares, César 19–20, 24
censure: and certainty 73; expressions of 16, 27; and separation 49; of society 45
certainty 9, 69–74, 100, 115
child abuse 38
civil commitment, sex offenders 85–6
civil society: and state 44, 49; virtuous 44, 45, 116
claims-making 48
Cohen, Stanley 5–6
collective action, political calls for 13
collective concern 9, 13, 15–17, 26–7
collective dimension, references to 15
collective discourse 96
collective level, and personal level 13
collective morality 91, 107, 109
collectivity 22–4, 24
Collini, S. 103
commentary: Anglo-America compared to Latin America 95–6; overview of study 3–4
commentators, as spectators 115
communicative action 111
community, concern for 27–8
compassion 27
concern: collective 9, 13, 15–17, 26–7; for collectivity 22–4; for community 27–8; as expression of emotion 39; individual and collective 15–17; levels of 28; for offenders 17–18; organizational 16; for others 17–20; regional variations 28–9;

concern *continued*
  for response 24–6; for self 20–2; summary and reflection 26–9; superficiality 16–17
conflict, language of 40–1
containment 98
control: language of 59; prescription 83
Cooper, Carnell 76–7, 93
Corbey, R. 38
corporal morality 6
corruption: governments 99; police 65–6, 67, 99; state 43, 67
Creba, Jane 17
crime: amoral accounts 2; areas of concern 54; collective concern 9; commentary 3; demographic factors 59–60; as different from civilization 44; drivers of 59; and identity 48; as local issue 22–4; locations 61–2; presentation of data 63–4; responses to 40, 45; spatiality 55–6, 98; war against 40–1
crime prevention 79
crime rates: New York 14–15; and policing 59; reporting 1–2; responses to 53–4; statistical data 51–3
criminal justice ethics 114
criminal justice system: collective concern 24–6; criticism of 42–3, 77–8
criminality, state 43
criminology 102
culture 68–9
cynicism 106

Dallas Morning News 47
damned insecurity 45–6
data reporting, bureaucratic 15
deliberations, moral 84–9
democratization, of risk 28
demographic factors 59–60
demonization 47
denunciation 117–18
descriptions, of crime 70
determination 40, 42, 44
deterrence 91
disagreements 70–1
discourse: collective 96; experimental 4; moral and factual 50–1; natural 3–4
discourse ethics 111
discursive morality 6
distant suffering 117
Distant Suffering: Morality, Media and Politics (Boltanski) 117–18
distrust, of state 99
Dixon, Sheila 76

Domanick, Joe 25
drivers, of crime 59
drug trafficking: as cause of crime 66–7; and crime 59; power of 65–6; using military to combat 87–9
Dupuy, J.P. 114
Durkheim, Emile 116
Durrell, Lawrence 114
dynamics, of crime 58–9

Earle, P.G. 104
effectiveness, of action 5, 89–91, 92–3
El Nacional 2; on insecurity 21; locations of crime 61, 62; solidarity 19; use of statistics and anecdotes 15
El Universal 3; calls to action 80–1; evidence 101; failures of criminal justice system 42–3; Gertz Manero essay 30–2, 43–4, 45; police corruption 65; regional lawlessness 87; young people as victims 18
Elbert, C. 102
elections, Mexico 31–2
Elizabethport, as location of crime 55–6
emotion 38–9
empathy 40
empirical doubt 115
empirical perplexity 114
Entman, R.M. 4
Ericson, R. 47
essays 104–5
ethics 114–15
ethnography, discourse in 4
evidence 100–2
experimental discourse 4
experts 105–6

facts 50–1, 70–1, 86–7, 100–2
Facundo. Civilization and Barbarity (Sarmiento) 34
failure to act, as moral weakness 81
fear: of future crime 56–8; generalized 21
Firpo, Norbert, on "Damned insecurity" 45–6
first person plural, significance of 13–15
foreknowledge 114–15
Foucault, Michel 35
Fox, James Alan 1
fragmentation, of social interaction 22–3
framing 4–5, 6, 27
Frost, N.A. 47
Frye, Victoria, letter to *New York Times* 95–6
funding, law enforcement 59

gangs 17, 24, 41, 45, 47, 53, 55–6, 58, 79
Gans, Herbert 112
Gertz Manero, Alejandro 78; *El Universal* essay 30–2, 43–4, 45
Globe and Mail 2–3; child abuse 38; on effectiveness 90–1; evidence 101; on gun crime 17–18; review of research 102–3
governments: characterizations of 41–2; corruption 99; criticism of 42–3, 78; dissatisfaction with 98; failure to act 67; moral weakness 81; as part of society 44
Grinbaum, A. 114
gun crime 76
gun ownership 76–7

Habermas, J. 111–12
Haen-Marshall, I. 102
Harper, Stephen 24, 53, 57
Hegel, Georg 114
Heilman, R.B. 114
Henderson, Elijah 55–6
Himmelfarb, Gertrude 103, 110
history 9; and cultural differences 110; of the present 78–9
Huhn, S. 110
humanity, and voice 37
humility 40
hyperbole 73–4

identity: and alterity 38; collective and individual 44; and crime 48; and melodrama 97; of moral community 9; within moral community 116; and morality 32; personal moral 45–6, 49; and public moral discourse 8–9; we the good 38–44
ideology, and prescription 83
image presentation 26
imagined social world 7, 9
immigration 59
impunity 42–3, 67
Index of Fear of Crime 63
indignation 39
individual action, as ineffective 14
individual concern 16
individual responsibility 20
individual rights, vs. health and safety 76–7
inequality 68, 70
insecurity: and business 24; condition of 20–1; terms used 22
issues, types of 110–11
Ivarrola, Lucas 42, 45

journalism: investigative 111; melodrama 112; simplicity 70

Katz, J. 113
knowledge, and action 48–9

La Nación 3; causes of crime 66–7; criticism of criminal justice system 77–8; cultural change 68–9; evidence 101; failures of criminal justice system 42–3; on insecurity 21–2; letter from Liliana Cánaves 11–13; letter on neighborhood violence 95; locations of crime 61–2; police corruption 65–6; prescription 82; volume and affected population 64
Lakoff, G. 48
language: of censure and approval 16; of collective concern 27; of control 59; of emotion 39; of essays 104–5; and expression of morality 2–3; hyperbole 73–4; moral imagery 58; responses to crime 40–1; use of metaphor 57–8, 66, 72–3, 98; vocabulary 71; *see also* prescriptive text
Latin America, moral outlook 61–9
law enforcement, funding 59
lawlessness, regional 87
Leerssen, J. 38
Lindblom, C.E. 70
lived experience, and moral discourse 100
Los Angeles Times 1–2; evidence 100; Males' article 74; minorities as victims 18–19; murder rates 78–9; Rampart Scandal 44; responses to crime 25–6; spatiality of crime 55; state and civil society 44
Lovett, B. 103
Lowney, K.S. 48

Males, Mike 51, 70, 71–3, 74, 100
Manichean world 32, 47, 97, 108, 111
Manning, N. 99
Marston, G. 101
Mayorca, Eduardo, and Cristina Martí 61
meanings, poetic and semantic 73
media, absence of offenders 47
melodrama 9–10; characters in 102–6; contextual understanding 106; denunciation and sentiment 117–18; depiction of crime 112–13; facts and evidence 100–2; journalism 112; overview 95–7; perspectives on 97–8; preferred moralities 114

metaphors 57–8, 66, 72–3, 98
"Metro Briefing," New York crime rates 14–15
Mexico: elections 31–2; Gertz Manero essay 30–2; kidnappings and violence 19–20, 24–5
military, combating drug trafficking 87–9
minorities, as victims 18–19
moral agency 9; as aspect of talk 116; calls to action 80–1; deliberations 84–9; drug trafficking 87–9; overview 76–9; prosaic morality 81–4; sex offenders 84–7; summary and reflection 91–4
moral community 8, 9, 116
moral deliberations 84–9
moral discourse: consequences of variation 115–16; and lived experience 100; stability and variation 111
moral health 28
moral outlook: Anglo-America 51–61; as aspect of talk 116; certainty 69–74; expression of 50; Latin America 61–9; overview 50; summary and reflection 74–5
moral panics, research on 5–6
moral paralysis 115
moral philosophy 91–2
moral sensibility, and virtue 39
moral shortcomings, identification of 41–2
moral significance: of newspapers 3; of utterances 7
moral space 13
moral universes 33, 46
moral weakness, failure to act 81
moralism 103
morality: affirmed by public discourse 8; and choice of language 2–3; conceptions of 6–7; corporal 6; as determinant of social phenomena 7–8; discursive 6; full 48; and identity 32; invocation 80–1; locus of performance 46–7; media attitudes to 103; prosaic 81–4; and sensibility 38–9; sociological perspective 6–7
moralizing 70; expression of 107; topics of 110
motives, for violence 54–5
Mugwumps 104

narrative, presentation of data 63
nations, concern for 28
natural discourse 3–4
natural moral discourse, study of 6
neighborhoods, as locations of crime 55–6

Nelson, Taj 17, 36–7
New York Times 3; Baltimore report 76; collective dimension 15; on crime rates 16; criticism of criminal justice system 78; evidence 100; letter on female homicide 95; murder rates 55; Newark shootings 23, 45; prescription 81–2; responses to crime rate 54; on sex offenders 85; state and civil society 44
Newark, as violent city 55–6
Newark shootings 23, 34, 45
newspapers of record 108
newspapers, quality of 108–9
newsprint: as ephemeral 3; moral significance 3; and public discourse 3
Niemöller, Martin 11
notables 30
nowhere to go 56
numerical data 63–4

offenders: absence from accounts 47; characterization 33–4; concern for 17–18; demonization 47; featured in texts 37; lack of voice 47; one-dimensional referents 35, 47; under- or unconstructed 48; police as 66; as silent 37; as victims 60
organizational concern 16
organized crime 66–7
Ortega y Gasset, J. 105
other side 113–14
Otherness 38, 46–7, 58–9, 66
others, concern for 17–20

Patterson, Orlando 60
personal level, and collective level 13
personal moral identity 45–6, 49
personalization of crime 64
personas, expressed through writings 45–6
Phillips, N.D. 47
poetic meanings 73
polemic 65
police: corruption 65–6, 67, 99; criminality 66; image 99–100
policing, and crime rates 59
political opinion research 110–11
political system, collective concern 24–6
politics, and prescription 83
position issues 110–11
poverty 59–60, 68, 70, 83
prescription 16
prescriptive text: research 93; sex offenders 84–7; specific action 81–3; see also language

problems, shaped by solutions 79
propriety, of action 5
prosaic morality 81–4
public discourse: as commentary 3; overview 108
public intellectuals 104
public moral discourse: as affirmation of morality 8; censure 8; certainty 9; and identity 8–9; and moral panics 6; reasons for study 7; scholarly use of 4
public moralists 103–4, 105
public perceptions, of risk 62–3
push factors, mitigation of 83

Quarantelli, E.L. 70

Ramos Garcia, José María 24–5, 26
Rampart Scandal 44
reason, in response to crime 41
Regent Park Project 35–6, 38, 40
regional lawlessness 87
repentance 36
reporting, tone of 15
research: audience for 74; detachment 96; distancing 74; moral significance 92; nature of 101; political opinion 110–11; position of 101–2; prescriptive text 93; and public utterance 70; role of 51–2; on sex offenders 85–7; significance of 106–7; as specialized 70
research study: focus of 116; overview 3–4; potential approaches 111; sampling 109; sources 9–10, 108–11
resolve 41
responses to crime: concern for 24–6; levels of 19; proactive and reactive 11
responsibility, individual 20
risk, and concern 27–8
Rodríguez, Fernando 42, 45
Ruiz, Lidmar 61

Sacco, V.F. 47
sacrosanct spaces 61–2
Sarmiento, Domingo Faustino 34
secret histories 113
security, importance of 22
Segovia Arancibia, C. 99
selves, concern for 22
sensibilities 38–9
sentiment 117–18
separation 49
severity, of problem/danger 5
sex offenders 84–7
shock 39

shortcomings 41–2
sickness, of society 45
Simon, J. 102
simplicity, in journalism 70
Skirius, J. 104
Smith, James 97
social action, and research 70
social class 62
social criticism 60–1, 104
social development 68
social factors 67–8, 83
social interaction, fragmentation of 22–3
social schizophrenia 31, 32
societal arrangements, concern for 28
society: concern for 28; criticism of 45; defining 44–5; failure of 68–9; sickness 45
sociology, perspective on morality 6–7
solidarity, as basis of concern 19
solutions, shaping problems 79
spaces, violation of 61–2
spatiality 35, 55–6, 98
state: characterization of 48–9; and civil society 44, 49; corruption 43, 67; criminality 43; critical views of 98–9; distrust 99; law-abiding 44; as separate from society 42–3
statistics 15, 51–3
stirring morality 80–1
structural factors 67–9
struggle 48, 56
Styzens, Rex 40
sympathy 19, 27
symptom, crime as 60
systemic factors, concern for 28

tabloids 108–9
talk: moral adequacy 117; moral outlook and moral agency 116
talking into being 9
tenacity 41
them and us 47
they the bad 46–7, 48
Thompson, C.Y. 47
threat, as constant 62–3
Titus, J.J. 70
Toronto, Regent Park Project 35–6, 38, 40
toughness 40
tragedy 112, 114
trends: controversy over 70; perspectives on 72; reporting 64–5
trust 99–100, 106–7
trying to turn their lives around 36–7
Tuirán, Rodolfo, opinion column 20–1, 22

ubiquity 62–3, 98
uncertainty 2, 70, 115
unemployment 83
universalization, of social problems 28
urban development, and crime 57
urban living, and crime 62
urgency, of problem/danger 5
us and them 47
utterances, moral significance 7

valence issues 110–11
validity, of statements 69
value judgements 16–17
values, and virtue 40
variability 10
Vasilachis de Gialdino, I. 47
Venezuela, kidnappings and deaths 38–9
victimization, rates of 63
victims: minorities as 18–19; offenders as 60; and victimizers 30–2, 33; young people as 17–18
violence: causes 66–7; concern over 54; motive for 54–5
virtue: of action 77, 92; locus of performance 46–7; meaning 7; and moral sensibility 39

vocabularies: of motive 5; of report and debate 71
voice: giving 113; and humanity 37; offenders' lack of 47
vulnerability 27

Waisbord, Silvio 111–12
war, metaphor of 40–1, 48
Watts, R. 101
"we," significance of 13–15
we-talk 27
we the good 48; alterity 33–7; identity 38–44; overview 30–3; summary and reflection 46–9
welfare, prescription 83
Wetzel, D.L. 99
Wexler, Chuck 53
what works 92
Willie, Monica 17–18, 33, 40
Wilson, Samantha 38
witnesses 96

Young, Joyce 35–6, 37, 38
young people: lack of care 67; nowhere to go 56; seen as brutish 54–5; as victims 17–18
youth violence 46

Taylor & Francis

eBOOKS
FOR LIBRARIES

ORDER YOUR
FREE 30 DAY
INSTITUTIONAL
TRIAL TODAY!

Over 23,000 eBook titles in the Humanities, Social Sciences, STM and Law from some of the world's leading imprints.

Choose from a range of subject packages or create your own!

Benefits for you
- Free MARC records
- COUNTER-compliant usage statistics
- Flexible purchase and pricing options

Benefits for your user
- Off-site, anytime access via Athens or referring URL
- Print or copy pages or chapters
- Full content search
- Bookmark, highlight and annotate text
- Access to thousands of pages of quality research at the click of a button

For more information, pricing enquiries or to order a free trial, contact your local online sales team.

UK and Rest of World: online.sales@tandf.co.uk
US, Canada and Latin America:
e-reference@taylorandfrancis.com

www.ebooksubscriptions.com

ALPSP Award for
BEST eBOOK
PUBLISHER
2009 Finalist

Taylor & Francis eBooks
Taylor & Francis Group

A flexible and dynamic resource for teaching, learning and research.